*Contemporary Garden
Aesthetics, Creations and
Interpretations*

*Contemporary Garden
Aesthetics, Creations and
Interpretations*

*Contemporary Garden
Aesthetics, Creations and
Interpretations*

*Contemporary Garden
Aesthetics, Creations and
Interpretations*

Dumbarton Oaks Colloquium on the History of Landscape Architecture XXIX

Held at Dumbarton Oaks May 5–7, 2005

Contemporary Garden Aesthetics, Creations and Interpretations

edited by Michel Conan

Published by Dumbarton Oaks Research Library and Collection
Washington, D.C.

Distributed by Harvard University Press, 2007.

Published by Dumbarton Oaks Research Library and Collection and
Spacemaker Press. Distributed by Harvard University Press, 2007

Library of Congress Cataloging-in-Publication Data

Dumbarton Oaks Colloquium on the History of Landscape Architecture (29th :
2005)
Contemporary garden aesthetics, creations and interpretations / edited by
Michel Conan.
p. cm.
"Dumbarton Oaks Colloquium on the History of Landscape Architecture XXIX
held at Dumbarton Oaks May 5/7, 2005."
Includes index.
ISBN-13: 978-0-88402-325-8
ISBN-10: 0-88402-325-7
1. Gardens--Design--Congresses. 2. Landscape architecture--Congresses.
I. Conan, Michel, 1939- II. Title.
SB472.45.D86 2005
712--dc22
2006035923

Printed in China

Contemporary Garden Aesthetics, Creations and Interpretations

Contemporary Garden Aesthetics, Creations and Interpretations

Contemporary Garden Aesthetics, Creations and Interpretations

Contemporary Garden Aesthetics, Creations and Interpretations

Contemporary Garden Aesthetics, Creations and Interpretations

In Defiance of the Institutional Art World

Michel Conan

Why does contemporary Garden Art receive so little attention from art critics, even less than Land Art, Earthworks or Landscape Design? This is somewhat extraordinary since gardens have been more numerous and ubiquitous in contemporary western cities over the last fifty years than at any previous time in their history, and tourist attention for historical gardens has prompted an important surge in historic garden renovation. One may say that gardening is one of the very few arts that has been practiced on a large scale by amateurs, as opposed to painting, sculpture, or any of the new visual arts during the last forty years, and sometimes with a degree of success that earned their authors local or even world-wide recognition.

So, garden art deserves scholarly scrutiny in its own right and should be studied in its own terms without any pretense at imitating critical discussions of the contemporary art world since it has remained alien to its critical discourse. New scholarly endeavors might reveal something about the specificity of gardens as an art with a public dimension that is nevertheless unfit for presentation in museums or art galleries, since, unlike so many works of Land Art or Installations that exist, like garden art, only outside the walls of the museum, it remains beyond even the reach of photographic or video representation in museums. There are interesting exhibitions of photographs, or videos and models of gardens, some of which deserve to be considered as works of art themselves, but cannot be mistaken for the gardens in which we like to walk, dream, or look for the first spring blossoms. We can neither mistake paintings by Claude Monet for haystacks, nor garden representations for the gardens themselves. Thus the art of the garden remains foreign to the rooms of the museum, and for that reason it may teach us something about art in the contemporary world that museum art does not.

You may be tempted to object to a praise of gardens as a buoyant form of art since the growing consumption of garden design in western cities and of garden images world-wide does not warrant its significance as a contemporary artistic development. We all know many forms of commercial art, like the comic strip, the advertisement board, or interior decoration that display great inventiveness and that are ignored by art criticism, even though they are widely consumed and appreciated. In similar fashion, the success of residential gardens and the flurry of recent garden festivals cannot be considered for sheer reasons of number, cost, or popularity with tourists, a demonstration of the pertinence of gardens as forms of contemporary art. This is precisely why this volume engages in a discussion of the contributions of several contemporary designers to the production of new aesthetic experiences provided by gardens.

There is a very simple reason for taking garden experience as the starting point of our presentations. Gardens are places that we enjoy as part of our dwelling in the world. They belong to our everyday life, and they impinge upon it. This is true of home gardens and of public gardens where we withdraw for a moment of leisure during the day, or of any of those gardens that we enjoy as part of our walks to work, to a shopping mall, or even to a museum; but it is also true of the historic gardens that are visited by tourists during their holidays, even though it is not immediately apparent that these visits belong in the same way to their everyday life. Yet, a visit to a historical garden is usually a vicarious experience of somebody else's life, or at least an entertaining moment of make-believe that enables visitors to paint their own lives in new colors. Gardens are undoubtedly about everyday life, at the same time that they offer moments of aesthetic enjoyment. Paraphrasing Arnold Berleant, garden aesthetics must establish themselves on the basis of artistic activities and aesthetic experiences.[1]

More precisely, gardens allow us to dwell in nature. This is not a definition of gardens since there are all sorts of other amenities that allow us to dwell in nature and would not qualify as gardens, but this provides a horizon of understanding of gardens in general and of the domain opened to the creation of gardens, a domain that it would be as vain to try to enclose in a definition as it would be vain to attempt a precise definition for the other arts.

In fact gardens have changed over the centuries as human societies invented new ways of dwelling in the world and developed new ideas of nature. Roman gardens, in which it was possible to dwell in close contact with the family gods and the gods of nature, belonged to a way of engaging with nature that has disappeared. The monastery gardens belonged to another mode of relation to nature, as did the humanist gardens in Renaissance Italy.

All of these were attached to a single dwelling, but how different the groups of people who lived in these dwellings: a family with its slaves, a single sex community, and an aristocratic court. The same changes can be discovered about the sense of nature for these different groups: nature inhabited by protective gods, nature inhabited by the devil and temptation, and nature as an embodiment of harmony as imagined since Pythagorus. Of course these quick evocations of differences do not attempt to propose a summary of the history of gardens. They only seek to underline that, as societies and the characters and the groups that make them change, the experiences offered by gardens to individuals keep changing.

As we know, during the nineteenth century, after the formidable changes brought to human societies by the creation of political states supposed to be managed according to reason rather than faith, all sorts of new gardens were created: public gardens for general welfare, allotments of villas with a garden to give each homeowner the imaginary pleasure of living in a rural domain, garden-cities to allow each citizen to live in a garden, garden allotments to encourage family virtues in the working classes, spas for comforting the well-to-do, gardens for soothing the mind of hospital patients and visitors, kindergartens for opening children's minds to the world of nature, conspicuous gardens to impress visitors of official buildings, sports fields for bodily improvement, parkways for family leisure, and many more. All of these gardens afforded new types of experiences for the groups that were dwelling there. Much changed during the twentieth century, and we can expect to discover that some contemporary gardens have been created in response to contemporary existential problems or to changing relationships with nature by artists and designers, thus enabling a cultural response to these issues to be articulated by their users, dwellers or visitors. In a word, we want to know whether the creation of gardens has enabled contemporary dwellers to engage in new experiences that prove significant for the present time.

Rather than adopt a systematic approach, we have to engage in different kinds of explorations since we cannot assume that we already know in which domains or with respect to what idea of nature or in the context of what kind of practice gardens would procure new and significant experiences for contemporary dwellers of this world. A number of lingering issues must be open for discussion: what is a garden; what is an aesthetic experience of a garden; what are the significant changes of our times that lead to the creation of gardens or to the introduction of creation in places that make them into new types of gardens; what are the new ways of experiencing gardens that are invited by each contemporary creation; to what extent do these experiences qualify as aesthetic experiences?

Several years ago Pierre Bourdieu noted that there would not be any possible expression of disagreement in public discussion without some shared agreement on contextual matters; in his cryptic use of Latin it became: "no *dissensus* without a prior *consensus*."[2] This applies to the chapters of this book. In order to explore their different understandings of what constitutes a garden or a contemporary garden, and what are the ways of dwelling in nature that emerge in the contemporary world, the authors agreed on three broad conventions that frame most of the chapters. First, they address a single place or a single designer or creator; second, they seek relationships between a contemporary creation and the kinds of experience it was meant for; and third, they turned to an American philosopher, John Dewey, as a possible reference for the study of aesthetic experience.[3] As you will see, each of these conventions has been seriously challenged by at least one of the authors and yet they weave a common background, allowing debates among very different perspectives on garden art to emerge!

Brief Presentation of the Content of the Volume

In the last book he contributed to the development of philosophy in America, John Dewey proposed a new approach of aesthetics starting from an examination of the aesthetic experience rather than the work of art which it addressed. This meant focusing attention on the conditions of reception as well as upon the conditions under which the creator of the work of art responded to his own work as it developed. He proposed that these two aesthetic experiences were comparable:

> For to perceive, a beholder must create his own experience. And his creation must include relations comparable to those which the original producer underwent (…) Without an act of recreation the object is not perceived as a work of art. The artist selected, simplified, clarified, abridged and condensed according to his interest. The beholder must go through these operations according to his point of view and interest. In both, an act of abstraction, that is of extraction of what is significant, takes place. In both, there is comprehension in its literal significance—that is, a gathering together of details and particulars physically scattered into an experienced whole. There is work done on the part of the percipient, as there is on the part of the artist.[4]

This is only a quotation from a book-length approach of aesthetics, but it gives a sense of the discussions of relationships between creation and reception that a common reference to John Dewey would bring to the study of contemporary gardens.[5] It certainly precludes speaking of people experiencing the gardens as mere users, or visitors, since they are exposed to a work that challenges them to respond. I shall call them "patients" in this text since they are not only invited to struggle against the difficulties imposed by the experience, but are called to an epiphany if the aesthetic experience is met with success. Susan Herrington, rather than insist on the mutuality of experience between the designer and an individual patient, lays stress on the reception by a group of elderly dwellers in a residential area of the gardens designed for them to share.

In "When Art is a Garden: Benny Farm Gardens by Claude Cormier," she attempts to demonstrate how Dewey's aesthetic theory provides an instrument for describing and understanding the experience of a garden. In that respect, her text is much more methodological than monographic. She stresses the sensual and emotional beyond any cognitive response that is the hallmark of a garden experience, and underlines the importance of collective appropriation of the garden as a place in the process of aesthetic experience by the dwellers. Relying upon information provided by the 'tenant relations coordinator,' she sees this process as conducive to a socialization of the experience of the garden which allows isolated and alienated elderly people to transform into an active group of neighbors engaging with one another.

The next two chapters show how a mid-twentieth century designer in Japan and a late-twentieth century designer in India engaged in the modernization of their culture while attempting to afford renewed experiences of their past culture to patients engaging with their work. In "The Re-enchantment of the Maegaki residence by Shigemori Mirei," Christian Tschumi presents a garden created in 1955 as an example of a philosophy of garden design that spans the years 1934 to 1975. Mirei, like Cormier, was concerned with the alienation of his contemporaries from nature. He entertained, however, a completely different view of nature, and constructed a personal narrative of the origin of Japanese culture rooted in spiritual encounters with the spirits of nature. His garden art aimed at restoring this relationship according to modern means of expression, such as abstract design, and materials such as concrete or colored gravels. Tschumi introduces us to the variety of people who live in this house and to the different ways they engage with the garden as well as to the variety of directions of interpretation it invites. There is clearly a sense that the garden offers several horizons of interpretation and imposes none. Priyaleen Singh's chapter "Culture, Tradition, and Contemporary Indian Landscape Design: Mohammed Shaheer at Sanskriti Kendra," discloses the alienating impact of materialistic attitudes and picturesque aesthetics upon large city dwellers' experiences of nature in India. She then presents the landscape design of a craftsmen village meant to afford its dwellers and visitors new experiences of nature in the context of a modern facility geared to the development of cultural tourism and contributions of Indian arts and crafts to everyday life. As opposed to Mirei, Shaheer's return to tradition does not proceed from a philosophical interpretation of human relationships to nature, but from a return to ancient practices. This does not imply a return to a supposed essence of Hindu cultural ideas of nature: Shaheer draws upon practices of space-making that includes Moghul as well as ancient Hindu practices. He thinks of Indian culture as highly pluralistic and yet, as in Japan, the resulting place frames all residents' and visitors' experiences in an unusual way without imposing a particular interpretation of these experiences. Craftsmen respond to these experiences in their own work and visitors respond to the experience of place and to the works of craftsmen in an infinite circulation of interpretations and responses. Landscape architecture does not promote a new perspective on nature; it enables people to achieve one. It does not produce messages, but communicative interaction.

Udo Weilacher also presents the dialogue between architecture and nature as a central concern in "The Garden as the Last Luxury Today: Thought Provoking Garden Projects by Dieter Kienast (1945-1998)," and stresses the need for landscape architects to address the disjunction between present Western practices and issues about the relationships of humans to nature. These issues—sustainability, privatization of public spaces, environmental pollution, changing perception of time, image and realities—are altogether different from the issues considered either by Mirei or Shaheer, and yet they led Kienast to seek a return to fundamental perceptions of nature as well. Unlike ecologically-minded landscape architects such as Ian McHarg, he did not want gardens to emulate nature, or landscape architecture to persuade visitors—thanks to the supposed force of living examples—that abandoning nature to itself would solve practical and cultural problems of contemporary societies. He wanted his gardens to defamiliarize the elements—water, earth, plants—and to engage patients' attention into observing nature's processes. He did not want gardens to preach a new faith, or to persuade of the truth value of a new attitude, but like the two preceding designers, he wanted them to open new perspectives for public debate. This is why his designs privileged the fragmentary, the transparent, the unfinished, and instead of expressing a particular viewpoint in his work he made it ambivalent and ambiguous. The theme of ambiguity is even more present in my presentation in the next chapter: "The 'Garden of Seasons' by Bernard Lassus: Coming to Terms with Fleeting Encounters in a Decentered World." In Lassus' gardens for the Colas corporation at Boulogne-Billancourt, garden and architecture engage in a clear dialogue, and yet it is impossible to decide whether it proceeds from deep agreement or ironical challenge. In fact, it proposes an ambiguous experience of the relationships between nature and artifice, real and imaginary, as well as interior and exterior of the corporation domain to stimulate all patients' imaginations. Lassus, like Kienast and even more than Shigemori, calls upon abstraction in order to introduce a source of resistance to the immediate perception of the patient. And, like Shaheer, he creates landscape experiences that stimulate communicative action in a way that is completely embedded in the functions and practices of the corporation for which the gardens are built. The ambiguities of multicultural encounters in this corporation are echoed in the aesthetic experiences of the gardens. Here again the gardens are *opera aperta*.

Peter Jacobs develops the discussion in a completely different context in "Echoes of Paradise: Fernando Chacel's Gardens in the Coastal Plain of Jacarepaguà." We pass from very small European to large Brazilian projects that aim at the reconstruction of coastal mangroves in a rapidly urbanizing area of Rio de Janeiro. Social and ecological tensions, issues of sustainability, loss of a sense of the beauty of the local flora and fauna among city dwellers are some of the tensions to which Chacel attempts to respond. Yet in the same way that Shaheer sees in the traditional craftsmen a creative source of the renewal of culture, he sees the vibrant multicultural diversity of Brazil that fosters a development of its music, arts, and architecture as a force capable of responding creatively to new landscape experiences. Xin Wu provides a further example of a landscape designed to enable its users to develop a sense of place in "Walking through the Crossing: The Draw at Sugar House Park by Patricia Johanson." Even more than Shaheer's or Chacel's landscape, this is a place designed with an obvious urban function, and yet the focus of the design is elsewhere. It enables passers-by and joggers who go through an underground passage to engage in a vicarious experience of the arrival of the founding fathers of the city, the Mormons who entered the Great Salt Lake valley along the creek to which it links. Wu describes the design strategy used by Johanson to capture the attention of park users and lead them in many different ways to engage with the landscape of the whole valley in the distance, and to wonder about the meanings of seemingly unrelated cues that are proposed by the artwork. As in the preceding chapter, the design does not propose a meaning attached to this landscape, or preach a sense of local history, but it creates a situation conducive to debates between local users, some of whom are very concerned with the history of this place. Michael Spens' "The Garden at Portrack Designed and Created by Charles Jencks (1986-2004): Entrapment and Release" introduces a very different approach to garden design and its purpose, even though Jencks proceeds, as the previous designers, from a deep concern with contemporary existential issues. In order to retrieve the harmony of the universe, Jencks turns to scientific descriptions of nature and life. Visitors are challenged to make sense of their emotional responses to a series of visually independent earthworks and gardens within a garden that announces itself as a representation of the cosmos. The question of unity is left for the visitor to decide. Returning to earlier examples of garden design, Spens suggests that Jencks' work explores a new aspect of the sublime, a contemporary sublime.

At this point of the book it is clear that in spite of the differences between the forms of these garden designs, the cultural contexts in which they are set and the scales and functions of the amenities they all provide, they share two important features: they shun didacticism, and they invite their patients to work through an unusual sensual experience. The chapter, "To Make the Stone[s] Stony: Defamiliarization and Andy Goldsworthy's Garden of Stone," by Jacky Bowring, not only proposes an in-depth analysis of the strategy of Andy Goldsworthy to create such an unusual experience leading to a personal meditation, but she uses her own understanding of the methods of defamiliarization advocated by Viktor Shlovsky (1914), a Russian futurist, to give the reader a sense of estrangement in front of images of a project already so well-known that they may fail to capture attention. She agrees with Dewey that such a work of art should call the patient to an existential engagement, but rather than lead to closure, as Dewey proposed, it should leave the patient perplexed, at the edge of a void. Thus her chapter moves from the discussion of the Garden of Stones by Andy Goldsworthy to a defense of a formalist approach to garden design, and to a garden criticism that distances itself from the study of authorial intentions to concentrate on the conditions of reception. In the next chapter Jacques Leenhardt pursues an opposite course in "The Planetary Garden, Garden Unknown: On the Work of Landscaper Gilles Clément." He seeks to reveal through a philosophical analysis of a novel written by Clément, a French landscape architect, how this designer seeks a style of representation, a picture or figure model for twenty-first century gardens, that would provide a bridge between the scientific knowledge of the indivisibility of the earth's ecosystem and cultural representations of local places. The chapter concludes, however, by suggesting that the works of Gilles Clément have not achieved the Idea of a Planetary garden even if they aim, each differently, at realizing it.[6]

Massimo Venturi Ferriolo approaches the debate about the role of contemporary landscape architecture through a different philosophical reflection in his chapter, "Cardada by Paolo Bürgi: The Experience of the Gaze." Cardada in the Apennines is a place through which passes the Insubres line, the fault between the African and European tectonic plates. The whole text is a summation of his experience of this place, of his transportation into the realm of the numinous: a poetical account of the philosophical reflection upon aesthetics that this experience suggested to him. Even if he shares the choice of reflecting upon his personal experience with Bowring, the perspective he brings to landscape appreciation is significantly different. He certainly expects, as she does, that the works of art, the paths, terraces, promontory designed and constructed by Bürgi, will invite contemplation and a sense of standing on the brink of a void; but unlike Bowring's position, he does not expect the works of art to defamiliarize but to bring the patient closer to an understanding, an appropriation of the landscape. And he describes the experience of place as an epiphany through which the patient becomes reunited with the poetic knowledge of nature and time before they were differentiated, without ever losing his foothold on the present time, place and knowledge. In a rather surprising way, even though Ferriolo does not share Dewey's attention for experience as art, he sees the patient's experience as parallel to the creator's experience, inspired by the landscape to draw upon his mastery of techniques, knowledge and artistic skills to express a human relationship to nature that precedes cultural development. The debate about the proper direction of interpretation to be adopted when accounting for the aesthetic experience of a contemporary garden between Spens, Bowring, Leenhardt and Ferriolo reveals different attitudes with respect to the respective roles of cognition and the senses, or science and the visual arts. Stephen Bann broadens the issue in "A 'Garden of the Hesperides:' The Landscape initiative of the Musée Gassendi, Digne, and the National Park of Alpes de Haute-Provence," suggesting that we might ask ourselves whether contemporary gardens achieve a distinctive synthesis between nature and culture, science and the visual arts. His discussion rests upon the idea that landscape is precisely such a synthesis that can be made into a subject for art in painting or gardening. He suggests, as examples, a landscape by Turner which he discusses for painting, and the gardens of Versailles, the sculpture garden of Villa Celle near Pistoia and the Réserve Naturelle Géologique at Digne. Leenhardt would add literature as an art able to present landscape, but Bann's demands for a successful synthesis agrees neither with Leenhardt's nor with Spens'. He sees, like Lassus or Finlay, landscape as inherently heterogeneous and resulting from syntheses that call upon a multiplicity of cultural intentions. In sculptural parks this is pursued by the interventions of multiple artists, but it demands from Bann's perspective that each artist engage in a coherent way with the site, that he transform it into a landscape, not a disconnected set of places, even if each of them displays great aesthetic interest in its own right. Yet it is not the diversity of intentions or their interlacing alone that makes the Réserve into a remarkable contemporary garden, but the bodily engagement of visitors with the whole site, as Bann clearly demonstrates in a study of the refuges built by Goldsworthy, displacing Ferriolo's stress from the gaze to the whole body.

There is, beyond any doubt, a renewal of garden design and a renewed intensity of critical debate about contemporary garden art. Is there also a renewal of garden aesthetics? Or in other terms, do contemporary gardens contribute to the creation of new aesthetic experiences or do they simply pursue the exploration of the aesthetic of the beautiful, the sublime, the picturesque or the gardenesque in new forms and situations? There is a general agreement among the presentations about the renewal of aesthetic experiences afforded by gardens as can be gauged by the debate about the appropriate relationships to be sought among nature culture and science in contemporary gardens. Yet such a simple observation begs another question, maybe more elementary: what is an aesthetic experience of a garden? Unless we can answer this question, there is little hope for a critical discussion of garden reception—that is, of the aesthetic experiences afforded by gardens to diverse people—and even less hope for a history of garden reception.

The Aesthetic Experience of a Garden

Each chapter presents different aspects of a garden experience and I shall not try to propose a conclusion, but rather a personal synthesis of these points of view. I think that the definition of an aesthetic experience of a garden is a question open for debate. As a whole, this book suggests to me a new set of assumptions that may help to understand how garden art differs in some profound respects from art that is presented in museums, and how gardens contribute to cultural debates at present.

It is difficult to present and analyze the experience of a garden. Even if artists intend to procure a new kind of experience they do so by layering it upon other intentions about the materials they work with, the history of their art, and the physical and cultural context of their creation. All of the intentions that contribute to the making of the artwork have to be unfolded before the new experience the artist seeks to bring about can be meaningfully presented. This makes my own reading of the presentation of garden experiences in these chapters tentative, at best, and I shall present it as a group of five assumptions. Dewey's perspective was a great help in structuring some of the presentations, but I do not wish to adopt his point of view without reservation. First, I shall stress the importance of the anticipation that we bring to any experience, as a pre-condition to any perception of the world, and as a limitation to achieving new experiences: any perception is framed by a particular horizon of perception that anticipated the perception itself.

Assumption One: *The importance of framing*
Edgar Allan Poe brilliantly made the point I am trying to raise in the story of the *Purloined Letter.*[7] As you remember, the Prefect of the Parisian Police assumed that the Minister had hidden the letter in his house, and that it would not escape scientific examinations—with the help of a microscope—of any possible hiding place in the house. The Perfect failed, however. Dupin, who later found the letter in plain view in "a trumpery filigree card-rack of pasteboard, that hung dangling by a dirty

blue ribbon, from a little brass knob" explained that the Prefect had mistakenly anticipated the kind of person the Minister was. The Prefect acted in a most thorough manner, "but says Dupin, he perpetually errs by being too deep or too shallow, for the matter in hand." Instead, Dupin himself adopted a different perspective, a different frame of mind, if you will, according to which "the Minister had resorted to the comprehensive and sagacious expedient of not attempting to conceal it at all." Whereas the horizon of expectations of the Prefect enabled him to pursue a thorough search of the Minister's home, but led his experiences of search to failure, the horizon of expectations of Dupin lead his own experience to a very satisfactory closure. The horizon of expectation, whether unreflectively embraced or willingly adopted, is crucial to the success of an experience.

Assumption Two: *Garden experience is a process*
Wu, in her presentation of Johanson's design strategy, has insisted on the way her work of art calls attention to itself and then leads to a shift towards engagement with nature. Thus, the jogger's ordinary experience of running through a passageway from the shopping mall to a public park leads him first into an exploration of the work of art out of curiosity. It eventually leads to immersion in the contemplation of nature, which will enable him later to engage in reflection about the whole experience with others. Thus we are presented with a succession of experiences that have different objects. My own presentation also highlighted the passage between the attention for the social event of a cocktail party and the attention for some conundrums posed by the artwork in the garden, and then the passage to a moment of reflection with others on the validity of multiple perspectives brought to the interpretation of the same object. Further examples were provided by Jacobs on the gardens of the coastal plain of the Jacarepaguà by Chacel. The aesthetic experience of a garden appears, as Dewey would have it, as a process with a beginning and an end, during which the patient experiences suffering or tries to overcome a difficulty. This is underlined by Weilacher with the "thought-provoking gardens" by Kienast, or by Bann's analysis of the challenges set by by Goldsworthy's nine refuges to visitors of the Réserve. Certainly Ferriolo insists upon "the intelligibility of the whole in a single glance" but he also refers to a full day's experience on site starting with a cable car ascent followed by a series of explorations on foot, and he presents a very sophisticated reflection on the content of this experience, allowing moments of transcendence within the scope of a longer experiential duration.

Assumption Three: *Bodily engagement and resistance are central to the development of the process*[8]
Bürgi's Cardada, presented by Ferriolo, invites great contrasts in the bodily experiences it affords between the passive transportation in the funicular, the active exploration of nature by all the senses under the cover of woods, and the exposure to the open panorama severed in two by its invisible fault. Leenhardt also reminds us of the body's fundamental importance in the initiatory experience of Thomas garden by the scholarly traveler, the Voyager, in Clément's novel: "Each blade offered itself up to being received or stroked, crushed, pushed back, brushed over or halted; each behaved differently on me, on my body, and sometimes I put my hand there to get a better understanding—to get closer to the encounter." Wu underlines that it is through the body as a kinesthetic sensor that Johanson's linear gardens can be experienced. Bann stresses the bodily effort that has to be overcome before the *Ferme Belon*, this work of art that incidentally celebrates the idea of resistance from four perspectives: historical, political, geological, and aesthetic. The mayor resisted the use of a place that embosomed memory of the local *Resistance* during WWII, and: "The way up the hillside traverses an area where the ground has the consistency of a dark sand, hard to walk upon and dramatically molded into wave-like shapes by erosion." Many points of view can be brought

to the experience of this construction by Goldsworthy in the mountain, but all of them bring the body of the visitor into the foreground. This is also made visible in the stills taken out of a video of Mirei raking the garden of the Maegaki residence reproduced by Tschumi in his chapter. The cultural distance to Japan allows us to see, in this case, to what extent the body is made of cultural flesh. This raking is neither an artistic gesture, nor the pursuit of an artistic form; it is the transformation of the self-centered body into a self-less instrument through which the spiritual energy of nature gives form to the abstract waves that the rake breaks into the sand. This is precisely the cultural distance to ourselves through an awareness of our bodily engagement in the world that Shaheer's or Lassus' works are inviting. The experience of a garden makes this more likely when it has achieved the estrangement that Bowring has skillfully analyzed in another work by Goldsworthy in New York City, even though she does not call attention to the bodily experience that echoes the sense of the stoniness of the stones, or the lightness of stones and visitors' bodies on the cantilevered terrace of the museum.

Fig. 1. Lullaby Garden, courtesy of Cao/Perrot studio

I should include here a mention of the works of two garden artists who attended the symposium and whose work was discussed: Dan Graham and Andy Cao. The garden works of Dan Graham are most conducive to reflection upon the experience of a garden since they invite the visitor to critically observe both the frame that one brings to a situation and the

Fig. 2. Vortex in Lullaby Garden, courtesy of Cao Perrot studio

trappings of representation that ensnare one's own relationship to the world.[9] One could also build upon another aspect of Dan Graham's works: the way they highlight the impossibility for the visitor to divorce his body from the experience of the place. Maaretta Jaukkuri in her presentation of "No Title," a mirror room set in the landscape of the Lofoten islands by Dan Graham, quotes a local girl's remarks: "What is extraordinary about the sculpture is the special glass that makes you look very fat close up, whilst you look very thin from a distance. If you remove yourself from the mirror, the mountain takes on a completely unbelievable shape, and if you are so lucky that you see the sun at the same time, it becomes even better."[10] Cao's work at Cornerstone, in Sonoma, California, "Lullaby Garden" invites visitors to remove their shoes and walk on undulating waves of monofilament carpet hand knit by sixty villagers in Vietnam.[11] (Fig. 1) A dark vortex beckons with the gentle music of Vietnamese lullaby. (Fig. 2) It takes "the visitor on a journey over golden field and into ocean waves that draw one deeper toward a dark whirlpool emanating soft Vietnamese lullabies,"[12] bringing him from ear to toe in contact with the Vietnamese women who spun those sheets. As in the case of the young teenager looking at herself and the mountain in "No Title" the sense of being wrapped up in these sheets between the voice and the hands of Vietnamese women may bring a certain sense of unease that conflicts with the pleasures of the whole experience.

A brief step further, the gardens we live in, near our home, with their pleasant places and familiar plants, would be very dull indeed if nature were not constantly destabilizing our expectations, challenging our willingness to resist her choice of weeds, deceiving our expectations of eternal life of the trees, or producing extraordinary blooms, fleeting moments of sensual bliss. The gardens by contemporary artists that were presented here differ mostly from these in their capacity to bring us face to face with the unexpected, and to destabilize our expectations of bodily engagement with our environment. They resist our temptation to take nature for granted. Bowring's parallel between the stones of Magritte and Goldsworthy did not establish a line of descent from surrealism that he denied, but rather the equal power of destabilization of bodily references that resides in Magritte's and Goldsworthy's works. All of these points seem to specify Dewey's model of interpretation for garden experiences by stressing the bodily engagement of the patient with the materiality of the garden, confirming the distinction between the art work that issues from the hands of its creators and the art that resides in the experience of the art work.

Assumption Four: *There is a dialectical relationship between experiences of everyday life and aesthetic experiences of gardens*
Contrary to Dewey's point of view, the acknowledgement of the cultural perspective inscribed in the body itself calls into question the universality of the language of art that he envisaged, and, more importantly, there is no continuity between an experience of everyday life and the aesthetic experience, but rather a discontinuity, a change of frame. It is only when the patient follows the example of Dupin rather than the stubbornness of the Prefect of the Parisian Police that he or she may take the path towards an aesthetic experience. This calls to mind Martin Heidegger's position about the radical difference between an everyday experience and an aesthetic experience.[13] David Marie points out how obvious Heidegger thought this difference was since we go to the museum to engage in aesthetic experiences, and elsewhere for everyday experiences.[14] Heidegger thought precisely to reveal a fundamental difference between the experience of an ordinary thing in everyday life and the aesthetic experience of a work of art.[15] And yet the presentations at this symposium belie the approach proposed by Heidegger. This should not be too surprising, since going into a garden is not going to a museum. The aesthetic experience of a garden is not reached by suspending any expectation to become immersed in the object, or to share in the flesh of the world as Maurice Merleau-Ponty proposed in a complement to Heidegger, but rather by relinquishing the horizon of expectation with which one came into the garden and framing attention towards new objects. Thus these aesthetic garden experiences follow a process that neither Dewey nor Heidegger, nor Merleau-Ponty envisaged.

Yet the experience comes to a closure only when we come back through a further change of horizon of expectation to the world of everyday life. This is what makes the aesthetic experiences of the gardens of Mirei, Cormier, or Shaheer seemingly so difficult to disentangle from experiences of everyday life. They can be enjoyed daily and thus bring a new horizon of understanding to everyday life through an endless number of cycles between experiences of daily activities and garden experiences, demonstrating the importance of the embedding of aesthetic experiences of gardens in everyday life. Other garden experiences for which this cycle takes a longer time seem to evince more clearly the importance of the mediation of exchange with others.

Assumption Five: *Garden experiences contribute to cultural changes*
Even when the discovery of a garden is a solitary affair, garden experiences come to a closure through interaction with other persons in a joint effort to come to terms with the meaning or the value of the process of discovery of the garden as a whole. The gardens by Johanson, Kienast and Lassus seem to lead to the establishment of a shared frame of interpretation that results

from the confrontation of perspectives between parties who have undergone different experiences of the garden and tried to come to terms with them. It issues into a process of communicative action that yields a tentative frame of interpretation shared by a group of persons. So, garden art seems to be open to the production of new modes of engagement with the world. It seems true for Chacel as well. Jacobs has called attention, however, to the difference between the frame of the experience of nature that results from the gardens of Chacel and the kind of experience of nature from which Chacel himself proceeds. Chacel does not expect the general interpretation of the presence of beautiful tropical plants on the coastal fringes of the city to lead to the kind of ecological knowledge he puts into practice, but rather to new cultural attitudes towards nature. Which ones? This is a question he leaves to be answered by future historians, because the achievement of new cultural attitudes towards Brazilian nature calls into play the interactions of cultural, social and political life in the city, and this is neither within the power of his will nor open to prediction. The same emphasis on both the openness of garden reception and its importance in the dynamics of cultural changes is foregrounded in Leenhardt's presentation of Clément's work, or Weilacher's presentation of Kienast's gardens.

Contrary to studies in critical reception of literature,[16] we cannot expect the reception to be solely determined by formal qualities of the gardens, in spite of the eloquent plea for a return to formalism by Bowring. Two important mediations prevent this mechanical relationship to prevail: the cultural body that imposes its own perspectives towards gardens, and the dynamics of cultural change that impinge upon the framing of garden experiences. This critical relativism does not mean that the works of art are irrelevant to the course of cultural change, but it locates their relevance in the directions of cultural exploration that they open for the contemporary world rather than in the cultural changes that they achieve. This is an important distinction in an age where planning attempts—predicated upon the anticipation of cultural attitudes, by institutions and commercial interests—frame almost every aspect of our active lives.

So the discussion of aesthetic experiences of gardens has led many speakers to highlight the embedding of these experiences within developments of everyday life, and the importance of bodily engagement with nature in the garden. Moreover, several of them called upon art and cultural history in order to sustain their analysis of contemporary garden experiences, encouraging us to see the contemporary world as part of a long history and to look to history again to understand the present. This demonstrates large differences between contemporary garden art and art presented in the museum world: it also explains why the experience of the representation of gardens in museums is altogether different from any garden experience. This vindicates a singular place for the art of gardens in present and future societies.

A Fundamental Return to Local Place

The irrepressible urge to move experienced by humans since immemorial times has always contributed to the circulation of persons, ideas and artifacts. The present trend towards economic globalization may seem to be just another instance of this phenomenon. Yet it may be more than a mere acceleration of Western colonization that started with the great European voyages around the world. The development of global fashion, crazes for music, films, garments, make-up, architecture, cars, computers, and video games, introduce an ever growing number of people to a tension between the idiosyncrasies of local culture in which they were born and the world culture of everyday life and fantasies into which they are drawn by newly invented collective desires. It is a world where disembodied communication challenges our notions of time and distance, and the growing circulation of representation in everyday life seems to threaten our ability to distinguish between virtual and real worlds.

Many works in the institutional world of art explore virtual worlds either because they exploit new forms of expression, such as computer and video art, or because they are committed to the development of an art world detached from any tie to other domains of culture or praxis. To the contrary, most gardens presented during this symposium aim at providing a renewed experience of the material world, a bodily engagement of place, and a sense of being rooted in local specificities and practices. This is not true, however, of all the works presented in this book. We should be cautious not to give the illusion of agreement when instead we are observing innovative explorations. The presentation of the Garden of Stones by Bowring suggests a strong link to the Museum of Jewish Heritage in Manhattan, but it seems that it could have been in another city, or in another country without any of its qualities of *ostranenie* being modified. In a similar way, the garden of Portrack presented by Spens proposes innovative land forms that seem to depend entirely on metaphors of contemporary science and not at all on local specificities of the Scottish landscape at Portrack. These two gardens are nevertheless profoundly different from one another, and they serve to remind us of the diversity of contemporary garden art. The other works discussed in this book, however, share concerns for a fundamental return to local place that can only be outlined here. An example may be helpful. Johanson's garden presented by Wu may seem at first sight to call upon figures—the Sego-lily and the rattle snake—arbitrarily imposed upon the ground. Yet we learn that both figures are condensations of memories of the arrival of the Mormons into the Great Salt Lake valley precisely through the same river bed where the project is located, of this region ecology and of its canyon landscape, and that they respond to the erasure of these memories by urban growth. Thus the figures so patent on the drawings for the project are camouflaged on the built site, demanding, in order to be revealed, close attention to details of the sculptures by walkers and joggers, a free play of their imagination, and exchanges of opinions between them and local inhabitants keen about the history of the creek. The landscape project demands a bodily engagement with local meanings aimed at changing current attitudes of urban dwellers who live there. Two hundred meters away from its site it would be out of place, merely decorative, and it would loosen its potential grip on the mind. In these projects, a renewed experience of the material world is clearly evidenced in the attention for water, stone, gravel, concrete, wood or metal as in the works of Shigemori, Shaheer, Johanson, Kienast, Lassus, Bürgi and Goldsworthy; as well in the attention for plant material in Cormier, Shaheer, Johanson, Lassus, Clément, and Chacel. This attention to material is meant to lead to experiences of bodily engagement. These engagements can take many different forms: exploration of the large planters in Cormier's project; or communicative interaction between residents or members of an institution as in a Kienast project; ritual practices and appropriation of traditional uses of thresholds between interior and exterior spaces in Shaheer; aporetic debates between members of an international group in Lassus; contemplation and meditation at La Cardada by Bürgi; efforts at bringing together contradictory impressions at Digne such as pain and delight during the walk, light and darkness in the refuges, geological evidence and irony about the willingness to accept facts as science. They respond to all sorts of contemporary issues that impinge upon the present, including transformations of relationships between humans and nature and the difficulties of establishing a multicultural world. Almost all of these projects are concerned with links between the past and the present, albeit in very different ways. This is obvious for the projects concerned with aesthetic experiences of geologic times, but it is as true of the projects by Cormier or Clément so deeply involved with the passage of seasons. Of course these are two completely different ideas of time. Shaheer's attention for the long time association of Hindu literature and myth and trees reaches for still another conception of time, quite different from Lassus' play with the history of modern architecture and municipal gardening. Johanson's project is involved with local history, and Mirei with myth and garden history. There is no unity among these contemporary gardens in the forms of time with which people are invited to engage, but we should see that time is ever present as a possible source of artistic and poetic intervention on nature. It always ties more deeply the bodily experience of material and local place to personal lives, anchoring them in the diversity of not only materials but also temporalities of the world. In all of these respects, garden art develops in directions of its own, unrelated to concerns of the institutional art world, and it contributes to a renewal of significance of our being in the world. Is it against the museum world? I do not think so. It is defiant only in its claim to be elsewhere—or everywhere—and still an art.

NOTES

[1] The perspectives proposed here owe much more to Arnold Berleant than can be mentioned in footnotes.
Arnold Berleant, *Art and Engagement*, (Philadelphia: Temple University Press, 1991). The source of the paraphrase is at the top of page 3.

[2] Pierre Bourdieu and Jean Claude Passeron, *Reproduction: In Education, Society, and Culture*, translated by Richard Nice, with a foreword by Tom Bottomore (London & Beverly Hills: Sage Publications, 1977).

[3] John Dewey, *Art as experience* (New York: Perigee Books, 1980, c 1934).

[4] Dewey, *Art as experience,* 54.

[5] Further analysis of John Dewey's ideas by Thomas M. Alexander also served as shared reference. Thomas M. Alexander, *John Dewey's Theory of Art, Experience & Nature, the Horizons of Feeling* (New York: State University of New York Press, 1987).

[6] Readers who are disappointed not to find in this chapter a detailed criticism of a particular work by Gilles Clément may find a thorough analysis of the Parc Citroën, evoked in this chapter, by a well trained landscape designer and botanist in Dagennais, Danielle, "The Garden of Movement: Ecological Rhetoric in Support of Gardening Practice," *Journal of Garden and Designed Landscapes*, Vol 24, #4, 2004 (313-340).

[7] Quoted from: Edgar Allan Poe, *Eleonora, The Fall of the House of Usher & The Purloined Letter.* Vol X, Part 3. Harvard Classics Shelf of Fiction. (New York: P.F. Colllier & Son, 1917). http://www.bartleby.com/ebook/adobe/3103.pdf

[8] These ideas are repeatedly expressed in *Art as Experience*. See for instance: "But in art the resistance encountered enters into the work in a more immediate way than in science. The perceiver as well as the artist has to perceive, meet, and overcome problems; otherwise, appreciation is transient and overweighed with sentiment. For, in order to perceive aesthetically, he must remake his past experiences so that they can enter integrally into a new pattern. He cannot dismiss his past experiences nor can he dwell upon them as they have been in the past." (Dewey, *Art as experience*, 138)

[9] See in particular the last chapter, "Garden as Theater as Museum," of Dan Graham's *Rock My Religion*, 1993, and the book on his works published by Phaidon (Pelzer et al, 2001). Dan Graham, *Rock My Religion, writings and art projects, 1965-1990*, edited by Brian Wallis (Cambridge: MIT press, 1993). Birgit Pelzer, Mark Francis, Beatriz Colomina, *Dan Graham,* (London : New York : Phaidon, 2001)

[10] Lene Kristin Westeng, Marie Aga Jørgensen, Tine Hansen quoted in Maaretta Jaukkuri, *Artscape Nordland* (Nordland county: Forlaget Press, 2001) (120)

[11] The Lullaby Garden by Andy Cao & Xavier Perrot, Cao|Perrot Studio.

[12] Quoted from http://www.cornerstonegardens.com/pages/cao.htm (January 30, 2006).

[13] The discussion here follows that analysis of relationships between everyday experience and aesthetic experience in Heidegger and Merleau-Ponty by David Marie. David Marie, *Expérience quotidienne et experience esthétique chez Heidegger et Merleau-Ponty, L'inattendu* (Paris: L'Harmattan, 2002).

[14] Marie discusses Heidegger's analysis of relationships between everyday and aesthetic experience in part II "Phénoménologies de l'expérience esthétique" (109-143). His discussion refers mostly to 'The Origin of the Work of Art' in Martin Heidegger, *Off the Beaten Track,* (Cambridge, Mass: Cambridge University Press, 2002).

[15] This calls for a long discussion of Martin Heidegger, *What is a thing?* Translated by W. B. Barton, Jr., and Vera Deutsch, with an analysis by Eugene T. Gendlin (Chicago, H. Regnery Co., 1968, c1967).

[16] See Hans Robert Jauss, *Toward an aesthetic of reception,* translation from German by Timothy Bahti; introduction by Paul de Man.(Minneapolis: University of Minnesota Press, c1982) and my own discussion of his ideas with respect to studies of garden reception in Conan, Michel (ed.) *Baroque Garden Cultures, Emulation, Sublimation, Subversion,* (Washington D.C.: Dumbarton Oaks, 2005) (17-19).

Contemporary Garden Aesthetics, Creations and Interpretations

Contemporary Garden Aesthetics, Creations and Interpretations

Contemporary Garden Aesthetics, Creations and Interpretations

Contemporary Garden Aesthetics, Creations and Interpretations

When Art Is a Garden: Benny Farm by Claude Cormier

Susan Herrington

Emerging from the fertile debate surrounding John Dewey's pragmatism are his theories of aesthetic experience denoting where art is attended and the effects produced in the experience. This paper charts these theories and how they are evident in gardens designed by Claude Cormier for elderly veterans at Benny Farm in Montreal. Cormier belongs to a new generation of designers who are reinstating landscape architecture as a practice responsive to other contemporary art forms. His temporary and permanent garden designs have consistently challenged us with both how gardens look and the experiences they invite.

His temporary work, like Blue Stick Garden at Jardins de Métis in Quebec (2000) and resurrected at Hestercombe Gardens in England (2004), confronts with optics the privileged status of sensorial perception experienced in herbaceous border gardens. Upon entering Blue Stick Garden one is enclosed in a field of blue painted garden stakes "planted" to define the walls of an outdoor room (Fig. 1). The reduced pallet of mass-produced wooden stakes in repetition evokes experiences with minimalist sculpture with its enchanting quality of manyness. Likewise, the readymade nature of the stakes, common garden elements used for the practical purpose of supporting vegetative life, when painted blue and planted en masse, are redeemed as transformative elements. Their slender, identically shaped forms serve as the compositional device, while their sheer number physically encloses the space, offering only glimpses out to the surrounding landscape. When one turns around to leave, however, the garden magically changes to orange because the fourth unseen sides of the stakes are painted orange (Fig. 2). The optical effects in this garden are visually different from the herbaceous border garden, yet the experiences and feelings prompted by both gardens are strikingly similar. Both herbaceous gardens and Blue Stick link color changes with perceptual and emotive states (Fig. 3-6). The aesthetic experience offered by Blue Stick Garden conveys how subtle manipulations of visual phenomena as well as the position of the viewer can cause a misinterpretation of the physical scene. An awe-inspiring work, it draws into question not only the materials used to create gardens, but the important role they play in eliciting feelings of amazement and joy.

The garden as an experience and experience as an art is a central feature to Cormier's permanent gardens as well. Cormier's designs for the Nissan Design Creative Studios courtyards in Detroit and the Montreal Convention Centre Winter Garden have been awarded for their emphatic quest to elicit experiences of surprise, enchantment, and humor in the daily lives

1. Entering the Blue Stick Garden at Jardins de Métis in Quebec (2000) (photo: Claude Cormier Architectes Paysagistes, Inc.)

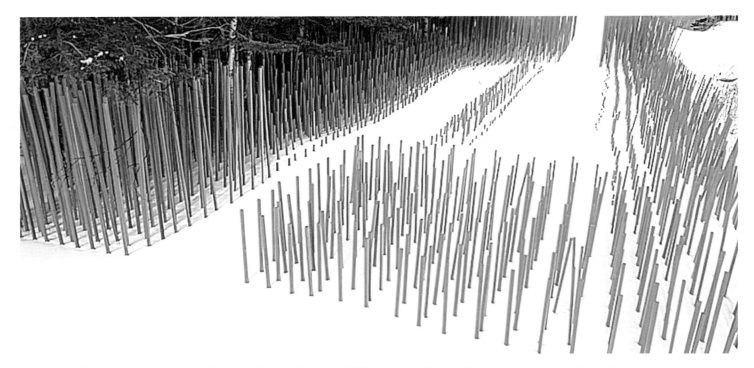

2. Exiting Blue Stick Garden at Jardins de Métis in Quebec (2000) (photo: Claude Cormier Architectes Paysagistes, Inc.)

3. Blue Stick Garden at Jardins de Métis in Quebec (2000) (photo: Claude Cormier Architectes Paysagistes, Inc.)

4. Blue Stick Garden at Jardins de Métis in Quebec (2000) (photo: Claude Cormier Architectes Paysagistes, Inc.)

5. The herbaceous border garden by Elsie Reford Jardins de Métis in Quebec (photo: Reford Gardens)

6. Looking past Gertrude Jekyll's and Sir Edwin Lutyens's garden to Blue Stick resurrected at Hestercombe, England (2004) (photo: Claude Cormier Architectes Paysagistes, Inc.)

of people (Fig. 7–8). Yet a relatively unknown project by the flamboyant landscape architect is his garden design at Benny Farm. Built in 2002–2005 for elderly veterans in a newly renovated housing project, Cormier's gardens subscribe to a growing oeuvre that reveals a set of aesthetic experiences important to understanding the role of gardens in contemporary society. The gardens' location in subsidized housing for the elderly reflects Dewey's concern for where art should be experienced. Likewise, the effects produced in the experience of these gardens points to provocative ways in which the garden can enhance social interaction and offer unique aesthetic experiences unattainable by experiences with other art forms. The following describes the Benny Farm project and Cormier's design in reference to Dewey's theories pertaining to where and when art works, socialness in aesthetic experience, and resistance and expectation in aesthetic experience. It accounts for the aesthetic experiences that

7. Nissan Design Creative Studios courtyards in Detroit (photo: Claude Cormier Architectes Paysagistes, Inc.)

Benny Farm gardens avail, finding them exemplary of art when it is a garden.

Dewey: Where and When Art Works

In *Art as Experience,* Dewey advocates that aesthetic experiences can be embedded in daily life from practices of work to casual recreation. For Dewey the relegation of art to museums coupled with the "gulf between producer and consumer in modern society operates to create also a chasm between ordinary and esthetic experience."[1] This is one of Dewey's major contributions to understanding art when it is a garden. Locating aesthetic perception outside the museum walls enables art to reach more people and shape interests that are instrumental to their daily lives, but it also expands the types of works to be considered aesthetic experiences. Likewise, Dewey's observation of "the gulf between producer and consumer" underscores his critique of modern consumer society in the early twentieth century. Echoing other critics of modern consumerism, such as Walter Benjamin and Peter Bürger, Dewey is troubled by the modernist project whereby authors, producers, and consumers are alienated, and the material conditions fabricated from this alienation serve only to represent and reinforce this disjuncture. In contrast to European critics who concluded that trapped within the clutches of modern consumer society art could be reintegrated into daily life only as propaganda or fetishized commodity, Dewey envisioned an immersion of modern society in art through experience.

At the heart of Dewey's connection between experience and art is his theory of when art works. "The product of art—temple, painting, statue, poem is not the work of art. The work of art takes place when a human being cooperates with the product so that the outcome is an experience."[2] Here art works, not by its success or failure as an object or mimesis, but in its ability to contribute to an experience. Dewey's cultural praxis that values art in everyday life and human experiences with art, over art's achievement as a material object sequestered in a museum, unlocks where and when aesthetic experiences can

8. Montreal Lipstick Garden in Montreal (photo: Claude Cormier Architectes Paysagistes, Inc.)

happen. This praxis includes gardens, which have been primarily appreciated outside the institutionalized art world during the twentieth century. As we know, Dewey's pragmatist aesthetics contradicted the course charted for art theory and appreciation, which privileges the autonomous art object in the museum. By the mid-twentieth century many of Dewey's ideas were rejected by philosophers and the art world. Furthermore the understanding of art when it was an outdoor experience was relegated to nature appreciation and later environmental aesthetics. These movements are largely concerned with nature or gardens as manifestations of nature. Subsequently, studies of human engagement with outdoor environments have been approached as scientific enterprises based on preference questionnaires and consensus building, leaving the garden as an imaginative endeavor behind.

The consequences of ignoring Dewey are not only felt in the exclusion of gardens from the institutionalized art world, but when art is excluded from daily life. Richard Shusterman contends that the removal of aesthetic experiences from everyday life also implies the "dismal assumption that ordinary life is necessarily one of joyless unimaginative coercion" and "provides the powers and institutions structuring our everyday lives with the best excuse for their increasingly brutal indifference to natural human needs for the pleasures of beauty and imaginative freedom."[3] This rationale is precisely what made the lifeless

9. Figure/ground diagram of Benny Farm in context (Claude Cormier Architectes Paysagistes, Inc.)

10. Evolution of Benny Farm (Claude Cormier Architectes Paysagistes, Inc)

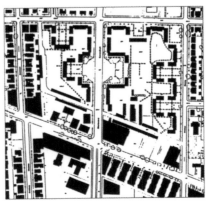

1947

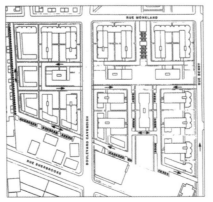

1992

institutional environments, criticized by Jane Jacobs, the necessary counterpart to public housing designed in North America during the second half of the twentieth century. In essence "housing" is the apex of everyday life, so why should it need to offer aesthetic experiences? It is for this reason that gardens in social housing should offer aesthetic experience, and why the Benny Farm gardens signal emergent contributions of the garden in contemporary existence.

Benny Farm

The Benny Farm housing complex was first built between 1946 and 1947 in Notre-Dame-de-Grâce, southwest of downtown Montreal. Known for its farms, which thrived on the land's fertile soil and flowing creeks, Notre-Dame-de-Grâce was by the 1930s a bustling Montreal neighborhood. Covering eighteen acres (approximately seven hectares), Benny Farm was created to house World War II veterans. Like many North American experiments in social housing, several blocks of nineteenth- and early-twentieth-century housing and an ornamental farm were removed to accommodate the modern project (Fig. 9). The fifty-two housing structures that comprise the original Benny Farm exhibit the hallmark features of modern garden–city landscape planning. These features include low uniform buildings clustered at the edges of the site, framing a series of unused courtyards replete with grass and low-maintenance plantings, and scattered islands of playground equipment and

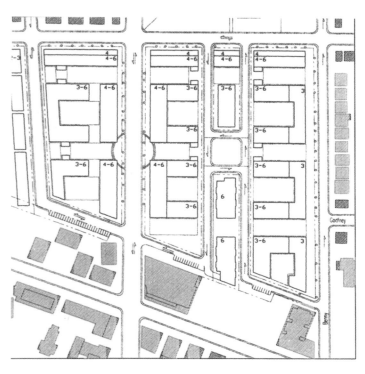

1997

2003

swaths of parking interjected throughout the site. Translated and modified from its European origins to North America, the ideas rendered by garden-city plans like Benny Farm aimed to create ample open space for its residents. Thus, the role ascribed to the "garden" in many North America garden-city schemes was primarily spatial. Although this is a subtle distinction, the failure to create gardens, for pleasure and utility, in these developments has contributed to the demise of these complexes. By the 1990s, Benny Farm had a high vacancy rate, and its open spaces were neglected and unused. The Canadian government sold Benny Farm to the Canada Lands Company. In 1994 Canada Lands was given approval to demolish and sell a part of Benny Farm and use the financial gain to renovate twenty-three of the

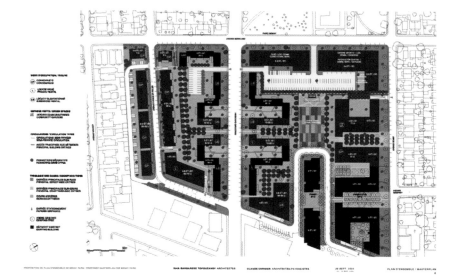

11. Evolution of Benny Farm (Claude Cormier Architectes Paysagistes, Inc.)
12. Benny Farm master plan showing gardens, paths, circular planting areas, and *petites forêts* (Claude Cormier Architectes Paysagistes, Inc.)

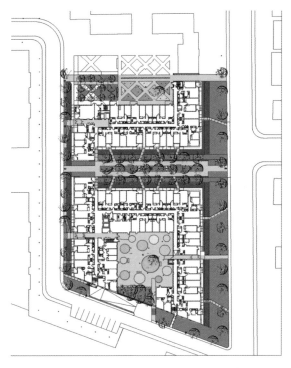

13. Benny Farm garden courtyard plan (Claude Cormier Architectes Paysagistes, Inc.)

14. Benny Farm entrance allée.

existing buildings to accommodate seniors, young families in financial need, people with limited mobility, and single mothers. Four renovated structures and two courtyards were set aside for the remaining veterans to inhabit.

Montreal design teams Daoust Lestage, Le Consortium Atelier BRAQ/Atelier in situ, Saia et Barbarese architectes/Claude Cormier architectes paysagistes, and L'OEUF (L'Office de l'éclectisme urbain et fonctionnel) were selected to produce master plans and first-phase design proposals for the renovation of Benny Farm. The project goals mandated by the Canada Lands Company focused on social programming and integration of Benny Farm within the existing neighborhood, leaving questions of physical form and conceptual direction up to the designers. The winner, Saia et Barbarese/Claude Cormier was the only team to focus on the emotional needs of the veterans who would be displaced during the construction process and then relocated to the renovated buildings on site (Fig. 11-12). In fact, they were the only team to include gardens for the elderly veterans as part of the master plan (Fig. 12).

Cormier's team was also unique in using contained perennial plants and landscape elements such as trees and accessible paths to remedy way-finding problems caused by the 1940s scheme. Furthermore, they designed these landscape and garden features as the core experience with Benny Farm and the heart of communal interaction.[4] While maintaining the garden-city layout, Claude Cormier's scheme entails a network of interlocking pathways connecting structures to courtyards to parking and out to the surrounding neighborhood. He also proposed 400 new trees, reminiscent of the previous orchard on the nineteenth-century site, eighteen garden courtyards, a central community garden, and thirty-five *petites forêts*—circular planters containing flowering perennial plants and wild grasses. In 2004, forty-eight veterans moved into the completed first phase of development. The first phase included not only the renovated structures, but also two courtyard gardens, an entrance allée, and a community garden (Fig. 13-15). The courtyard gardens are of particular interest here. Many shared courtyards in post–World War II North American garden-city housing complexes have evolved into problematic "fish bowls" that are rarely used and enjoyed.[5] The following distills how Cormier's specific redesign for the courtyards responds to this predicament.

The Garden in the Garden-City

The garden courtyards are distinguished by a series of circular planting areas, the *petites forêts*. There is no attempt to mask the act of design here. Rather, the disarmingly simple forms bustling with the splendor of life confront people and raise expectations of an imaginative encounter. Reinforcing Dewey's emphasis on art in everyday life and on the human

15. Pathways connect garden courtyards at Benny Farm.

experience with art, Cormier's courtyard gardens are the experiential imperative of the housing's organizational scheme. The apartments have at-grade doorways and windows opening up onto the gardens, where veterans experience an intensity of light and shadow, smells, colors, textures, as well as seating. Upper-story units have large windows and balconies that look onto the gardens as well. It could be argued that Benny Farm merely addresses a growing societal need to house the elderly respectfully and that the concept of garden serves as a leitmotif echoing the nostalgic theme of farm as housing complex. Yet it is Cormier's specific design for the gardens that brings into existence a set of valuable aesthetic experiences that lend gravity to the role of the garden in life and its potential for philosophical inquiry.

According to Allen Carlson, a key reason why outdoor environments lost their importance as a subject of philosophical inquiry in the twentieth century was the absence of a designing intellect in the features of these environments.[6] Although historically gardens have been an object of aesthetic interest, and a central interest during the eighteenth century, twentieth-century aesthetics catered almost exclusively to the fine arts of painting, sculpture, music, poetry, and to some extent architecture. These are works that invite an "emotionally and cognitively rich engagement with a cultural artifact, intentionally created by a designing intellect, informed by both art-historical traditions and art-critical practices, and deeply embedded in a complex, many facet art-world."[7] Although gardens can certainly entice these experiences, many North American art critics and philosophers of art ignored gardens as a subject of inquiry. Gardens were aligned with disinterestedness whereby a concern with their purpose and the pleasures they offered was replaced by their role as a representation of nature. Although modern era gardens by Isamu Noguchi, Ian Hamiliton Finlay, and Bernard Lassus contribute to the arts, the conception of gardens as manifestations of a designing intellect informed by art-critical practices was overlooked by much of the institutionalized art world.[8]

By the 1970s artists like Michael Heizer, Robert Smithson, and Mary Miss began to explore territory outside the museum's walls. Recalling Dewey's pragmatics, conceptual artists sought to dissolve the barriers between their work and the audience. For those artists working in the urban realm, the experience of the public was the subject of their art.[9] Likewise, in the 1980s this situation was challenged by both designers of gardens and artists. In particular, Peter Walker and Martha Schwartz revived the garden as a subject of aesthetic exploration in landscape architecture. They challenged landscape architects to revaluate the materials used to create gardens and how materials can extend meaning in gardens. For inspiration, Walker and Schwartz advised students of landscape architecture to experience the work of Robert Irwin, Robert Morris, Carl Andre, or Andy Warhol. "Insightful, poignant and sympathetic to our common culture they feed upon its energy and rawness … with which they illuminate the stuff of our everyday lives."[10] These permutations of where art can happen in both landscape architecture and the art world encouraged designers like Cormier to treat the materials of the garden as an artistic medium. Cormier studied with Martha Schwartz at Harvard University's Graduate School of Design, later working in Schwartz's office before opening his own studio in Montreal. The garden intentionally created by a designing intellect, informed by art-critical practices, does not suggest that every material experience of the garden is dictated by the designer. On the contrary, for Ian Hamilton Finlay, the author "embark(s) on a garden with a vision, but not a plan,"[11] framing, ordering, or anticipating its processes and the experiences it offers. It is also important to distinguish Cormier's gardens at Benny Farm from outdoor environments created for seniors. The design of "open spaces" for seniors has received considerable attention from environmental psychologists and behavioralists in regard to comfort and safety.[12] However, this work exhibits an ambivalence toward the designing intellect and is largely grounded in disinterestedness where the garden is a banal retreat for, at best, passive contemplation instead of a transformative aesthetic experience. The social dimension of aesthetic experiences is key to its transformative outcome, particularly for elderly men. Gerontologists and social workers note that social interaction is vital to reducing loneliness and despair in elderly men, who often lack the social networks established by many elderly women.[13]

Socialness in Aesthetic Experience

The ability of gardens to offer transformative experiences, in other words, to work in the way art does, is explored by Stephanie Ross in *What Gardens Mean*. Using Arthur Danto's definition of aesthetic experience as "interpreting the material counterparts" of art, Ross contends that the "garden-as-art is a certain arrangement of terrain, water, flora, sculpture, and architecture which possess aesthetic and expressive qualities and which make a statement and requires interpretation."[14] This aesthetic denouement described by Danto and Ross emphasizes the cognitive mode of experience: the accretion of factual knowledge, relations, affinities, and likenesses. Yet the material counterpoints of the Benny Farm gardens, as with many gardens, are overwhelmingly visceral and are felt when experiencing the gardens. The vicissitudinous conditions of color, wind, light, smell, and sound heightened by the design appeal to our senses and emotions (Fig. 16-19). Nestled in the everyday lives of veterans living at Benny Farm, the experiences aroused by the gardens promote dialogue, socialization, and shared meaning.

During the design process Cormier ignored conventional practices to use plants as buffering devices at the street edge

16. Benny Farm garden courtyard initial planting (photo: Claude Cormier Architectes Paysagistes, Inc.)

17. (right) Benny Farm garden courtyard after plant growth (photo: Claude Cormier Architectes Paysagistes, Inc.)

18. (left) (Benny Farm garden courtyard after the bloom (photo: Claude Cormier Architectes Paysagistes, Inc.)

Fig.19. (below) Ground view of Benny Farm garden courtyard for elderly veterans (photo: Claude Cormier Architectes Paysagistes, Inc.)

or as foundation plantings in front of the housing. Instead he insisted that plants foreground the experience of the garden itself.[15] By placing the circular planters throughout the center of the courtyards, he announces their importance in the experience of the gardens, and potentially enriches the social life of elderly people who are increasingly isolated from themselves and society (Fig. 20-21). Residents' experiences of changing scale, color, shade, and light brought about by the gardens' design provide a dynamic source of social exchange. This correlates with Thomas M. Alexander's interpretation of Dewey's aesthetic experience that "expresses everything which makes shared life human and worthwhile … and in which participation rather than decoding or autonomous self realization is the key idea."[16] In fact, some philosophers argue that building community is the very meaning of aesthetic experiences.[17] Benny Farm is not a mute piece; rather, it seizes the condition and moment of collective appropriation by providing art that residents experience within their daily lives.

20. Benny Farm garden courtyard for elderly veterans (photo: Claude Cormier Architectes Paysagistes, Inc.)

21. Benny Farm gardens for elderly veterans (photo: Claude Cormier Architectes Paysagistes, Inc.)

In Dewey's Laboratory School in Chicago he introduced gardening for this very reason. While he was Professor of Philosophy at the University of Chicago, Dewey founded the school as a tangible expression of his theory that learning is a profoundly social process. His school also embraced "learning by doing." Children worked in groups creating gardens, plaster cities, and other works to build a community as a foil to the regimented and alienated forces of society.[18] For Dewey, gardening in particular brought a social connectivity to the children, and this socialization structured meaning between children and their teachers. In *School and Society*, Dewey notes that "the whole community was interested in starting a garden, using every available ground."[19] Although

Dewey's model involves the act of gardening, designed gardens also encourage socialization because of their rich visceral qualities and the emotive effects they invite.

Experiences that arouse emotions can provoke a verbal "venting" of that experience, which can give shape to attitudes expressed by others. The aesthetic value of this exchange is not so much invested in the semantic truth of the statements made as it is nested in the particular physical and temporal location of the exchange."[20] When Cormier employs the wild grasses and flowering perennial plants at Benny Farm as the key material counterpoints of the gardens, which not only arouse cognitive interpretation but emotive venting, he simultaneously enhances the sociability of the gardens. For example, the dramatic changes to Benny Farm gardens regarding space, scale, color, texture, light, and sound from winter to spring indexes the shift in seasons, a cognitive observation. Changes in temperature when wind filters through the grasses are visceral sensations, and feelings of sadness when the plants go dormant are emotive responses. Because these changes are dramatized at Benny Farm, they entice veterans to converse, leading to increased social exchanges that are integral to the aesthetic experiences provided by the gardens.

It's significant to note that Dewey's aim to recover "the continuity of aesthetic experience in the normal processes of living"[21] locates a way of grappling with life in an increasingly alienated world. Pragmatism is a response to capitalism's divestment of art's social capacity. For Dewey, this divestment not only deprives people of moments of shared meaning, but simultaneously hides and reinforces inequities among people, such as age, gender, and class distinctions. Dewey asserts that his theories of aesthetic experience are for all people, and the initial actualization of his theories involved children; however, pragmatism is particularly relevant to elderly people living in group housing. People who are "retired" do not have a place in market capitalism. They are themselves alienated from the producer-consumer equation. Since group housing created for elderly people is both a symptom and a source of this alienation, the integration of art into the experience of these facilities, where it can become a source of shared experience, is crucial.

Based on the veterans' current engagement with the gardens at Benny Farm, these gardens are more about attaching than detaching, promoting a socialization that did not exist before construction of the gardens. According to Micheline Charland, the Tenant Relations Coordinator for Benny Farm, the gardens designed by Claude Cormier are not only instilling a sense of togetherness, but they are the places veterans and their visitors relish the most. The circular planters, vigorous plantings, and fountains not only provide privacy for the veterans both in the courtyard gardens and inside their apartments, but the gardens also stimulate interactions: "This is where people meet, converse, play a game. The gardens are occupied as early as six o'clock in the morning and late into the evening. They move with the sun. When family and friends come to visit this is often where the veterans entertain them."[22] People want to see what is in bloom, what has died, and what has taken over. The Benny Farm gardens, sites of life and death, are also sites of resistance and anticipation, which offer important, if not unique, contributions of art when it is a garden.

Resistance and Expectation in the Garden Experience

Time. The one thing that's never given to you.

—Louis G. Le Roy[23]

Aesthetic experiences stimulated by the growth, life, fight, death, and decay of plants resonate with Dewey's "biological common places" that humans share with other organisms. The shifting experiences of scale, color, sound, smell, and temperature triggered by the perennial plants and grasses articulate Cormier's design approach to heighten the sense of time. By telling time rather than denying it, the gardens provide insights for residents who have a fuller grasp of the meaning of the passing of time. The quest for meaning becomes increasingly intense and poignant in later life, and this search is encouraged among the veterans as a therapeutic activity to prevent despair.[24]

Like a chord that is about to follow in a musical phrase, the changes in the garden offer aesthetic experiences that involve expectation as much as reflection. These experiences also connect with Friedrich Fröbel's pedagogical use of the garden in his kindergartens. Fröbel was deeply moved by the transcendental qualities he found latent in plant life. Observation of natural processes, like the life cycles of plants, inspired analogues that anticipated children's growth. However, an understanding of gardens was always tempered by the acknowledgment that there was an unknowable dimension of their processes.[25] Both Louis Le Roy and Fröbel's theories point to a keen interest and active engagement with the real existence of the living garden, challenging the notion of gardens as aesthetic experiences forged from disinterestedness. Although the role of expectation in aesthetic discourse has traditionally been ascribed to experiences with music,[26] it is also present in garden experiences. For example, Le Roy acknowledges the role of the garden designer in setting the stage for experiences that capture the intervals between change, whether geologic or in a moment. Intervals are the time between instants, events, or states that prompt expectations in the work. Likewise, Fröbel contends that children's experiences with the changing nature of gardens are in expectation of other changes: in seasons, bird migration, and even their own physical growth.

It is important not to underestimate Cormier's use of primarily ornamental grasses and perennial plants as materials that avail aesthetic experiences. Considering Quebec's short growing season, the voluminous amounts of sheer biomass produced by these plants on a daily basis create a narrative of survival (Fig. 22). Traditionally, gardens have been designed with the intention to demarcate and control the voracity of their plant life. However, at Benny Farm the vigorous plants are materials that not only resist each other in a struggle for water, light, air, and space, but also resist conventional expectations of gardens as places of retreat. Lassus notes a similar approach, relatively unexplored in garden design, originated by Louis Le Roy, who "staged fights between plants."[27]

In *Art as Experience,* Dewey argues that resistance is the essential contour in the "outline of every experience clothed in meaning."[28] For Dewey resistance is critical to the way art works because people must have an awareness of how their experience with works deviate from what they believe. If people are unable to engage with art in a way that challenges beliefs, then this experience can lack significant meaning.[29] Resistance is a condition in both the generative processes of the artist and the imaginative engagement with art: "The perceiver as well as the artist has to perceive, meet, and overcome problems; otherwise, appreciation is transient and overweighted with sentiment."[30] Gardens are often critiqued for perpetuating sentimental experiences, so this is particularly relevant to discourse on aesthetic experiences with contemporary gardens. This can be demonstrated in other arts as well, such as experiencing poetry. Sentimental poems recall conventional emotive states invoked through verses and words that comply with predictable stanza and assonance. Readers are not challenged; rather they "get" what they expect. On the other hand, with a turn of a word or phrase, poems that offer resistance challenge readers by putting into question what is expected, opening up unrealized possibilities and beliefs.

Dewey contends that resistance can launch aesthetic experiences, for it "calls out thought, generates curiosity and solicitous care, and, when it is overcome and utilized, eventuates in elation."[31] However, it is argued here that at Benny Farm gardens, when resistance commences experience, it leaves a residue of thought beyond the encounter. In fact, the garden outside a veteran's apartment discloses an aesthetic experience that is distinct from the aesthetic experiences offered by the painting on his wall. This difference is due not only to the fact that the material attributes of the garden will change more than the painting, continually challenging what is expected, but that this is the garden's aesthetic appeal.

22. A narrative of survival at Benny Farm garden

This teleological understanding of art through its expression in the garden is where further exploration of Dewey's aesthetics may reveal how gardens contribute unparalleled aesthetic experiences when compared to other works. A debated definition in Dewey's aesthetics is "completion" and the difference between a complete duration of experience versus the idea that expectations are being resolved (completed) in the work itself. The idea that 'expectations are being resolved' was later questioned by George Dickie, who argues that "fulfillment of the expectation is not an effect, as the expectation itself is."[32] This is an interesting distinction because one of the beauties of most gardens is that they are never finished, and what we expect is always challenged by what is not known. Furthermore, we seek aesthetic experiences from gardens precisely for this reason, and this in fact is their unique aesthetic contribution.

NOTES

[1] John Dewey, *Art as Experience* (New York: Putnam Capricorn, 1958), 10.

[2] Ibid., 214.

[3] Richard Shusterman, "Pragmatism: Dewey," in *The Routledge Companion to Aesthetics*, ed. Berys Gaut and Dominic McIver Lopes (New York: Routledge, 2002), 102.

[4] L'OEUF proposed an intensive farming program for the entire site that assumes that all residents wish to garden. See www.bennyfarm.org/en/redevelopment/project.htm.

[5] See "Typology as Policy," in *Architecture California* 16, no. 2 (1994): 42–48. Here, we describe the shift in social housing from small-scale apartments with gardens to large multiple unit structures surrounded by unused courtyards after World War II.

[6] Allen Carlson, "Environmental Aesthetics," in *The Routledge Companion to Aesthetics*, ed. Berys Gaut and Dominic McIver Lopes (New York: Routledge, 2002), 425.

[7] Ibid.

[8] This should not be confused with the rise of sculpture gardens in the twentieth century. See Elizabeth B. Kassler, *Modern Gardens and the Landscape* (New York: Museum of Modern Art, 1984). In this classic, Kassler wrestles with the role of the garden in modernism.

[9] See Rosiland E. Krauss, "Mechanical Ballets: Light Motions, Theater" and the "Double Negative: a New Syntax for Sculpture," in *Passages in Modern Sculpture* (New York: Viking Press, 1989; first published 1977), 201–88. John Beardsley, *Earthworks and Beyond* (New York: Abbeville Press, 1984).

[10] Martha Schwartz, "Landscape and Common Culture," in *Modern Landscape Architecture: A Critical Review*, ed. Marc Treib (Cambridge, MA: MIT Press, 1994), p. 264. Also see *The Vanguard Landscapes and Gardens of Martha Schwartz*, ed. Tim Richardson (London: Thames & Hudson, 2004).

[11] Ian Hamilton Finlay, "Unconnected Sentences on Gardening," in John Beardsley, *Earthworks and Beyond* (New York: Abbeville Press, 1984), 133. "Unconnected Sentences on Gardening" was originally taken from *Nature over Again after Poussin: Some Discovered Landscapes*, exhibit catalog (Glasglow: Collins Exhibition Hall, University of Strathclyde, 1990).

[12] This refers to the work of environmental psychologists and behavioralists. See Rachel Kaplan, Stephen Kaplan, and Robert L. Ryan, *With People in Mind: Design and Management of Everyday Nature* (Washington, DC: Island Press, 1998) and Clare Cooper Marcus, *Healing Gardens: Therapeutic Benefits and Design Recommendations* (New York: Wiley, 1999).

[13] Dorothy Jerrome, *Good Company: An Anthropological Study of Old People in Groups* (Edinburgh: Edinburgh University Press, 1992), 76.

[14] Stephanie Ross, *What Gardens Mean* (Chicago: University of Chicago Press, 2001), 179.

[15] Claude Cormier, "Fake or Artificial," Light Source Lecture, Vancouver, 2004.

[16] Thomas M. Alexander, *John Dewey's Theory of Art, Experience and Nature: The Horizons of Feeling* (Albany: State University of New York Press, 1987), 124.

[17] Ted Cohen, "Metaphor, Feeling, and Narrative," *Philosophy and Literature* 21 (1997): 223–44.

[18] Williams Harms and Ida DePencier, *Experiencing Education: 100 Years of Learning at The University of Chicago Laboratory Schools* (Chicago: University of Chicago Press, 1998), 4.

[19] John Dewey, *School and Society* (Chicago: University of Chicago Press, 1942), 99.

[20] See Eddy M. Zemach, *Real Beauty* (University Park: Pennsylvania State University Press, 1997). This is only one facet of Zemach's account of aesthetic value, the concluding thrust of his book contends that great art holds truths and should be considered an aesthetic merit.

[21] Dewey, *Art as Experience*, 10.

[22] Special thanks to Micheline Charland, the Tenant Relations Coordinator for Benny Farm, who spoke with my students and me at Benny Farm in May 2004 and by telephone on 8 February 2005.

[23] Sacha Bronwasser, interview with Louis Le Roy in *de Volkskrant*, 22 January 2003.

[24] Rose Dobrof, "The Search for Meaning in the Later Years: The Views of a Seventy-four Year Old Gerontological Social Worker," in *Changes of the Third Age: Meaning and Purpose in Later Life*, ed. Robert S. Weiss and Scott A. Bass (New York: Oxford University Press, 2002), 176.

[25] See Susan Herrington, "Garden Pedagogy: Romanticism to Reform," *Landscape Journal: Design, Planning, and Management of the Land* 19, no. 1 (2001): 30–47; and Susan Herrington, "The Garden in Fröbel's Kindergarten: Beyond the Metaphor," *Studies in the History of Gardens & Designed Landscapes International Quarterly* 18, no. 4 (1998): 326–38.

[26] See Leonard B. Meyer, *Emotion and Meaning in Music* (Chicago: Chicago University Press, 1956).

[27] Udo Weilacher, "The Invention of Espace Propre," in *Between Landscape Architecture and Land Art* (Basel: Birkhäuser, 1999), 110.

[28] Dewey, *Art as Experience*, 60.

[29] I thank Michel Conan for directing me toward an exploration of this term during the symposium at Dumbarton Oaks, May 2005. Dewey also argues that resistance is critical to scientific thought as well, but "in art the resistance encountered enters into the work in a more immediate way than in science" (ibid., 138).

[30] Ibid.

[31] Ibid., 60.

[32] George Dickie, "Beardsley's Phantom Aesthetic Experience," *Journal of Philosophy* 62 (1965): 132.

Contemporary Garden
Aesthetics, Creations and
Interpretations

Contemporary Garden
Aesthetics, Creations and
Interpretations

Contemporary Garden
Aesthetics, Creations and
Interpretations

Contemporary Garden
Aesthetics, Creations and
Interpretations

The Reenchantment of the Maegaki Residence by Mirei Shigemori

Christian Tschumi

Mirei Shigemori created gardens in Japan between 1933 and 1975, but he refused to reproduce traditional gardens because they lacked any sense of modernity and refused to imitate European gardens because they were out of touch with Japanese culture. Thus he anticipated the concerns of many contemporary artists who feel the urge to embrace all aspects of modern culture and yet wish to remain true to their own regional or national culture. In this sense he sets a very interesting example for contemporary artists.

Caught between tradition and modernity, Shigemori would always argue that art was the main focus (Fig. 1). Art for him meant to engage with life, and, in the case of the garden, with nature, which by definition was undergoing continuous change and constant renewal. This view of art left little room for imitating past styles, a practice he viewed with great suspicion. Shigemori wrote: "One can make gardens according to the ancient meanings or according to the ancient shapes, but actually the person who is designing the garden and building it, is from no other than the present time. The significance of the fact that we are people who live in the present is that we aren't able to make gardens that carry the meaning of the old times or have the shape of those times. So, in this case, we can only make a garden that is an imitation and this is meaningless."[1]

This shows how much Shigemori saw art as rooted in the present, drawing from the current life-world. In his view gardens should connect to people's everyday experiences and reflect modern times (Fig. 2). In this way art would be pregnant with meaning as it mirrors what people deal with and creates a specific moment in time. As a person looking into the future, Shigemori felt it was wrong to imitate past forms at the cost of present artistic inventiveness. Although, in general, this was an attitude not unlike the modernists' of the West, it did not imply that Shigemori advocated the adoption of European garden styles in Japan (Fig. 3). Quite the contrary, in fact; he argued that Western garden culture was not relevant for the Japanese garden's renewal, as Western thinking did not engage at all with the culture of the place nor build on its long history.[2]

On top of his fierce opposition to simple imitation of the past or assimilation of European styles, Shigemori pointed to what he saw as an enormous deficit in contemporary Japanese gardens: a notable loss of spirituality, usually replaced by interchangeable and meaningless form. People in the modern world had lost this most important connection to the world of

1. Sumiyoshi Jinja, Suminoe no Niwa (Suminoe Garden), Sasayama City, Hyōgo Prefecture, Japan, built in 1966.

the gods, a link to which the ancient Japanese gardens had formed a testament. The old references had been dropped or simply forgotten, and new ones contained no spiritual dimension. To Shigemori most new gardens were dull, often unimaginative reiterations of past forms. Hence, he saw this desecration as resulting in much poorer gardens, places clearly lacking the deep aesthetic experience of their predecessors.

Shigemori affirmed that forward-looking invention, a quintessential artistic act, had been replaced by a backward-looking imitation of past examples, and visual delight had been substituted for the creative personal engagement with the gods. This realization is what motivated him to work on the modernization of the Japanese garden himself, in the role of a creative garden maker.

To understand Shigemori's work, it is necessary to look briefly at his formative years. While studying painting from 1917 to 1919 at the Tokyo Fine Arts School, he became interested in art history and Japanese aesthetics. Next, Shigemori (Fig. 4) took a class in Indian Philosophy at Tōyō University and pursued studies in the tea ceremony, *ikebana,* and the Japanese garden. This eventually led to a strong involvement in the avant-garde *ikebana* movement, where, together with Sōfu Teshigahara and Bunpo Nakayama, he drafted the New Ikebana Declaration, rejecting fixed forms and nostalgic feelings. All

2. Tenrai-an Teien (Garden at the Hermitage for the Enjoyment of Nature's Sounds), Kibichūō-chō, Kaga-gun, Okayama Prefecture, Japan, built in 1969 (photo: Chisao Shigemori).

this is testament to his deep interest in traditional culture and marks the start of a lifelong struggle for the renewal of these inherited native arts.

The devastating Muroto typhoon of 1934 then turned a page in Shigemori's life. In an effort to document the country's rich but frail heritage, he embarked on a survey of approximately 250 of Japan's historic gardens and subsequently published the results as a twenty-six-volume encyclopedia. This experience laid the base for his career as a revolutionary garden maker and resulted in his devoting the rest of his life to the renewal and revitalization of Japanese garden culture.

The gardens of the Maegaki residence (Fig. 5), which he designed in 1955 and which will be the focus of this paper, are deeply representative of the new aesthetic he proposed. They were meant to make daily life in the residence a poetic encounter with nature and, at the same time, prove the potential for renewal inherent in the dry landscape garden style.

Shigemori's philosophical interpretation of the roots of the Japanese garden starts with the advent of people moving into more permanent dwellings. He argues that as human beings spent more time indoors, they became more and more segregated from nature and the spiritual experience connected with it, and that this in turn eventually would foster a desire for

3. Yūrin no Niwa (Yūrin's Garden), Kibichūō-chō, Kaga-gun, Okayama Prefecture, Japan, first built in 1969 in Kyoto, then moved and rebuilt in 2002 at its current location.

the outdoors and a longing for nature's beauty. In ancient Japan, nature had always been occupied by gods. According to Shinto beliefs, tall mountains are places inhabited by deities, and those *kami*[3] were thought to visit regularly stone outcroppings and lofty old trees (Fig. 6). Hence these became places to meet with the other world and eventually developed into objects of worship. In time, people started to add stones to such an existing *iwakura* (Fig. 7),[4] and this is where Shigemori saw the very origin of the Japanese garden. According to him this is the root of the now prominent tradition of stone settings in the garden. Another example are the ancient *kami ike,* literally "god ponds," also places enhanced or created for the visit of *kami.* Thus these can be seen as predecessors to the later pond gardens. As people eventually desired to bring nature, and therefore gods, into their dwelling places, the garden really came into being. Ponds were created and stone settings erected. Where before nature had been a world made by the deities, man had now put himself on a par with the gods and re-created nature in the form of these early gardens.

Although the Shigemori family had traditionally followed Tendai Buddhism, Shigemori eventually converted to Shinto, the original religion of the Japanese archipelago.[5] It must have been Shinto's close connection to nature that so appealed to Shigemori, as he confessed: "The only thing we can trust is nature, and there is no other way than to leave everything in nature's hands."[6] Hence from Shigemori's point of view, Shinto was much closer to nature, and therefore the ancient *kami,* than Buddhism ever could be, and that is why he changed his religion. Unusual as this step might seem in the intermingled religious landscape of twentieth-century Japan, with it he manifests his deep appreciation of the spiritually infused nature and hence relates back to the old roots of the Japanese garden.

Shigemori's own garden creations, often situated somewhere between tradition and modernity, have to be seen in light of this spiritual experience that nature in the form of the ancient gardens provided for the early Japanese. This is why he argued that in the recent profanation of the Japanese garden these original mythological roots had been lost. Consequently, in his own written as well as created works, Shigemori came to see the

4. Mirei Shigemori, portrait c. 1970 (photo: Haruzo Ohashi).

Japanese garden as a spiritual place, an arena for the *kami* to come and visit. His cultural studies and the aforementioned survey had persuaded him that gardens were an essential part of the Japanese dwelling as they allowed metaphysical encounters with nature. This interpretation of the garden as a place for the *kami* therefore manifested itself in some of his most interesting designs. A case in point is Shishin Sōō no Niwa, the garden of four gods at Sekizō-ji (Fig. 8), based on an ancient Daoist idea that a land area is protected by four gods assuming the form of a blue dragon, white tiger, red phoenix, and black tortoise. It has a quite remarkable design and is probably Japan's first dry landscape garden featuring four colors of gravel. Another garden that effectively illustrates Shigemori's religious interpretation of the Japanese garden, even across denominational borders, is the south garden at Zuinō-in (Fig. 9). Here the scene in the garden depicts Buddha with twenty-five Bodhisattva as they come to fetch a deceased person to take him or her to paradise.

Shigemori also understood the Japanese garden as an abstraction of an area's natural and cultural landscapes. In fact, that was not just his personal interpretation but was a rather widely shared concept among traditional garden makers in Japan, even today. The famous *Sakuteiki,* written in the Heian period (794–1185), already advises that when making a garden, one should "think over the famous places of beauty throughout the land, and by making your own that, which appeals to you most,

5. Maegaki Garden, Juen-tei (Garden of Joyful Long Life), Higashi-Hiroshima, Hiroshima Prefecture, Japan, built in 1955 represents the new aesthetic Shigemori proposed for the dry landscape garden style.

design your garden with the mood of harmony, modeling after the general air of such places."[7] This strong connection to their place and the local landscape used to be one of the distinct characteristics of Japanese gardens and was at least partly responsible for their unmistakable feel of atmosphere and harmony. The aesthetic experience provided was completely rooted in the natural and the cultural basis of the place.

Shigemori had not only read the *Sakuteiki* but was able to learn directly from hundreds of examples when working on the survey. In the 1949 book *Gardens of Japan,* he ultimately concludes: "The influence of nature is particularly strong on the garden, because … it is a man-made landscape, and also because it is made up of the component parts of nature such as land, water, rocks, trees, etc. This however does not mean that the garden is a photographic copy of nature, for there are many in which the interpretation is symbolic, idealistic or even fantastic."[8] This is exactly where Shigemori saw numerous opportunities to renew and further develop the traditional Japanese garden. In his view there was still much more possible within these interpretations, as to an innovative mind many options had not yet been explored. A typical example of a garden design based on an abstract landscape is the south garden at Zuihō-in (Fig. 10), where a seaside scene complete with waves washing up to a

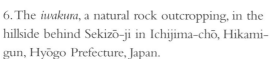
6. The *iwakura*, a natural rock outcropping, in the hillside behind Sekizō-ji in Ichijima-chō, Hikami-gun, Hyōgo Prefecture, Japan.
7. An *iwakura* likely to be extended by man, Kibitsuhiko Jinja, Ichinomiya, Okayama city, Okayama Prefecture, Japan.
8. Masshō Honzan Sekizō-ji, Shishin Sōō no Niwa (Garden of Four Gods), Ichijima-chô, Hikami-gun, Hyōgo Prefecture, Japan. View from north to south with the black turtle stone setting in the foreground.

peninsula next to an inland bay are depicted. An example more likely to fit the category of a fantastic interpretation is the western garden at Tōfuku-ji's Ryōgin-an (Fig. 11), featuring a dragon rising from a sea of black clouds. Where with Zuihō-in Shigemori remained within the traditional set of design elements, with Ryōgin-an he clearly pushed the limits of what a dry landscape garden and its alleged experience can be in the cultural landscape of contemporary Japan.

Last but not least, Shigemori saw the garden as a major artistic achievement, which by definition was a product of its time. To re-create gardens in traditional styles was, as stated above, mere imitation of the past and therefore meaningless. Art, also in the form of a garden, had to be contemporary and novel; otherwise it was ineffective. Shigemori had a very clear idea

9. Zuihō-in, Shōju 25 Bosatsu no Niwa (Garden of 25 Bodhisattva), Ōtsu, Shiga Prefecture, Japan, built in 1956.

10. Zuihō-in, Dokuza no Niwa (Garden of Solitary Meditation), Kyoto, Japan, built in 1961.

of where the designer's efforts should be directed when he suggested that "in most cases the artistic value of the garden is proportionate to the degree of simplification carried out."[9] This indeed was an important realization for him, one that he increasingly followed in his own work. With regard to the proper style to be chosen for a design, Shigemori had a definite favorite in the form of the *karesansui,* or dry landscape garden, a garden style he valued highly for its level of abstraction and apparent timeless modernity. Among a large number of projects that could be cited here, I will single out just two that illustrate the range of his artistic interpretations of this style. One is the garden at Kishiwada Castle (Fig. 12), a design representing the layout of the castle's old fortification walls as a bird would have seen them from the air. The theme of the stone settings is most appropriately Zhuge Liang's eightfold battle camp formation, with the central camp here taking center stage. The other garden I want to point to as a rather artistic reinterpretation of the Japanese garden is his early masterpiece at Tōfuku-ji's main hall (Fig. 13). The north garden with the square stones scattered over a plane of moss has reached iconic status, but when built in 1939, for many observers it seemed to go beyond the limits of what a Japanese garden could be (at least that is how many of the local Kyoto gardeners felt). They were not able to accept a garden so visibly modern and allegedly disconnected from tradition.

One specific analysis of the state of the Japanese garden stands at the beginning of Shigemori's career as a garden maker, when over the course of working on the survey he deduced that "the gardens after the middle of the Edo period lost their artistic character and turned into form only."[10] An insight undoubtedly helped by his background as a painter, providing for a different, if not broader, understanding of what the garden as an art form could be, this conception is what stood at the beginning of a garden like the one at Tōfuku-ji's main hall.

What do these gardens tell us about Shigemori's understanding of the Japanese garden's relationship with nature? Obviously there is a strong connection, despite that the supposedly naturalistic garden is, in effect, a rather abstract construct based on the above described religious, cultural, and artistic considerations. First of all, nature was the spiritual home of the garden. It was a world full of deities, *kami*, an enchanted place as well as the link to the universe of the gods. On a more practical level, nature was the material basis for the Japanese garden. Without it, not only would there not be any plants and rocks to work with, but there would be no famous landscapes to refer to. So in Shigemori's view, nature is the physical and intellectual basis for the Japanese garden. He saw the Japanese garden as an abstract and condensed version of nature, the degree of which was determined by the abovementioned parameters. Where cultural and artistic considerations were naturally subject to constantly changing times, it is the religious aspect that adds and maintains a certain aura and myth to the place. In our aesthetic experience of the garden, these characteristics eventually are

11. Ryôgin-an Hōjō Teien (Garden at the Main Hall of the Temple of the Chanting Dragon), Kyoto, Japan, built in 1964.

12. Kishiwada Castle, Hachijin no Niwa (Garden of Eight Battle Camp Formations), Kishiwada, Osaka Prefecture, Japan, built in 1953.

unified and resolved. Above all, this is an experience of being in close harmony with nature, and therefore with the spiritual side of our human existence.

13. Tôfuku-ji, Hassô no Niwa (Garden of Eight Views), Kyoto, Japan, built in 1939. The garden to the north of the temple's main hall depicts a grid (*ichimatsu*) fading out toward the northeastern corner.

14. Maegaki Garden, Juen-tei (Garden of Joyful Long Life), Higashi-Hiroshima, Hiroshima Prefecture, Japan, built in 1955. View from the main room into the South Garden.

The Maegaki Garden

Shigemori believed that people were really alive only if they existed with nature (Fig. 14), in other words, if they had their own garden. He was convinced of its benefits for physical health as well as its soothing influence on the mind, the latter also being a necessary result of creating refuge for the *kami* nearby one's own dwelling.

It is this intended experience of living with a garden that I now want to investigate in the example of the one for the Maegaki residence, designed and built in 1955 (Fig. 15). The residence, located next door to the family's sake brewery, consists of three main parts: the front garden, the courtyard garden, and the south garden. The entrance from the street is located to the north of the property, and access to the door is through the front garden. The south garden is the largest part and is enclosed by a *kura,* a traditional storage house, located on the south side of it and visible in the background. It extends along a corridor of the *shoin* rooms, creating a U-shaped space that reaches into the center of the building. This entire residential garden is designed in the *karesansui* style, where areas of sand or gravel traditionally symbolize water.

Shigemori's design for the garden contains two main themes. One is the garden as a place for the gods, the Shinto *kami,* creating a space for the spiritual part of the Maegakis' existence.

Hence the garden creates a godly atmosphere that pervades the house. The other is an ancient Daoist belief, the boat on its way to Mount Hōrai,[11] a symbol of the islands of the immortals. He transferred this scene from its mythical origin somewhere in the East China Sea to the Japan Inland Sea, further simplifying and condensing this myth (Fig. 16).

前垣氏庭園平面圖

昭和三五年二月実測
本庭二〇〇坪
前庭二〇〇坪
中庭一三坪

15. Maegaki Garden, site plan scale 1:50 (plan: courtesy of the Shigemori family, Kyoto, Japan).
16. Sketch of the Maegaki South Garden by Mr. Kokeji, November 1960 (sketch: courtesy of the Shigemori family, Kyoto, Japan).

17. Maegaki Garden, room directly adjacent to the south garden.

For most members of the Maegaki family, the experience of the garden's construction stood at the very beginning, and laid the basis for a deeper appreciation, of their own cultural traditions. Not all family members are old enough to have witnessed it, but certainly everybody in the family has been told about it. So, looking out at this landscape, they are reconnecting to those moments when Shigemori was living among them, teaching them about renewing tradition, while creating this work of art. In doing so, moments of great cultural achievement and social glory are being recalled. Consequently, the shared experience of the garden's construction, of learning from Shigemori about its cultural context and references as well as the personality and status of the designer himself, are all still important parts of the current experience of this garden for most members of the Maegaki family. From their point of view, the continuous well-being of the garden mirrors the state of the family and reflects the level of economic achievement they have made over four generations in this dwelling place.[12]

On a sunny winter afternoon, the Maegakis would serve their guests a bowl of tea in the room directly adjacent to the south garden (Figs. 14 and 17). The sun would warm the room through the glass of the sliding doors, and the visitor, sitting on

18. Maegaki Garden, overlooking a grandiose landscape.
19. Maegaki Garden, the waterfall stone setting with a river flowing toward the ocean.

20 and 21. Maegaki Garden, a special stone presented by Michiko Maegaki's parents at the occasion of her wedding and joining her new family.

the *tatami* floor, could enjoy the great scenery of the garden. One of the most memorable experiences of my time in Japan was, when on my first visit to the Maegaki residence, Michiko Maegaki kneeled down on the *engawa,* facing the garden, and prepared a bowl of *macha* for me. It was the afternoon of 15 November 2001; the garden was spotless and flooded with sunlight. The 77-year-old lady performed the task with an evident grace that puzzled me. Appropriately, she used a bowl with a chestnut design, a present from Shigemori, designed to be used in a special autumn tea event. The water came out of a *kyūto-ki,* or often just called *poto,* one of those contemporary conveniences that the more modern-minded Japanese seem, without much hesitation, to accept and willingly integrate into their cherished tea culture. Whereas it is usually confined to backstage, Michiko Maegaki felt no reluctance to bring it out of the kitchen and use the device right in front of her guest, remembering what she had learned about the renewing of culture from Shigemori. The *poto* was a proof that she had accepted the challenge posed to her and was willing to continue renewing tradition.

"For to perceive, a beholder must create his own experience. And his creation must include relations comparable to those which the original producer underwent."[13] So it was stated in *Art as Experience* by John Dewey. Shigemori almost certainly would have agreed with that, and in the *Shin-Sakuteiki* he even provided us with the necessary steps to get there: "When we bring something that we have found in nature into the garden, it is each gardener's task to decide how to reduce it in scale, how to abstract it, and how to translate it in a meaningful way. However, we have to stay focused when considering fundamentals, for example, the meaningful translation into modern [design] language. Nature is tolerant of many points of view."[14] So by reducing, abstracting, and translating historical landscapes and other cultural references, Shigemori creates a garden experience that the viewer has to decode to have his or her own experience. The very idea of the garden is abstract and hence resists easy consumption. For viewers to have an experience, they must make an effort to discover it. Once uncovered, the viewer reproduces the experience of the garden maker.

The experience created by Shigemori is that of overlooking a grandiose landscape (Figs. 16 and 18), not knowing if one is in a dream state or a moment of conscious real life. You are seeing cosmic mountains and mythical islands, separated by oceans, an image based on Daoist mythology, but executed with stone settings in such a way as also to accommodate for the *kami*. If you imagine sitting on a mountaintop, looking down at the ocean scattered with rock islands, you are seeing a picture similar to the Maegakis' view of their garden. This is the same view one would have from atop one of the neighboring mountains that are part of Hiroshima Prefecture's coastal range. Hence, the garden is a highly conceptual miniature landscape that reminds the Maegakis of the larger region in which they live. This technique is called *shukkei* and is a good example of how abstraction works at the very heart of the Japanese garden.[15]

But abstract landscapes and a place for the gods are not, as previously suggested, the only content of this garden. There is in addition a significant story being told—a narrative on life. The setting for the story is a condensed landscape consisting of a waterfall and a subsequent river that flows to the ocean (Fig. 19), an allegory for the unfolding of life.[16] A Mount Hōrai stone arrangement (A), located at the back of the garden, resembles the imaginary waterfall, making a noteworthy reference to the famous garden at Daisen-in in Kyoto.[17] The respective stone setting, in appearance not unlike an ancient *iwakura,* consists of seven stones, six set clearly vertically and one set horizontally. The last, placed right in front of the *Mizuochi-ishi,* is the one where the imaginary water splashes down on. This being the *Daiza-seki,* the base or foundation stone, it visually provides a basis for the waterfall and a welcome contrast to all the vertical lines within the composition. The small stones to the edges of the group are placed for accent to the left and to balance out the right side. It is at the right corner where the water from the waterfall eventually meets the main stream, as is indicated by the two small stones. Looking at this composition, every connoisseur of the Japanese garden hears the thundering sound of masses of water tumbling down the side of the mountain. The more spiritually inclined would also be able to see the *kami* come and visit at times.

The waterfall suggests the mountains at the back, as the origin of the ocean's water, and if we look at the sketch, it becomes clear how the stream then winds its way toward the sea that spreads out right in front of the house. From this viewpoint, it is clearly visible that when the river flows by the rock islands (E and G), it finally enters the ocean. François Berthier's description of Daisen-in matches this garden's aesthetic experience perfectly and illustrates the kinship of the two: "The torrent has become a river with a slow and majestic flow; it spreads out into a vast plain from which hills rise up. A boat unhurriedly follows the current of the pacified waters. Having run its course, the great river empties into an infinite ocean."[18] This is exactly the same in the Maegaki case. Gazing into the far distance, to the back of the garden, almost at the horizon, you may recognize the tallest of the islands—Mount Hōrai rising high from the waters. Looking at this entire scene you observe an ocean dotted with numerous rock islands. It echoes the experience that Shigemori had when he looked at the sea from Hiroshima Prefecture's coastal mountain range.

The boat featured in both scenes is another metaphor all by itself: a boat on its way to the islands of the immortals, as symbolized by a longish low stone (H) pointing in the direction of Mount Hōrai. The boat seems to have just left the shore, turning toward the open sea. The journey is one well known by many Japanese. The boat is embarking on a journey to the other side of life, taking the recently deceased to paradise, a trip that allegedly takes several days, with Mount Hōrai as its final destination. It reminds beholders that some day in the future, they too might be on the boat, moving from this world to another one, in continuation of a long journey. This of, course, is an allusion to the changing phases of human existence, a fact much appreciated by Shigemori and easily deciphered by any viewer of this garden. And naturally all beholders create their own experience as they follow the journey the boat undertakes.

Writing about the famous *karesansui* garden at Ryōan-ji, François Berthier well describes the experience of looking at a garden of gravel and rock: "All one has to do is to sit at the edge of the garden and stop up one's ears. Then the miracle happens. In the great silence that is thereby regained, the spontaneous beauty of these rough rocks surges forth, and their immortal chant ensues, the substance of which is this: Beyond the weight of matter there is Spirit, without which one can never truly live."[19] It is this kind of spiritual experience, added by the ancient rocks, together with the narrative of life that attach a touch of eternity to the experience of this garden, for the Maegakis as well as for all others open to perceive it.

For Michiko Maegaki, there is one very special stone in this garden (Figs. 20 and 21). As is often traditionally the case in Japan, she had officially changed families and therefore moved in with her husband's family the day she got married. As one of many gifts, her parents presented a sizable rock to her new family. This very stone was then part of the previous garden at the current site for a number of years. When Shigemori learned about its origin, he decided to reuse it in his new design. This is not something he would usually do, as he disliked using stones that he had not selected himself. But considering the importance of the stone to Michiko Maegaki, he apparently felt it was better to make an exception and include it. Consequently, he placed it close to the house, for Michiko Maegaki to access it as a connection to her former home. She explains her experience of the stone as follows: "Whenever I looked at that stone, I remembered that I was not alone and that my parents were always with me. It was a symbol for my old family. When I was in a difficult situation or there was something I wanted to talk to my parents about, I looked at that stone and thought or even talked to it. That made me feel better." In a more quiet and relaxed moment these days, Michiko Maegaki enjoys sitting on the *engawa* in a comfortable lounge chair, reading a book. This contemplative space next to the garden provides for some "of the most peaceful moments in my life," she admits—hardly a surprise, considering the experience of the scenery, with all the references and memories it contains. In a way, it must feel a little like sitting on a cloud, looking down on a scene of everyday life.

The house completely embraces the garden, hence making it the center and focus of everyday life (Fig. 15). As a result the rooms next to the garden provide the desired space for many more aspects of daily life in the house. Besides being a place for making tea for visitors and reading books, it is a place to get important work done. Kazuhiro Maegaki, for example, often meets with clients or suppliers at the little table with a view out to the garden. The negotiations sometimes continue for hours and include meals supplemented with a lot of sake—no doubt a place chosen for the consoling influence of the garden. Kayo Maegaki, Michiko's daughter, on the other hand, likes to write a letter to a friend or a poem while sitting at the table with a view of the garden. When she feels like doing calligraphy, she brings paper, ink, and brush to the very same place. Kneeling on the *tatami* mats, for her the garden then becomes the ideal background for an art project.

On a more basic level the garden requires a certain level of maintenance work, resulting in rather physical interaction

22. Maegaki Garden, stone setting as an abstract art.
23. Maegaki Garden, *suhama* in the form of a dramatically undulating line.
24. Maegaki Garden, peninsulas in the garden help create a sense of depth.

with its elements. First is the weekly raking of the gravel, currently done by Kazuhiro's father, with the son in careful observance. Then there are the less glamorous tasks of picking up dead leaves and branches, weeding, and pruning, all of which are mainly shared among the older family members, who enjoy this type of work for its pensive and relaxing effect and are provided a sensual escape from other more mundane tasks of the house and business. This too seems especially true for the watering of the garden: a welcomed chance to feel the cool fluid in one's hands in anticipating of another hot summer day. After the tiresome garden work, the older folks enjoy a bit of meditating in an armchair, or napping in the afternoon sun coming through the sliding glass doors. This is the moment the youngest ones have waited for, as they can now finally play with the gravel and climb the garden's stones, actions otherwise immediately prohibited when discovered by the elders.

Day after day the garden is the place where the Maegakis connect with the outside world upon waking—watching a bird jump from stone to stone while eating breakfast or contemplating the first snow on an early winter morning. Most ritualized practices of daily life are reenchanted by the simple presence of the garden. The garden allows the dwellers of the home who take care of it to live in proximity of the gods, and thus to access a deeper relationship to nature throughout all of their daily activities.

What role does abstraction play in all this? Abstraction is an inherent characteristic of the *karesansui* garden, Shigemori's favorite type of Japanese garden. But why was this style so dear to him? Shigemori approaches the issue this way: "Why should

we make gardens similar to nature? This is my query. It is unnecessary and unnatural to copy nature."[20] Abstraction is neither natural nor realistic. It functions as a buffer and resists immediate comprehension. In the process of abstraction the essence of nature has been extracted and translated into the language of modern design. The resulting form therefore qualifies as art. Looking into the history of Japanese arts such as painting, it becomes clear that abstraction is not a new phenomenon by any means. Some scholars even argue that it is an inherent characteristic of Japanese art altogether. Irmtraud Schaarschmidt-Richter, for example, argues that abstraction in modern Japanese art "had roots of its own that can be

25. Maegaki Garden, the *karesansui* garden as an ideal paradigm for modernized residential gardens in the second half of the twentieth century.

traced back to a very specific view of art, to uniquely Japanese modes of vision and aesthetic codes." She further points out that "Japanese artists retained a fundamental position of their own that played a significant role in later developments. This position is evident, and has been since the classical period, in an unmistakable tendency toward the abstract, toward a unique kind of asymmetrical surface configuration."[21] It is this fondness of the abstract that we find, for instance, in many paintings of artists belonging to the Rinpa School, such as Kōrin and Sōtatsu, a body of work of which Shigemori was keenly aware.

In the context of Shigemori's work, abstraction becomes a way of being Japanese and being modern at the same time, while neither falling prey to nor divorcing oneself from tradition. But from an artist's point of view, it may just be one of several ways of creating art, of encoding an aesthetic experience for others to decipher. For Shigemori, art, especially in its more abstract forms (Fig. 22), is the result of an intense struggle between the artist and matter, trying to resolve the problem of artistic creation by renewing matter itself in a new way. In his gardens this often results in recovering the ancient roots of the Japanese garden and reintroducing the presence of the gods. When successful, as I would like to suggest in the case of the Maegaki residence, this results in a reenchantment of the human dwelling place.

By comprehending the different aspects of this garden, the viewer is re-creating the experience that the original producer of that garden underwent. In doing so, one is extracting from this garden what is significant, and the result is a comprehension of its literal significance. Pieces of the beholder's experience have merged with the encounter provided in the garden. A new understanding of the garden has been reached, resulting in a conclusion of the experience.

Engaging with Tradition and Innovation

Now, shouldn't we see the Maegaki's garden as a rather traditional Japanese garden after all, following a tradition of abstraction, *karesansui* garden making, and mythical iconography? Compared to some of the initially presented designs, such as the gardens

26. *Maegaki Garden, video sequences from Bairon Shigemori,* Ishibashi's Garden, *a film produced as the author's graduation work from film school (Tokyo: Tōkyō Sōgō Shashin Senmongakō, 1971); used with permission*

at Ryōgin-an and Sekizō-ji, it does look more traditional, at least from afar. And in the case of the Hōrai concept as well as the *iwakura*-like stone settings, Shigemori indeed embraces tradition and works with a historic concept. But with regard to the *suhama* (Fig. 23),[22] which comes here in the form of a dramatically undulating coastline, he breaks with tradition and takes a very different approach. This edge of the paving stones under the eaves along the house is built of red *kurama-ishi* with the joints filled with red mortar. Thematically it is as an abstraction of the coastline, hence the *suhama* form, but formally it is a bold artistic statement.

Pebble beaches sloping gently into a pond have a long tradition in the Japanese garden. But here in the Maegaki case real pebbles were not used, nor is it really a sloping beach. In fact, rather the opposite is true. The beach shows a real edge to the gravel, and the stones are angular rather than round. Moreover, it is not a long, slightly bending curve, like the traditional examples would stipulate, but an ostentatiously undulating line, recalling the shape of waves. So Shigemori's coastline is not just any beach, it is an artistic interpretation of the traditional concept of the *suhama,* rooted in his background as a painter and possibly inspired by similar shapes that his idols Kandinsky and Kōrin liked to use in their abstract paintings. The use of red concrete in the joints between the stones can serve as further testimony to the artistic intention and the character of this intervention.

This edge is undoubtedly one of the most flamboyant undulating lines that Shigemori ever designed, and he was to do many more later in his career. Not only is this Shigemori's first use of this surprising and innovative design element, but also up to this point nobody had dared to juxtapose elements of a traditional Japanese garden with an artistic statement of such gravity and impact. To be sure, this was not only because of the geometry, but also the use of colored concrete, as its use as material in a garden was unprecedented. So, in effect, this use of geometry and color represents an important step in Shigemori's strategy of renewal and hence amounts to a small revolution in the world of the traditional Japanese garden at the time. As such it constitutes the basis and point of departure for some of the more radical designs that I showed earlier.

Intermediaries, in terms of both their radicalism as well as their location in the garden, are the two moss-covered peninsulas. They intrude upon the space from two sides, west and east, while their tips overlap in the center of the garden. Together with the white sand, this creates, as previously suggested, a landscape resembling the Japanese Inland Sea. Where in a traditional garden there would have been just one peninsula, making the usual reference to the famous landscape of Amanohashidate,[23] this garden features two of the longish peninsulas. Thus Shigemori cites a different reference, without really wanting to erase the memory of the earlier one. He explains: "Working on this design, I remembered that there were examples of mist-shaped center islands in the Kamakura period's *Sakuteiki*. Originally that referred to islands, but I used the idea for the peninsulas."[24] Creating in this garden a landscape resembling the Inland Sea, the image of islands and mist is actually quite close to the Maegakis' actual experience and memory of this very space. In addition, it is a reverence much celebrated in traditional Japanese paintings. Depending on the viewpoint, this layout of the land grants depth to the garden (Fig. 24). As with the *suhama,* here too Shigemori is playing with tradition in a very subtle way, using past samples as a source of inspiration, yet invigorating them with a slight twist. This leaves the peninsulas suggesting two possible meanings, further widening the connotations.[25]

And finally, the choice of style for a residential garden also reflects a substantial break from tradition (Fig.25). *Karesansui* gardens used to be built at temples and sometimes shrines, but few private gardens would traditionally fit that category. This departure also should be noted as a major part of Shigemori's strategy for the renewal of the Japanese garden tradition. He saw no apparent reason why the *karesansui* gardens needed to be restricted to a religious context only. Quite the contrary, actually; he recognized and used the great potential for abstraction inherent in this garden style as an ideal paradigm for modernized residential gardens in the second half of twentieth-century Japan. By placing again a strong emphasis on a role and place for the *kami,* Shigemori was able to reintroduce a spiritual experience to the gardens and the people that lived with them.

Let me end with one of the great moments of the weekly care of the garden: raking the gravel, as shown in this sequence (Fig. 26).

Shigemori is raking the gravel in front of his patrons in the garden that he just finished. In abstract fashion, he draws curls and waves of the ocean on a canvas of gravel and sand. Note the concentration he brings to this task, and the fluidity of his gestures as the body becomes fully engaged—to the tip of the teeth of the rake—in producing a gravel design inspired on the spur of the moment. As he rakes, the sea becomes alive and enters the experience of the beholder.

For years to come, the owners, time and again, will be raking their gravel, reenacting the experience of the garden's creation. Rejuvenating the abstraction of the sea, they become artists in their own garden.

NOTES

[1] Mirei Shigemori, "Shinsakuteiki," in *Shigemori Mirei Sakuhinshû: Niwa—Kamigami e no Apurōchi* (Tokyo: Seibundō Shinkō Sha, 1976), 292. This text was first published as a series of 11 essays in the *Kintaifu* pamphlets nos. 16 to 27 (with no essay in no. 19); after Mirei Shigemori's death his son, Geite Shigemori, compiled the abovementioned book and republished the essay for the first time in one piece.

[2] The quest for modernization in Japan has been ongoing ever since the Meiji Restoration (1868), when after more than 250 years of closed borders the country opened up and started to catch up with the West. Hence the tension between the traditional and the modern element in Japanese society has existed (and fertilized) the country for almost a century and a half.

Although a connoisseur of traditional Japanese culture, Shigemori was for most of his life an adamant proponent of cultural renewal. Already when as a young man he studied *ikebana,* he criticized how this art was caught in its traditional forms, a tendency he saw as mainly enabled by the hierarchical school system dominated by a single leader or *iemoto,* a position usually inherited over many generations within the same family. Here, as with the tea ceremony or the garden, Shigemori argued that the individual's creative act had to be the focus and not the following of a given (traditional) style. He claimed the establishment of the individual within the context of the rapidly changing art scene as well as all of society, and was therefore opposed to traditional ways of *ikebana.*

The same is true for the garden, where at Tofuku-ji's main hall, built in 1939, Shigemori created a manifest for the renewal of this very art. The image of the square stones spread out over a field of moss went around the world and became the icon for the modern Japanese garden. This early masterpiece alone is to guarantee Shigemori a place in history.

But although Japan experienced a strong wave of nationalism in the 1930s, ending only with its defeat in World War II, Shigemori's interest in the country's traditional cultural roots was never politically motivated and therefore did not stop after the war. Quite to the contrary, many of Shigemori's best and often still traditionally inspired designs appear in the 1960s and 1970s, the time of enthusiastic economic growth, now referred to as "the bubble," born out of a fascination with the new and modern.

[3] *kami:* god(s), of which there are about eight million in Shinto.

[4] *iwakura:* a shrine rock; often a large natural stone outcropping where in primitive beliefs a god is held to descend. They have been used since ancient times at prayer sites, as the *iwakura* is thought to contain a *kami* at certain times of the year, or to be a link to the world of the gods.

[5] One of the remarkable characteristics of Japanese culture is the readiness to find a place for all religious teachings and all forms of religious life in a comprehensive view of truth in the people's everyday world. This unique quality is still very noticeable in today's Japanese society. For example, it is not uncommon for people to go to a Catholic school or university, visit a Shinto shrine on New Year's Day, and have a Buddhist funeral ceremony, to mention just a few of many possible situations. Hardly any other culture has integrated so many different religions in people's everyday life. This has been the case ever since Buddhism came to Japan in the sixth century A.D. and has in the meantime led to great integration of Shinto, Buddhism, Daoism, and other religions.

In light of this situation Shigemori's official leaving of the Buddhist faith and returning to Shinto has to be seen as a statement. With it he said that he was more attracted to the very origin of Japanese spirituality and wanted to rid his spiritual life of the diluting influences of Buddhism and other religions. Consequently with Shinto he chose to go back to the very roots of Japanese culture and return to what he saw as the purest available form of religious practice in Japan.

Although this move was congruent with the government policy of the time (Shinto and nationalism), Mirei Shigemori was not a nationalist by any means but rather stated a very personal religious preference, a fact very visible in many of his gardens. But interestingly enough, when working on actual garden projects, his own denomination did not limit Shigemori to designing Shrine gardens only. Quite the contrary, in fact, as many Buddhist temples are to be found among his clients.

[6] Shigemori, "Shinsakuteiki," 313.

[7] Shigemaru Shimoyama, *Sakuteiki—The Book of Garden* (Tokyo: Town & City Planners, 1976), 1. This book constitutes a well-done early translation of the *Sakuteiki.* For a more recent and rather comprehensive translation see also Jiro Takei and Marc P. Keane, *Sakuteiki: Visions of the Japanese Garden* (Rutland: Charles E. Tuttle, 2001), 153. The *Sakuteiki* is said to have been written by Tachibana-no Toshitsuna sometime in the Heian period (784–1185).

[8] Mirei Shigemori, *Gardens of Japan* (Kyoto: Nihon Shashin Insatsu, 1949), 2.

[9] Shigemori, *Gardens of Japan,* 36.

[10] Shigemori, "Shinsakuteiki," 297.

[11] One of the sacred islands in the cult of immortality in ancient Chinese philosophy, together with Hōjō and Eishû islands. It is an imaginary island in the East China Sea where the immortals dwell. This is a theme often depicted in Japanese gardens.

[12] The author of this paper interviewed several members of the Maegaki family on their interaction with and experience of the garden. This afternoon-long conversation took place on Friday, 26 November 2004, at their residence in Saijō, Hiroshima Prefecture. Some of the statements made during that interview are also reflected here.

[13] John Dewey, *Art as Experience* (New York: Perigee Books, 1980), 54.

[14] Shigemori, "Shinsakuteiki," 301.

[15] Maybe the most famous example of this technique is the peninsula at the Katsura imperial villa representing Amanohashidate, a narrow pine-covered strip of land surrounded by the Sea of Japan. Another famous example of this technique can be found at Suizen-ji's Joju-en garden in Kumamoto city. Here not an island but rather a miniature reproduction of Japan's celebrated Mount Fuji is the main focal point throughout the garden.

[16] This is a traditional metaphor, used not only in the Japanese garden. Isamu Noguchi also was inspired by it when he designed the famous California

scenario in Costa Mesa near Los Angeles.

[17] The Daisen-in composition of a dry waterfall and river flowing to the ocean is also what inspired Mirei Shigemori's very first work, the garden that he made together with his father at his parent's house in Yoshikawa, Okayama Prefecture. The waterfall stone setting at the Maegaki residence is in fact almost an exact mirror image of the earlier one. The only thing missing is the stone bridge and the stepping stones through the water. Of course, the depiction of the waterfall, river, and ocean is a traditional set piece in the Japanese garden and has been used often, but nonetheless it is remarkable to find such similarities in Shigemori's first garden as well as in a major work he designed more than 40 years later.

[18] François Berthier, *Reading Zen in the Rocks: The Japanese Dry Landscape Garden* (Chicago: University of Chicago Press, 2000), 59.

[19] Ibid., 77.

[20] Shigemori, "Shinsakuteiki," 283.

[21] Irmtraud Schaarschmidt-Richter, *Japanese Modern Art* (Zurich: Edition Stemmle, 2000), 14.

[22] *suhama*: denotes a beach consisting of a sand bar jutting out into the sea; in Japanese gardens it indicates a pebbled beach sloping gently into a pond, serving both to protect the shore and to enhance the view.

[23] Amanohashidate is considered to be one of the three most scenic places in Japan. It is located on the Tango Peninsula in the north of Kyoto Prefecture at the Sea of Japan; the peninsula is 3.6 kilometers long, less then 189 meters wide, and covered with about 8,000 twisted pine trees. The Japanese name translates as Bridge to Heaven. The garden at Katsura Rikyū features a miniature version, including a stone lantern that has become quite famous.

[24] In the *Nihon Teienshi Taikei,* vol. 28, 77. For relevant English translations: Shimoyama, *Sakuteiki—The Book of Garden,* 10. In this earlier translation of the *Sakuteiki* the relevant sentence reads: "The Mist Shape: The shape of this island should look like the mist stretching over the lake under a clear morning sky, in double and triple folds, with narrow breaks here and there."

[25] The element of the earth mound, called *tsukiyama*, was, just like the undulating line, to gain great importance in Shigemori's later work, to the point where he even built it from colored concrete. Hence the action of first playing with its connotations is an initial step of a longer series of experiments with this very garden feature. For the most relevent examples see the gardens at Tenrai-an (1969) and Hōkoku Jinja (1972).

Contemporary Garden Aesthetics, Creations and Interpretations

Contemporary Garden Aesthetics, Creations and Interpretations

Contemporary Garden Aesthetics, Creations and Interpretations

Contemporary Garden Aesthetics, Creations and Interpretations

Culture, Tradition, and Contemporary Indian Landscape Design: Mohammad Shaheer at Sanskriti Kendra

Priyaleen Singh

There are some who are exclusively modern, who believe that the past is the bankrupt time, leaving no assets for us, but only a legacy of debts. … It is well to remind such persons that the great ages of renaissance in history were those when man suddenly discovered the seeds of thought in the granary of the past. The unfortunate people who have lost the harvest of their past have lost their present age.

—Rabindranath Tagore[1]

The past remains integral to us all, individually and collectively. We must concede the ancients their place. But their place is not simply back there, in a separate and foreign country, it is assimilated in ourselves and resurrected into an ever changing present.

—David Lowenthal[2]

Design in contemporary times has more often than not perceived tradition and modernity as polar opposites in a linear theory of social change, wherein the relationship between tradition and modernity is characterized as being one of perpetual struggle. The role of tradition in promoting and directing social changes is seldom acknowledged, and instead, from a very bounded binary perspective, it is commonly thought that as societies modernize, the significance of tradition declines or disappears.[3] The detraditionalization thesis is theorized as an inescapable aspect of the formation of modernity. However, as Raymond Williams explains, tradition is derived from the Latin root *tradere,* which means to hand over and deliver; the word has survived in the English language as "a description of a general process of handing down with a strong and often predominant sense of this entailing respect and duty."[4] This definition highlights the need for an alternative theoretical framework that reexamines these dualistic analyses and "either-or" frameworks of meanings and instead of seeing them as systems in conflict views tradition and modernity as mutually reinforcing. Tradition in this framework of understanding involves absorbing new features and inventions in the existing ways, thereby modifying both the new and the existing. In respecting the capacity of old and new cultures to exist without conflict and with mutual adaptations, tradition in temporal terms therefore is an active process, something that is created afresh at each moment of renewal.

Debates such as this acquire immense relevance in countries such as India where although "change" is too pressing to admit nostalgia, at the same time "tradition" is too vital to be ignored.[5] Change in the developing countries, in recording transformation from precapitalist to industrial societies, started under the colonial rulers but accelerated with the independence of these countries. It had many implications, both positive and negative. As described by Qadeer, "Cities in the developing world, particularly the large ones, have become centers of conspicuous consumption and imitative westernism. … They act as conduits for foreign ideas and practices and remain mired in dependency, inaction and inequality."[6] Although it is true that the visible "Western" or supposedly "modern" attributes of these cities belong to a small minority of the middle- and upper-class lifestyles, what is of concern is that in mediating change by establishing new frameworks of intervention, this minority helps in imposing alien schemes and practices over a larger majority. In this scenario what role tradition will play in the future in fact emerges as a critical issue. In facing the challenge of modernization, is this heritage of traditions to be preserved merely to remind us of our past, or will it have a decisive role in determining the nature of the future?[7] The answer in terms of design, which includes landscape design, clearly lies in combining valid propositions from the sphere of international knowledge with paradigms from the more indigenous traditions of design with nature that are still identifiable and relevant to contemporary lifestyles. The search for "roots" and their expression has to take place within the structure of a modern secular nation state. It is from this ideological position that one addresses this paper on "culture, tradition, and contemporary Indian landscape design."

Historically, cultures have differed in the nature of their sense of kinship with the natural world. Historical and geographical specificities produced in India a response to nature that was unique in many ways, giving India a very rich tradition of design with nature. The prominence of natural elements in religious iconography, mythology, secular art, music, literature, and architecture demonstrates that there was little dichotomy in the constructs of "nature" and "culture" in Indian thought and practice.[8] This relationship is perhaps best illustrated in the Ragamala and Barahmasa paintings, based on the premise that human moods and sentiments respond to nature and to natural phenomena. Indian classical music also acknowledges this quality wherein the melody interprets the spirit of the season, and the seasonal atmosphere echoes in harmony with the notes and the essence of that melody.[9]

As part of the same narrative, Indian art also viewed nature in essentially a protective role, a portrayal reflected in the gentle, benign faces of nature deities. Nature's maternal, procreative aspect is symbolized many a time by Ganges and Yamuna, the two major rivers in north India, as female divinities adorning the temple doorways and guarding the sanctuary, in the process also ensuring an integration of nature with ritual. Nature indeed inspired both the aesthetic and spiritual sensibilities, to result in landscapes replete with meanings and symbolisms. For example, water for physical purification, which led to spiritual rejuvenation, was a metaphor that found expression both in temples with water tanks for rituals and in urban landscapes with city forms reaching out literally to embrace the water edge. There were moral lessons also learnt from the acts of nature, seen in the motif of the lotus in Indian art and sculpture as a symbol of creation of a world of beauty, formed out of apparent waste. In precolonial India, a participatory relationship with nature was expressed in all aspects of design, architecture and landscape alike. This perception of nature withstood historical changes in both aesthetic taste and religious thought. For example, just as the concept of paradise as a garden was promoted in Islamic imagery and found expression in the Mughal gardens, the Hindu romantic tradition associated with the monsoon season found form in various other gardens such as Deeg in Rajasthan.

Attitudes to design with nature, however, changed in the eighteenth century with colonization and subsequent industrialization. Colonization by the Europeans brought with it a new vocabulary of design with respect to nature that essentially served a new people with a new ideology. It introduced an attitude to art and to nature that had developed contemporaneously in England, namely, "the picturesque." Nature as scenery, by giving primacy to compositional criteria, determined by the act of "seeing" only, sacrificed a wide range of sensory, emotional, and symbolic values inherent in the Indian landscape. In place of a natural world redolent with analogy and symbolic meaning was constructed a detached natural scene to be viewed only. For example, "the river front at Varanasi with its 'irregular' [sic] architecture and teeming pilgrims" was regarded by the British as one of the most picturesque spots in India and featured in many paintings of that time.[10] It was seen and understood purely in visual terms, devoid of the meanings and messages it still held as one of the most sacred spots in India.

The colonial period had already expressed a tendency to override existing indigenous forms of spatial organization wherein large parts of old cities were restructured according to notions of hygiene, order, and aesthetics as defined by a foreign ruling elite.[11] In landscape design too, where both visual and olfactory sensory preferences contrasted sharply with those of the indigenous culture, members of the colonial community were "repelled by the overpowering perfume in the native gardens," "detected a want of freshness in all the native gardens viewed," and were "offended by the straight walks of the Mughal gardens and their juxtaposition of unpruned trees and shrubs."[12] "In their selection of flowers, considerations of beauty have no influence with natives. For them, the prime consideration of a plant is that its flowers have a sweet smell, the second that they are of gaudy and distinct colors. Delicacy of shading, gradation of tint and grace of form, are unappreciated. … Landscape gardening is unappreciated, nay unknown among them."[13] The colonial legacy in introducing new, alien cultural responses to nature certainly disrupted, seemingly irrevocably, the ecological and cultural fabric of Indian society.

The shift in attitudes to design with nature persisted in the post-Independence period when all planning and design exercises continued to identify themselves increasingly with a wish to do away with traditional Indian urbanism, of which traditional patterns of design with nature were an integral part.[14] In exhibiting an unambiguous impulse to identify with Western lifestyles and institutional frameworks, where "Western" became synonymous with modernization and "progress" came to mean imitation of Western ways and adoption of Western vocabularies of design, the urban form was conditioned by the forms and images of what was generally known as the international style.[15] As a result contemporary Indian architecture and landscape design in the twenty-first century continues to stay as a tangent of global architectural activity in which the sources and forms of design are still largely unconnected to the dominant local cultural themes and traditions.

During the last century new building technologies, faster communications, and publication of professional journals have further ensured that design products, architectural fashions, and planning practices are increasingly advertised and then exported, imported, borrowed, copied. Being deliberately designed for international consumption, they reduce the possibilities for regional adaptations. Consequently, in the realm of landscape design today, although most schemes incorporate the trappings of nature like lawns, trees, and water bodies, they are designed with very little regard to the cultural responses to nature, resulting in virtually identical schemes of landscape design cropping up in urban India, in complete negation of the local contexts.

Nature as a product and its subsequent marketing has given rise to another phenomenon, that of nature for conspicuous consumption.[16] As social inequities become more complex, those who have more than the average, and more than they need, tend to express or flaunt such surpluses in the quality of their immediate living environments. With nature as a rare feature in the urban areas, "farm houses," owned by the wealthy and powerful residing in the suburbs, typify an existence in which the possession of nature is more important than the actual enjoyment of it. In these "farm houses" one finds immense wealth being expended to create natural environments artificially. In creating or rather caricaturing nature, products such as fiberglass rocks, silk plants, and concrete trees all help in creating "instant" nature for display. And the little nature that exists in the urban environment is there to be viewed only. Public places abound with signage and guards admonishing people not to touch anything.

This new aesthetic also has meant that nature is not just being marketed but is also used as a device for marketing, or as a packaging material for the promotion of various products. Promoters offer a remarkable range of housing complexes such as "the Forest," "Charmwood Village," "Green Meadows," "Green Fields," all rich in terminologies of traditional rural environments and natural landscapes. But the concern for resources, climate, location, and most importantly human responses to it becomes redundant, and nature, once conceived in both sacred and profane terms, is made into a commodity like everything else. "Landscape has some of the best packaging around, but it is not the product we are meant to buy. Landscape has been treated like incidental music, allowed center stage for effect, but usually treated only as a background element in the final presentation."[17] Clearly, design with nature has come a long way from being a "subject" replete with social meanings and intents, to an "object" for display.

In this scenario some landscape works stand apart, providing an alternative discourse in contemporary landscape design, a discourse rooted in the cultural context of India. With constant reference to and adopting of vocabularies from the rich repository of precolonial traditions of design with nature, these works reflect an understanding of both the natural and cultural ecologies, producing in the process an experience of a very contextual landscape. These designs do not make a plea for historicity or revivalism but rather distinguish historicism from the continuity and relevance of traditional idioms of design to help create more culturally responsive environments. Sanskriti Kendra, with the landscape designed by Mohammad Shaheer, is one such project that, in a manner of speaking, transcends imaginary boundaries, between "the past" and "the present," acknowledging at the same time the need to reinvent some of the expressions found in history to address the reality of present-day India. The design uses historical references as tools to understand how natural ecology and cultural ecology can work together to produce a very contemporary and distinctively Indian landscape.

Sanskriti Kendra is a cultural complex designed as a garden landscape providing a platform for craftspersons to live and work in a creative environment in addition to hosting a number of other activities. The site is a historically rich but geographically arid land at the foothills of the Aravalli range on the outskirts of Delhi, surrounded by what has earlier been referred to as "farm house" development. Although owned and managed by a private trust, the institution is very public in the kinds of activities it hosts. Located in an area of seven acres, its open spaces house an exhibition of everyday art and a display of Indian terra-cotta, along with residential studios and infrastructure such as kilns, conference facilities, a library, and an amphitheater. In visualizing the design of Sanskriti Kendra, the concept initially was that of design "in" nature rather than "with" nature. This was in keeping with the philosophy that design is inherent in nature and the artwork to follow should be

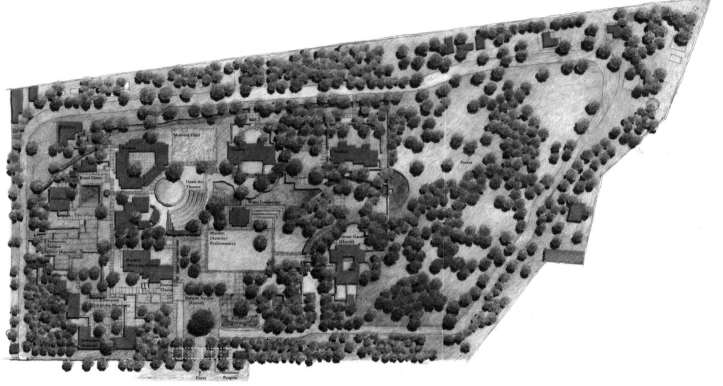

1. Sanskrit Kendra plan (plan: Shaheer associates)

inspired by it. A beginning was therefore made not with building plans or the formalization of a landscape layout, but with the planting of over a thousand indigenous trees. All the trees selected had associations with antiquity, finding mention in Indian epics such as the *Ramayana* and the *Mahabharata*. Asoka (*Saraca indica*), kadamb (*Anthocephalus cadamba*), amaltas (*Cassia fistula*), and arjuna (*Terminalia arjuna*) all are names that resonate through time but also continue to play a more contemporary role with qualities such as shade, climate modulation, soil binding, and aesthetically pleasing forms. This initial intervention guided the evolution of the landscape and subsequently was responsible for the site layout and landscape design twenty years later, by which time the barren, rocky terrain was transformed into an oasis (Fig. 1).

In its planning, the design is one of a continuing dialogue with space, where the natural landscape features all come together to form a series of structured spaces. In fact, the architecture and the landscape are so interwoven in the true spirit of a collaborative effort between the architect and the landscape architect that it is difficult to decipher territorially where architecture ends and the landscape begins.[18]

The site plan borrows extensively from traditional environments and their treatment of open spaces. Traditional settlement planning was far wiser than "modern" planning in its modulation of open spaces. With rooms centered around courtyards and narrow lanes with the mutually shading walls of the structures on either side of the streets that opened into pleasant squares, the concern of a design that wanted to respond to the climate was well articulated. Within these house courtyards and squares or *chowks,* as they are referred to in the vernacular idiom, using only the primordial elements of sun,

2. Entrance *chowk*

wind, water, and earth in very elemental ways, very vibrant environments rich in visual textures were created. These *chowks* and courtyards woven within the larger built-up urban fabric also allowed an effortless transition from indoor spaces to the outdoors. The courtyard was also one way of embracing and capturing the sounds and scents of nature within the four walls of the house to ensure a complete interaction with nature.

The distribution of these open spaces also spelt out a hierarchy both in function and scale. From the town square to the courtyard within the house was the transition from the absolute public realm to the more private domain, establishing several thresholds in the process. The highlight of this transition, paradoxical in terms of design, was that even though these thresholds were clearly established and treated in special ways, one saw a very smooth progression from one realm to another. This range of thresholds, whether from indoors to outdoors, rooms to courtyards, house to street, light to shade, water to land, are all adopted at Sanskriti Kendra in its open space planning (Figs. 2 and 3). In a robustly simple way the aesthetics of the site is derived more from the experience of open spaces than from the application of purely decorative features or the artifacts on display.

As one crosses the first threshold and enters the site, the space in its scale and form is reminiscent of a town square with the banyan tree in the center (Fig. 4). The tree in its symbolism of the world axis supporting the multiple worlds becomes a metaphor for the multiple worlds of activity centered around this space. These worlds are experienced through a circulation system that takes off and terminates in this *chowk*. In this journey through the various spaces are all the experiences one would have encountered in a traditional urban milieu. There are *chowks* with facades textured with visual detail, courtyards with water tanks, trees, and platforms. The forest at the periphery is evocative of the commons or groves that would have been at the edge of the settlement and would have sustained the habitation with food, fuel wood and timber (Fig. 5). Today it plays a more contemporary role by providing the important and vital link with untouched nature in an otherwise overcrowded urban environment that is completely alienated from nature.

The next threshold is provided by the changes in level and floor texture defining the entry into the more private realm that houses some of the terra-cotta exhibits. In the entire landscape, with the open and covered spaces merging seamlessly and in the relationships established between the built-open and solid-void volumes, a visual rhythm is created with the changing colors and textures through the play of sunlight as it falls on the various planes. The experience of the outdoors is achieved not just by being in the open space but also through intermediate courtyards and openings in walls that allow for vignettes of nature, thus renewing involvement with nature at every step. This experience is truly inspired by the courtyard vocabulary of traditional housing.

3. Water bodies as *kunds* and *ghats* (photo: courtesy of Shaheer associates)
4. Banyan square

5. Groves of *champa* trees
6. Courtyard within Terracotta museum

As one moves along, the spaces are not visible all at once but slowly unveil their qualities by the judicious placement of features that also give each space an identity. There is the sacred *tulsi* or basil pedestal reminiscent of the house courtyard (Fig. 6). This part of the circulation is an exploration that is more private in nature. It ends by opening out into the more public central space, which is a contemporary rendition of the *chahar bagh* or quartered garden of the Mughals (Fig. 7).

From the entrance *chowk* one may also make the choice to take the more public course, more in the nature of a processional route winding its way through the streets of the settlement. The scale and treatment of this path and the activities along it are also more extrovert in their character. Contributing to the experience are elements that elicit more vocal and less introspective responses. The cluster of Bankura horses waiting to take off, the raised platform inviting festivities, and the adjoining water tank or *kund* ready to host various events are some of these elements (Figs. 8–10). The platform is in fact created by cleverly placing the Museum of Everyday Art below it, allowing for a visual communication, filtered through trees, with the rest of this central space.

The spaces in their multifunctionality and multiple experiences also borrow from the traditional concepts of town planning, where the notion of a public open space set aside for exclusive recreational activity is absent. A central *chowk* in most settlements is used as a weekly market in the early morning hours, as a playground during the day, to hold public

7. *Char bagh* in courtyard of Terracotta museum

meetings in the evenings, and to celebrate festivals and conduct rituals on special occasions. These *chowks,* with a well, a tree, and a platform often with a shrine, are the focus of all community activity. Spaces thus acquire a social significance beyond the purely functional.

The spaces in Sanskriti Kendra through their design and presence of similar vocabularies such as trees, stepped tanks, and platforms encourage this multiplicity of usage, as a result of which all the spaces are perennially active. Groves of trees enclose the main open space where low walls further define spaces as both teaching and working areas (Fig. 11). The amphitheater through the use of a traditional façade at one end, while evoking the memory of several streets opening out onto the main central *chowk,* is again both a workspace and an arena for performances (Fig. 12). The *maidan* at the entrance is the traditional festival ground seen in historic settlements, used presently as a public gathering space for large meetings and for holding workshops with schoolchildren. It is through sensitive landscape design that the site is able to absorb a whole range of

8. Bankura horses on Terracotta terrace

9. Terracotta terrace (photo: courtesy of Sanskriti Foundation)

10. *Kund* court

diverse activities very successfully. Through their changing scales the spaces also allow for easy legibility and interpretation by all age groups. The comfort levels are established largely because of the use of everyday idioms of design that have been encountered sometime, somewhere, rendering them familiar, be it the glimpses of the mustard fields through the trees recalling the memory of a rural Indian landscape or the space with the cluster of pots in the image of a traditional courtyard.

   The nature of both the spaces and the activities within ensures that the site is not simply for visual exploration but is to be culturally experienced at many levels too, as it is a cultural setting where seasons, colors and textures, events and activities all overlap. Although colors and textures do play a major role in creating an experience, it is the users and the nature of activities encouraged by the spaces that transform the complex into a culturally responsive design. So although the rich earthen color is redolent of unspoilt natural landscapes and the mud-plastered Indian village, and the harmonious weave of soft and hard landscapes using essentially local materials creates a very pleasing and comfortable environment, what is of more significance is the manner in which the spaces are rendered active and alive.

   People from diverse cultural backgrounds relate to the site at various levels. Craftspersons and artisans invited by the Sanskriti Foundation to live and work there view the spaces as an extension of their workplace back home as they sit in the

11. Work spaces adjoining Terracotta terrace (photo: courtesy of the Sanskriti Foundation)

12. Open air theater (photo: courtesy of the Sanskriti Foundation)

shade of the trees weaving a basket, working on the potter's wheel in the courtyards, or simply painting the walls with motifs as they would in their own homes. For the performing artists, conducting theater workshops or giving music and dance recitals, the site is a familiar setting. In encouraging performances done in the tradition of street theater and street performances, so common in towns and village squares all over India, each open space acquires a new life with each performance. For the school children attending various workshops, the spaces as outdoor classrooms are vastly different in scale and form from the conventional classrooms found in schools. They allow for a novel and exciting experience as the children have their classes sitting on the banks of the water body or on the steps of the *kund* as they would in a historic urban settlement.

And for the more "contemporary modern" artists, it is absorbing all these activities as they unfold simultaneously on the canvas of the site and translating and expressing this experience through their works of art, be it painting, sculpture, or installations made in the sylvan setting of the groves of trees. For the visitors to the museum within the complex, it is an experience wherein they carry back memories of more than just the artifacts they see on display. These memories are those of a traditional urban setting with its variety of open spaces, vibrant activities, a richness of textures, and an abundance of nature in many forms and shapes.

The designer is also constantly looking for other paradigms from the rich tradition of design with nature and uses symbols as instruments of knowledge and tools of communication. However, the authenticity of the experience again is not in simply using symbols for ornamentation but in successfully conveying the meanings inherent in them. Although these symbols may be familiar motifs, they encourage an exploration of both the mind and of the site. "It is through symbols that one is awakened; it is through symbols that one is transformed; and it is through symbols that one expresses. Symbols are realities contained within the nature of things."[19] The presence of a "symbol" milieu with meanings, many introspective in nature, may seem romantic and unrealistic in an age characterized by incessant change and quick consumption. However, its appreciation can be rationalized as a healthy reaction to the lack of real psychic nourishment in a world otherwise weighed down by practicality and superficial stimuli.

A study of the Indian landscape indicates that a central feature of the traditional landscape design was its encapsulation of the metaphysical and the physical existence, the spiritual and the utilitarian interpretations imbuing natural elements with new meanings. For example, in a hot dry climate, planting of trees in groves was seen as a meritorious act and articulated in the sacred books of Hinduism as such, as an act from which followed wealth, power, longevity, and absolving of sins and from which followed the concept of sacred groves. The myth of the *kalpavriksha* or wish-fulfilling tree was another theme that entered literature, sculpture, and architecture and became a dominant artistic motif.[20] The tree that was meant to symbolize abundance has been amply suggested in all sculpture, in the luxuriance of its thickset leaves, each leaf rendered individually and robustly. The delineation of *vanadevatas* or tree deities in the sculpted panels at Bharhut showing the hands carrying food and water issuing from the clump of the boughs is perhaps the best explanation of a tree as a giver.[21]

The landscape design at Sanskriti Kendra employs all these metaphors and through adoption of various elements such as the groves on the fringes as sacred groves, or the banyan tree at the entrance in the image of *kalpavriksha,* enhances the cultural forms of representation of nature (Figs. 4 and 5). In Indian thought the tree figures as the total cosmos.[22] The tree in its location is also the sacrificial stake or the royal column venerated at the entrance to all traditional towns and villages.[23] The elegant proportions of the banyan tree in particular, in representing the vitality of nature, are also an expression of life, immortality, and wisdom. With all these cultural interpretations its location at the entrance makes a very powerful statement and underlines the sense of both arriving at and of being in a very special place. Similarly the grove of champa trees (*Plumeria alba*), traditionally associated with temple landscapes, helps create a contemplative and serene ambience (Fig. 5). In contemporary living, with an existence increasingly alienated from nature, a return to a time for which we no longer understand the iconography and symbols attached to it nor share the intrinsic beliefs the ancients had might not seem a valid proposition. But projects such as Sanskriti Kendra offer provocative alternatives in setting up an engagement with nature that is both enriching and fulfilling. Besides helping retrieve some of the meanings lost over time, it also adds new interpretations to the design, surprising many by even inviting poetic reverie within a larger setting of a very noisy and chaotic urban environment.

The artistic creations of the artists and craftspersons working within the site contribute as much to the symbolisms in the landscape as to the realm of arts and crafts. One of the objectives of the project was to develop a framework of spaces that would enable the craftspersons to contribute to the design within the complex and consequently help in its evolution. Even as they reveal the diverse facets of India's pluralistic culture, these creations by the craftspersons help set up a communication between the user and the landscape.

The encounter with the environment does not remain as a passive one but becomes one of interaction and exploration. So, although the exquisite textures of the screens create a more playful ambience inside, the banyan tree also becomes a part of the sculptural creativity constantly changing with time (Fig. 13). The bird feeder placed strategically at the edge of the water body as a vertical element visually connecting the spaces across also becomes an invitation as one is drawn in from afar, to then turn and move on, to take another path and enter another space. Spaces are also embellished with some other very traditional and culturally specific design gestures. The terra-cotta and metal basins, *urlis* in the vernacular dialect, artfully placed at the various thresholds provided by the design with water, rose petals, and leaves is one such profoundly simple and delicate gesture (Fig. 14). They indicate not just an auspicious beginning to a journey through the site but also contribute immensely to the aesthetics of the experience.

To consider these artifacts merely as objects in space would be to undermine both the creativity and the cultural role they play, because it is in these gestures that the landscape acquires an animated and spirited quality. In no way is there an attempt to create a museum of traditions. Instead new and multiple meanings emerge as each individual engages with the landscape at a personal level. The platform with terra-cotta sculptures, for example, elicits a range of responses and imagery from different age groups and different social backgrounds (Fig. 8). The commonly perceived impressions are those of a celebratory procession, a forecourt of a temple, a gathering of elders in an urban or village square, or even a forest grove with animals. It is clearly the landscape design of the space that enables and encourages such a range of interpretations as well as provides an ambience to savor these artifacts.

Other elements of nature such as water have also been treated in a very culturally specific manner. Throughout Indian history the utilitarian dimension to water saw the emergence of many important typologies of design. The step wells and *ghats* were two such architectural vocabularies. The wells were often rendered into large monuments of high architectural and artistic merit where the design not only enabled easy access to the water source, but also served as a cool retreat in the hot season. The *ghats* or steps along the water front were also employed at an urban scale with entire cities addressing the water source and in

13. Banyan tree as sculpture (photo: courtesy of the Sanskriti Foundation)

14. *Urlis* at various thresholds (photo: courtesy of the Sanskriti Foundation)

15. Water landscape of *ghats*
16. Water landscape as art (photo: courtesy of the Sanskriti Foundation)

the process integrating the *ghats* with the open space system of the city. Other design forms with water, as in the Mughal gardens, illustrate best how with only a scant amount of water and spirited design, the imagery of all the water in the world could be recalled to mind. Design with water engaged the best financial, intellectual, and aesthetic energies of the people and became an expression of well-being, of life, and of happiness.

The symbolisms in water are also many. In ancient texts water precedes creation and reabsorbs it and is thus associated with both evolution and dissolution implying both death and rebirth.[24] It symbolizes fertility as it sustains life, and though being formless itself, it is a reservoir of all possibilities of existence. Sanskriti Kendra in employing these vocabularies embodies all these meanings and many more within its spatial experience. The *kund,* the lotus pond, and the *ghats* are used, though in very contemporary forms (Fig. 3). Closely linked to water is the symbol of the lotus that has been used by Mohammad Shaheer in many of his other schemes as well. In Sanskriti Kendra it is the lotus ponds at the entrance and within the courtyard. At Astha Kunj, an unexecuted project, the designer makes extensive use of the geometry of the lotus petal. In Vir Bhumi, a memorial site, stone lotus buds mark out the floorscape. All this is in recognition of its importance in Indian myth, art, and ritual where the lotus becomes more than just an ecological statement of the processes of nature.[25] Indeed, if the motif of the lotus were to be excluded from Indian poetry, prose, music, dance, sculpture, or relief, Indian heritage would be impoverished beyond recognition.[26]

The design at Sanskriti Kendra also acquires ecological validity by incorporating the traditional wisdom of water harvesting. Conservation of water at the site was an early concern in the design. The site slopes were graded so as to direct the storm water where it could either be collected within the site or absorbed into the ground. The central water channel became

17. Edge of water landscape (photo: courtesy of the Sanskriti Foundation)

an important element of the scheme as it harvests the rainwater through a series of indigenous design forms such as *kunds* and *ghats* into a larger water body at the edge of the forest (Fig. 15). This water body when dry in the summer also becomes a canvas for artwork (Fig. 16). By placing activity spaces around the water bodies, the portrayal of water as a physical and spiritual oasis in a hot dry climate is further enhanced.

The concern for ecology is echoed in the entire design process. The materials used in the landscape are in conjunction with nature by being consciously natural, local, site specific, and environmentally appropriate. The philosophy of the Sanskriti Foundation, responsible for conceiving this project and administering it, is reflected in the very sensitive use of ordinary materials to create the extraordinary. Materials such as quartzite, sandstone, brick, terra-cotta, and stone grit finish not only help in creating a richly textured ambience but also connecting to the larger urban landscape of Delhi, where today they are still to be found in the monuments from the twelfth to the eighteenth centuries.

In employing elements and images that are known to most users, the design expresses a desire to go beyond an esoteric expression of art to one that communicates with all. The site in eliciting active and varied responses reflects the success of a design that is comprehended by everybody. Landscape design thus becomes both a powerful and poetic medium of

communication (Fig. 17). The intent to open the site to all literally and metaphorically is best expressed in the treatment of the boundary. The definition of the site is through a very transparent wall that allows for a visual connection into the site, inviting everybody to enter in and be part of the experience within.

Through this project the designer explores new terms of reference, other than those conventionally adopted, for developing contemporary landscape practice in India. It represents the design possibilities offered by a specifically Indian vocabulary for dealing with outdoor environments and landscape design. The blending of traditional features in a contemporary milieu has been done with sophistication so that even for the visitor who is unfamiliar with the traditional meanings, but is simply open to the experience, the journey through the site is a stimulating and enriching one. It is contemplative at times and robust at others, but at all times strongly indigenous in its flavor. This response reflects on the genuinely humane content of the design that appeals not just to the sensibilities of the indigenous population but to the universal human senses. It is a design that is vibrant and living and is as old as it is contemporary, as beautiful as it is functional, as complex as it is simple, and as Indian as it is universal.

The project also highlights that aesthetics in design is more than just a visual experience. It is a cultural statement wherein the landscape becomes a repository of both memory and of a living tradition. Within these cultural experiences are contained the other poetic, romantic, and mystical nuances to landscape design. At Sanskriti Kendra the designer calls upon the past to play a role in the present, not simply because of a nostalgic sentiment but because it is a representation of a more wholesome and meaningful existence and is rooted in the soil of life. The rationale for referring to the past depends on what one is looking for in the relationship, as well as the quality of communication with it. A sentimental nostalgic feeling where mistrust of the future fuels nostalgia for the past, a need for a sense of identity or valuing a sense of continuity, are all valid reasons for invoking the past.[27]

But perhaps the most pervasive reason to recall it is the lessons and the inspiration that it can aid us with, thus helping in constructing a better environment for today and the future. In adopting the vocabularies of the past much depends upon both the strength and relevance of the import and the resilience and cultural depth of the recipient.[28] In drawing upon the past perceptions of design with nature, the designer ensures that the manifestations are not to be considered as antiquities or museum pieces, but as useful references that represent a unique facet of a living Indian culture, philosophy, and symbolism. They are of particular relevance as they can continue to enrich landscape design concepts for urban spaces today. In viewing the past it is therefore not a question of historic indulgence or of traveling back, but of being aware of what is relevant today, what exists in the present, and what can travel into the future via the created present. "Traditional" in the context here also denotes a more humane landscape setting, one that has not yet lost contact with elementary perceptions and archaic needs of the human sensibilities. It is perhaps this quality that engages everybody in its experience, making "traditional" a universally appreciated dialect. And that perhaps is the strength of all traditional design anywhere in the world.

The "past," often expressed in and seen as synonymous with traditions, has invariably been invoked when a society is undergoing rapid transformations resulting in a sense of loss of what had existed a while ago in the "past." The loss is felt even more acutely when the "new" replacing the "existing" is perceived to be much inferior in its content and form. For example, Japan in the 1950s underwent rather aggressive and rapid change and transformed from a traditional to an industrialized society. The idea of "tradition" manifested itself in many forms, one such being the works of Shigemori Mirei discussed elsewhere in this publication. In contrast to Japan, India as a developing country, although also transforming significantly in the last several years, has done so at a pace not as disruptive as probably occurred in Japan several decades earlier. In mapping the transformations, it is observed that the change has been restricted to the larger towns and cities that present the interface between a fast globalizing world and the relatively smaller towns and villages, which even today continue to nurture traditional practices and lifestyles to a great extent.

In India it is only in very recent times that the positive aspects of indigenous patterns of development and building practice are beginning to surface among some professionals, in a conscious search for identity in their professional practice.[29] But here too, in relatively nascent disciplines such as landscape architecture, this search for "roots" is largely missing. It is also true that this search has many a time produced a self-conscious design in which historic references have been trivialized to become mere ornaments. Projects such as Sanskriti Kendra indicate the possibility of a more sophisticated and authentic synthesis between traditions and more "modern" living and illustrate that a genuine future in design may be found by combining them. It is also important to note that traditions will be sustained over time only if they are continuously re-embedded in new contexts and re-moored to face new challenges. The design of Sanskriti Kendra recognizes this and does not lack the vitality of innovations. And yet it continues to stay authentic in its cultural context.

In highlighting the possibility of an indigenous response to contemporary design, the project perhaps makes an even larger statement concerning all aspects of living in a developing country. It illustrates that an indigenous model of modernization that rationalizes, strengthens, and builds upon the developmental potential of its traditions and historical practices is possible. Such an approach does not exclude foreign ideas and technology but insists on assimilating them within a progressive, indigenous framework. In adopting such an approach it is hoped that Indian landscape design will cease to have its present indistinguishable character and begin to make emphatic statements that are more responsive to their own cultural backgrounds.

NOTES

[1] Rabindranath Tagore, *Creative Unity* (London: Macmillan, 1926), 195.

[2] David Lowenthal, *The Past Is a Foreign Country* (Cambridge: Cambridge University Press, 1985), 412.

[3] Etzioni, ed., *Social Change* (New York: Basic Books, 1964).

[4] Raymond Williams, *Key Words: A Vocabulary of Culture and Society* (London: Fontana, 1981), 268.

[5] A. G. K. Menon, *Cultural Identity and Urban Development* (New Delhi: Raj Press, 1989).

[6] M. A. Qadeer, *Urban Development in the Third World* (New York: Praeger, 1983), 28.

[7] A. G. K. Menon, "Conservation and Urban Development," unpublished paper given at national seminar on Urban Development and Management, Bhopal, 6–7 March 1992.

[8] Themes wherein nature serves to intensify the feelings and establish moods figure conspicuously in the works of Indian writers, Kalidasa in the fourth century A.D. being the most famous. His impact on Indian tradition was deep and influenced classical Sanskrit drama and poetry to a great extent. His most famous work, *Rtusamhara,* is a descriptive poem of the six Indian seasons. It contains brilliant depictions of the beauties of nature where the human feelings, whether of love, pangs of separation, sorrow, or serenity, are projected onto the world of nature.

[9] Classical treatises on music are based on seasons. They stress the importance of playing certain *ragas* (compositions) and *raginis* (subcompositions) in certain seasons. Indian classical music tradition recognizes six principal *ragas* and 36 *raginis,* the six *ragas* being often equated to six seasons. According to the Indian theory, there is an inherent quality in ragas and particular seasons that evoke same or similar moods or *rasa* and attune them to the atmosphere of nature prevailing during a given season.

[10] Mildred Archer, *British Drawings in the India Office Library* (London: Her Majesty's Stationery Office, 1969), 55.

[11] Anthony King, *Colonial Urban Development* (London: Routledge and Kegan Paul, 1976). In fact, there was almost a complete negation of the traditional patterns of development in all spheres of design. In 1886, John Lockwood Kipling, director of Mayo School of Art in Lahore, wrote of the institute established in Rourkee, "Rourkee training is now considered necessary for all who would attempt to design. … But surely it is a strange omission that in a college for Indian students there should be no Oriental department. Not a single native draughtsman turned out from this school has been taught the architecture of the country" (J. L. Kipling, "Indian Architecture of Today," *Journal of Indian Art* 1, no. 3 [1886]: 2–4).

[12] Ray Desmond, *The European Discovery of the Indian Flora* (New York: Oxford University Press, 1992), 282.

[13] R. W. Danvers, *Calcutta Review 49* (Calcutta: Government Printing Press, 1869), 202.

[14] In the years immediately following Independence most Indian nationalists drew a wholly different conclusion from the colonial experience, arguing that India's subjugation was a consequence of its intellectual and economic backwardness. "The central question in the debates on (design) style in the decades before Independence was: How much indigenisation of style could the British afford to indulge in without appearing to be making political concessions to a subject people? After Independence, the question changed to: How much indigenisation could a newly independent nation afford without appearing backward and weak in its own eyes and in the image it presented to the rest of the world?" (Moloy Chatterjee, "Contemporary Indian Architecture," in *India* [Delhi: Brijbasi, 1987], 83). In this perspective, its revitalization and modernization could come about only through a clean break with tradition by emulating the West. Nehru, the first prime minister of independent India, best articulated this vision in the design of Chandigarh: "Let this be a new town symbolic of the freedom of India, unfettered by the traditions of the past … , an expression of the nation's faith in the future," and "the site chosen is free from the existing encumbrances of old towns and old traditions. Let it be the first large expression of our creative genius flowering on our newly earned freedom" (Ravi Kalia, *Chandigarh: The Making of an Indian City* [Delhi: Oxford University Press, 1987], 12).

[15] Perhaps this view fits into the worldview where dramatic social changes wrought by industrialization and urbanization led to new attempts to understand both the past and the present. While in one nineteenth-century development, the Romantic movement looked backwards with nostalgia toward a simpler past and nurtured an intense interest in folk life and national traditions, on the other hand was developed an evolutionary hierarchy with Western civilizations at the top and primitive cultures at the bottom (Carolyn Merchant, ed., *Ecology: Key Concepts in Critical theory* [Atlantic Highlands, NJ: Humanities Press, 1994]). This no doubt signaled that the Western civilizations were there to be emulated and copied and primitive cultures to be looked down upon and abandoned on the way to progress. This perception has been retained and has become an integral part of most development ideologies in the "developing" world.

[16] The term "conspicuous consumption" was used by the American economist Thorstein Veblen in 1899 to describe the behavior of a new wealthy class in displaying their affluence. "In order to gain and to hold the esteem of men," he wrote, "it is not sufficient merely to possess wealth or power. The wealth or power must be put in evidence. The most obvious way of putting wealth in evidence is to be ostentatious in one's acquisition of goods" (quoted in E. Relph, *The Modern Urban Landscape* [London: Croom Helm, 1987], 89).

[17] Brian Goodey, "Spotting, Squatting, Sitting or Setting: Some Public Images of Landscapes," in *Landscape Meanings and Values* (London: Allen and Unwin, 1986), 82–99.

[18] The landscape architect worked very closely with the architectural firm of Upal Ghosh Associates toward evolving the site plan.

[19] Laleh Bakhtiar, *Sufi, Expressions of the Mystic Quest* (London: Thames and Hudson, 1976), 25.

[20] One of the earliest representations of vegetation in Indian sculpture is the *kalpavriksha* of Besnagar, which has been assigned to the third century B.C. and represents the mythical wish-fulfilling tree that produced food, drinks, dresses, and ornaments.

[21] C. Sivaramamurti, *Approach to Nature in Indian Art and Thought* (New Delhi: Kanak Publications, 1980), 73.

[22] Snodgrass has likened its branches to the heavens, the lower branches or the surface of the ground where it grows to the plane of the earth, the roots plunging into the subterranean levels as the hells. The branches and roots are thought of as the superior and inferior states of existence (Adrian Snodgrass,

The Symbolism of the Stupa [Delhi: Motilal Banarasi Dass, 1992], 180).

[23] Jeannine Auboyer, *Daily Life in Ancient India* (London: Weidenfeld and Nicolson, 1965), 137.

[24] In the Hindu conception of creation water is one of the five primary elements. In the evolution of the world, water was the fourth element to appear, preceding only *prithvi* or the earth, and at its dissolution the world is supposed to assume first the form of water.

[25] The lotus is regarded as the divine flower, symbolizing the earth with its eight petals as the eight quarters, and in blossoming with the rising sun is seen as a bestower of life. In mythical terms, the lotus emerges from the primeval waters, connected to the mythical center of the earth through its stem. It is mentioned several times in the Vedas, the ancient texts dating back to 1000 B.C. It symbolizes a miraculous birth since it comes into being out of water and is *swayambhu* or self-born. It also has moral interpretations. The lotus exists in the water and yet it remains above it; it can grow in slime and yet its beauty is untarnished.

[26] Kapila Vatsayan *Prakriti: The Integral Vision* (New Delhi: Indira Gandhi National Centre for the Arts, 1995), vol. 3, 147.

[27] As Lowenthal suggests, nostalgia is a memory with the pain removed that often comes when the rapidity of change is difficult for people to absorb and where change represents a loss more than a gain. "The past is integral to our sense of identity; the sureness of I was is a necessary component of the sureness I am" (Lowenthal, *Past Is a Foreign Country,* 41).

[28] William J. R. Curtis, "Modernism and the Search for an Indian Identity" *Architectural Review* 182, no. 1086 (1987): 33–38.

[29] A. G. K. Menon, "Vernacular Architecture and Colonial Legacy: An Indian Perspective," unpublished paper presented at the conference 'Future of Asia's Past' at Chiang mai, 11–14 January 1995.

Contemporary Garden Aesthetics, Creations and Interpretations

Contemporary Garden Aesthetics, Creations and Interpretations

Contemporary Garden Aesthetics, Creations and Interpretations

Contemporary Garden Aesthetics, Creations and Interpretations

The Garden as the Last Luxury Today: Thought-Provoking Garden Projects by Dieter Kienast (1945–1998)

Udo Weilacher

"It is quite simply a fact that our present social, political, and religious situation is hanging in the balance, and there is very little we can do about it."[1] It was the Swiss landscape architect Dieter Kienast (1945–1998) who in this way characterized the condition of our society in 1998, and there have been no fundamental changes to these conclusions in the past few years. On the contrary: at the beginning of the twenty-first century all disciplines concerned with designing and shaping the environment see themselves confronted with new, exceptionally dynamic development trends changing the image of the landscape and the city as well as our perception of nature and ideas of the environment far more radically and, at the same time, more subtly than could have been predicted in the last century. All of these changes are not without severe consequences for our contemporary way of experiencing the built and natural environments. If gardens today still reflect our understanding of the world, what are they supposed to look like in the twenty-first century? These questions conceptually reach far beyond the traditional boundaries of the garden. Current debate in Europe on the sustainability of cities, urbanization of cultivated land, increasing privatization and the ensuing disappearance of public space, urban decline and urban perforation—meaning the demolition of inner city building structures caused by a negative growth of population in many European cities—as well as worsening economic and ecological crises pose a variety of very difficult questions to contemporary landscape architecture and environmental planning.

There is decreasing confidence in the effectiveness of human attempts to make corrections in a complexly interlinked, heterogeneous environmental system. But in spite of all these dramatic changes, to most contemporary landscape architects the issue of renewal in garden design and landscape architecture appears merely as a formal problem. Many landscape architects and environmental artists cling to historical models, reproduce artistic patterns, develop conspicuous design graphics, or get caught up in superficial, formalistic approaches to design, constantly in search of a formal style to make into their own, readily recognizable trademark. Dieter Kienast viewed such trends as symptomatic of an acute, serious lack of theory and the renewal of garden culture as primarily being a problem of content, "as it is not possible to carry out an important aspect of landscape architecture on an emotional level."[2] He, however, did not see himself as a theorist let alone as the creator of pioneering theories in today's landscape architecture, but his extensive oeuvre sparked many significant developments in contemporary landscape architecture.

1. Ernst Cramer, Garden of the Poet with view of Lake Zurich, 1959. Piles of prefabricated concrete elements structure the area and many gardeners interpreted the concrete container with geraniums as pure provocation. (Copyright: Archive for Swiss Landscape Architecture, Rapperswil)

2. The large pyramid in Ernst Cramers Garden of the Poet was reflected in the pool and appeared to be much larger than it actually was. Visitors estimated a height of 10 metres but it was actually about 4 metres high. (Copyright: Archive for Swiss Landscape Architecture, Rapperswil)

3. The design plan for the Garden of the Poet, variant in adhesive foil on transparent paper. Four pyramids measuring 2, 2.8, 3 and 4 metres high and a stepped asymmetrical truncated cone with an overall height of three metres and a base diameter of about eleven metres formed an abstract earth sculpture in Zurich 1959. (Copyright: Archive for Swiss Landscape Architecture, Rapperswil)

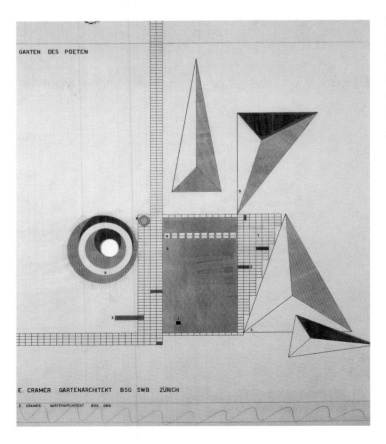

Just like the French landscape architect Bernard Lassus, whose theory-backed work he held in very high regard, Dieter Kienast was "one of the few landscape architects to discuss landscape architecture at a generalizing, theoretical level as well as describing their own projects."[3] Kienast's fundamental "10 Theses on Landscape Architecture," formulated for the first time in the mid-1990s, mark the theoretical coordinates of his oeuvre. In particular, his belief in an approach to discontinuity in a supposedly self-contained conception of the world and his penchant for heterogeneity in a landscape architecture "between Arcadia and leftovers"[4] pose interesting questions as to his own theoretical points of reference. But, above all, he provides worthwhile points of departure for exploring current theories in landscape architecture, including the question: What kind of aesthetical environmental experience might be adequate with regard to the contemporary changes in our society? Kienast's general aim was to make landscape architecture an expression of the spirit of the age, the garden as a place of meaning, intended to heighten awareness, awaken the senses, and open perspectives for new aesthetic experiences, especially including a higher sensibility for natural processes rather than for finished design objects. When he died in 1998 at the age of 53, he was one of the most influential landscape architects in Europe.

Marked interest in urban development and a special feel for architecture were particular features of his work, because Kienast was aware of the fact that the majority of the world population lives in urban environments. "Our work is the search for a nature of the city, which colour is not only green, but also grey" was one of the most important theses for him.[5] Beginning in the early 1980s, Dieter Kienast and his team cultivated the dialogue between architectonic severity and naturalness with outstanding consistency and skill. His inspiration was derived from his interest in not only the fine arts, in particular American Minimal Art, but also Swiss radical garden architectural works dating from the 1950s and 1960s, particularly those of the Zurich garden architect Ernst Cramer.[6] "The things that were relevant in the early eighties are not the same as those that are relevant in 1995, but, despite this, the works of Ernst Cramer still inspire me today"[7] Kienast explained in 1996. He greatly admired Cramer's modern landscapes and further developed Cramer's radical design approach, which gained international recognition for the first time with the abstract Garden of the Poet, built in 1959 and published by the Museum of Modern Art in New York in 1964 as one of the most visionary examples of modern garden architecture (Fig. 1).[8]

"You … bring a completely new landscape, you create a feeling of space that I have never experienced before in the open air. You prove that with an ingenious spirit and precise application of the craft it is not absolutely necessary to work with the costly material soil as the forces of the natural elements do. You do not create an imitation of a natural feature, but you create a work of the kind we abstract painters and sculptors have been striving after with concrete resources for years." (Fig. 2) This letter from Hans Fischli could have been aimed at the landscape architect of the Mountain Garden (*Berggarten*) at the 2000 International Horticultural Show in Graz, offering a new aesthetic experience, located in the stress field between art and landscape architecture, and discussing the contemporary concept of nature without imitating natural formations (Fig. 3). But, in fact, Fischli, the distinguished architect, painter, sculptor, and then director of the renowned Kunstgewerbeschule (Arts and Crafts School) and Kunstgewerbemuseum (Arts and Crafts Museum) in Zurich, was writing a tribute in 1959 to a brilliant work by Ernst Cramer at the First Swiss Horticultural Exhibition G|59 on the shores of Lake Zurich.

Decades after the G|59 show, Kienast was also able to benefit from his knowledge of land art, which had caused a sensation with spectacular earthworks in American deserts from the late 1960s onwards. Although Cramer's earthworks in the famous Garden of the Poet were still freestanding individual structures, in Graz 29,000 cubic meters of soil were used to create

4. The abstract pattern of folds in the Graz Mountain Garden by Kienast Vogt Partner can be made out clearly from the viewing tower at the International Horticultural Show IGA 2000 in Graz, Austria.
5. Particularly attractive spatial sequences appear between the earth pyramids of the Mountain Garden, while blooming lady's mantle nicely highlights the scenery in the background.

an extended earth sculpture that people could walk on as well as stroll through and experience the space in total (Fig. 4). For these kinds of sculptures, Manfred Schneckenburger, director of the *documenta 6* in Kassel 1977, once pointed out: "This sculpture asks to be used, entered, mounted, touched. In contrast to earlier works of art, it not only wants to be experienced in an aesthetic or intellectual dialogue, but—literally—wants to be lived. … Thus, psychology too has recognized that the whole body is an organ of spatial experience: and it is precisely this that sculpture not only uses as a form of action, but takes as its very subject and transmits into the various sensorial dimensions of the body. … The body is both used and experienced through this use. It is both an instrument and sensorium."[10] This understanding of art as a holistic physical experience is strongly connected to John Dewey's concept of art as experience.

Just like a *hortus conclusus,* the Mountain Garden in Graz is framed by a steep grassy rampart about five meters high like a monastery wall, which has two striking openings cut into it with runs of exposed concrete. Between the twenty-six large earth formations, which are accessed by a network of geometrically cut paths, are remains of a monotonous spruce plantation that was already on the site. Rather than stripping out this ecologically inferior vegetation, it was integrated in a radical new piece of contemporary landscape architecture (Fig. 5). Large individual trees, some newly planted, many found on site, are natural extras on the scene in the northern area of the garden, accentuating the various spatial sequences. The dialogue between the basic architectural concept and the natural quality that has become a distinguishing stylistic quality of Kienast Vogt Partner's projects also occurs at the centrally placed woodland pool in the Mountain Garden. Its basic form is geometrical, and it acts both as a reflecting pool and as a habitat, complementing the remarkable composition of art and nature (Fig. 6).

Unlike the temporary Poet's Garden, which the garden designers' community of the 1950s saw as mere provocation, the Mountain Garden was retained as a public park once the international exhibition was over. Its precision means that it needs to be tended as carefully and expertly as many a historical masterpiece. In a polemic against the widespread design loquacity of horticultural shows, Dieter Kienast expressed a wish for "everyday, intellectual, sensual, atmospheric, green and colourful, large and small, light and dark, open and closed, ordered and wild gardens, full of poetry."[11] He has made his own wish come true in Graz and revitalized the discussion about the right balance between art and nature in contemporary landscape architecture. The new aesthetic experience that the Mountain Garden offers derives from at least three different aspects: first, its uncompromising quest for a new contemporary formal language in landscape architecture beyond conventional ecodesign and at the same time closely linked to the culture of garden architecture. Second, one finds the questioning of traditional clichéd images of nature and, third, the intelligent unbiased incorporation of existing landscape elements. Setting new trends in evolved cultural landscapes without destroying existing identities is now one of the most common but also the

6. The little tree seems to part the earth masses effortlessly: graphic plant patterns emphasize the artificiality of the Mountain Garden in Graz by Kienast Vogt Partner.
7. Reflections in the woodland lake of the earthworks enhance the experience of landscape art in clear reference to Ernst Cramers Garden of the Poet from 1959.

most difficult tasks in current landscape architecture. Successful interventions stand out in many cases by combining old and new to make new connections in terms of meaning, without destroying each other's expressiveness (Fig. 7).

Since the early 1980s and particularly when garden design, rather defined as "design with nature," sought to imitate nature on purely ecological grounds reached its peak, landscape architecture was threatened to freeze into a "dictate of nature."[12] Many garden architects at that time offered a rather questionable "real" experience of nature by simply producing artificial illusions of nature in any given environment. Kienast knew that, based on the theories put forward by Basel-based sociologist Lucius Burckhardt, nature itself is invisible, and he understood that nature is only getting visible and accepted if the viewed image in reality matches an ideal image in the head of the spectator. Therefore his aesthetically radical—sometimes provoking, projects, questioning traditional images of ideal nature, had the effect of long-sought-after liberation for the young generation of European landscape architects. The sensational international competition successes of Kienast Vogt Partner made substantial contributions to an increase in thinking as to what a new balance between architecture and landscape, design and ecology, culture and nature in garden and landscape might look like. While still a young researcher, Kienast investigated the question of a conscious approach to dynamic processes and spontaneous development of urban vegetation.[13] What began as a doctoral thesis in the late 1970s led fifteen years later to the development of urban landscape and garden architecture projects that have been highlighted in the latest research work at the Leibniz University in Hanover,[14] as outstanding examples pointing the way ahead for a new approach to nature in the urban environment responding to contemporary existential problems.

As far back as 1981, Dieter Kienast pleaded for a critical questioning of the popular clichéd images of nature in an essay entitled "By Formation-Dictation to Nature-Dictation—or: Gardens against Human Being?".[15] In his view ecology was no longer a cure-all and nature no longer the sole designer,[16] but, nonetheless, projects and experiences derived from a conscious approach of ecology principles were by no means to be ignored. Kienast was, to use a term coined by Bernard Lassus in 2005, a truly post-ecological landscape architect, that is to say, a landscape architect who clearly transcended the ecological ideology of the 1970s and 1980s without banning ecology from his works. Almost every project by Kienast Vogt Partner shows a remarkable sensibility for the given environmental circumstances and ecological requirements as well as for the genius loci, without producing clichéd images of "ecodesign," images that meet the conventional expectations about the preferred naturalistic look of ecological design, but do not truly relate to the given environmental circumstances. The wetland biotope on the underground parking lot, for example, was such a popular fake image of nature, applied like camouflage to the surface of a building but not really touching the essence of the place. "I call this kind of new garden design ecodesign," Kienast stated,[17] and clearly turned against a very popular, naturalistic and decorative style of garden architecture in Europe, originating from the rising environmental awareness in the 1970s. Kienast believed this kind of ostensible design does nothing to improve the deeper understanding, to intensify the experience of nature or the public sensibility for the environment by concealing the true character of any given situation.

It was particularly Dieter Kienast's ability to combine seemingly divergent positions between preservation and design, orientation toward processes and awareness of form that guaranteed his work a central place in present international discourse. "Despite this renewed stressing of the diachronic over the synchronic, there are some designers who operate with equal facility in both areas. One of those landscape architects was Dieter Kienast," Marc Treib wrote in the 2003 *Landscape Architecture Journal*,[18] pointing out that Kienast, given his strong interest in garden history, never had any difficulties discussing his work as part of the past development in European garden architecture. At the same time—as stated in his sixth thesis "Garden Architecture as an Expression of Zeitgeist"[19]—he was convinced that contemporary landscape architecture should also be viewed and developed in strong relation to all contemporary forms of art and culture.

In particular, Kienast always attached special importance to the collaboration between artists and landscape architects, especially admiring the minimalist work by artists like Richard Long, Carl Andre, and Donald Judd, and working together with Jenny Holzer, Fischli/Weiss, or Ian Hamilton Finlay. In fact, it was Finlay who inspired the Swiss landscape architect to create some of his written interventions in gardens, like "ET IN ARCADIA EGO," formed as a concrete balustrade in a private garden near Zurich, providing a profound subtitle to the magnificent view into the Arcadian alpine landscape. Not only from Ian Hamilton Finlay but also from Lucius Burckhardt and Bernard Lassus, who had already developed his concept *l'intervention minimale* in the 1970s, Kienast learned that the successful transformation of a site does not depend on the range of physical transformations, but on the intervention suited to the perception of the user. With such minimal interventions, aiming at the idealized landscape images in the contemplator's mind rather than at the outward appearance of a garden, Kienast skillfully modified the reading, experience, and deeper understanding of the given environmental context, not only in private gardens.

With regard to a common tendency to interpret landscape architecture as a form of art, Kienast stated critically: "People who confine themselves to purely aesthetic works often appear to be fighting something of a rearguard action. Perhaps they make it a bit too easy for themselves. But their work does have

8. One of the four floors in the Kunsthaus Bregenz, built by the Swiss architect Peter Zumthor, was totally flooded by Olafur Eliasson and Günther Vogt for the exhibition *The Mediated Motion* in 2001 to contrast nature with architecture. (photo: Markus Tretter)

9. In this room of the Kunsthaus Bregenz in Austria the artist Olafur Eliasson and the landscape architect Günther Vogt covered the whole floor with rammed earth creating almost a Land Art atmosphere for the exhibition *The Mediated Motion*. (photo: Markus Tretter)

10. Kienast Vogt Partner in 1994 designed the private garden K., eleven metres wide and 40 metres long, in an almost minimalist manner.
11. In the garden K., Dieter Kienast integrated a 2.5 metres high, 60 centimetres thick and eleven metres long wall of rammed earth as a spatial enclosure and the most important design feature.

something of a refreshing, liberating quality. However, it's my opinion that we work in public open space and what we plan shapes part of people's everyday life. … Here we have a responsibility, which we can't simply avoid by references to freedom of the artistic or having to accommodate wishes of the general public. What matters much more is to keep looking at what one is doing in terms of its quality and validity, to develop mental alertness and to find new answers to Adorno's old question: How can a specific purpose be translated into space, using what forms and what material? Seen in this way, architectural imagination would be the ability to articulate space through its purposes, to let them become space, to build forms to fulfill purposes."[20]

One of the most important purposes for Kienast was the everyday experience of the garden as the last luxury of today: "And so we are strolling through the garden, we enjoy the shady chill of the old trees, the bewitched wilderness of elderberry, butterfly bush and vipers bugloss, we get infatuated by the incomparable scent of jasmine, we listen to the murmuring fountain, taste the dewy grapes, dream under the apple tree, wander through the rose arch, get to the sunny terrace and take a deep breath."[21] The landscape architect felt that the garden might be an antidote to our changing perceptive abilities as already characterized by the German philosopher Hartmut Böhme in 1989: "Our perceptive abilities are conditioned to identify the information content of images within a matter of seconds. The sensuousness to which we are attuned has, as it were, been decentralized by a frightening speed of our modern means of transport and the unrelenting onslaught of images in both cities and the media, has become restless, nervous, greedy, aggressive. Perception of nature requires a different relationship to time. … Perception of nature reveals entirely different time forms, rhythms, time figures in which natural processes are organized. Human time, societal and historical time, and the times occurring in nature only overlap in very few zones and are, otherwise, poles apart."[22]

Kienast's sensitive, almost romantic approach to nature and his unbiased cooperation with modern artists has been further developed by some of his younger colleagues in recent years and in exceptional cases has even achieved recognition in art museums of international repute. The exhibition entitled *The Mediated Motion* by the Danish artist Olafur Eliasson in collaboration

12. The idea of the rammed earth wall in the private garden Kienast was to make the invisible visible and to present a powerful image of nature that was living but not green.

with landscape architect Günther Vogt, a former partner of Kienast's, at the Kunsthaus Bregenz in 2001 was an outstanding presentation of art, landscape architecture, and architecture ultimately because of its successful symbiosis with the museum architecture of Peter Zumthor (Fig. 8).[23] Olafur Eliasson and Günther Vogt transformed Peter Zumthor's rigorously orthogonal architecture of concrete and glass on different levels by means of smell, fog, water, plants, and soil in a route of experience and of awareness of this experience. The estrangement effect played an important role in this concept: one room of the museum was completely filled with rammed earth, allowing the visitors to walk on it and experience architecture and nature in a completely unexpected way: muffled sound, perceptible higher humidity, and an earthy smell pervaded the gallery room (Fig. 9). In the same manner, Kienast preferred to create aesthetics from reduction and concentration. His earlier garden designs in particular, with up to two-meter-high walls of rammed earth in very small private spaces, addressed exactly the same kind of primary experience of nature: pure soil, pure dirt is not just a construction material but a medium with its own inherent history, mythology, and meanings, interacting with all other elements in the garden and reacting sensitively to changes in the surrounding microclimate: whenever the humidity in the air rises, the wall reacts immediately and intensifies its natural play of colors (Figs. 10, 11, and 12).

Dieter Kienast, like "Arte Povera" in the late 1960s, preferred to use cheap raw material such as pure soil, rusty steel, or plain concrete in sophisticated designed parks and gardens, contrasting the raw with the refined. The landscape architect obviously tried to reveal the elemental forces locked within these raw materials as well as the fields of energy that surround the visitor in the garden. For the owners of rammed earth wall gardens as well as for their visitors, the encounter with such a powerful, somewhat oversized and rather unfamiliar-looking earth element in a very small private garden is an intensive, deep

13. The garden for the Basler & Partner engineering office in Zurich was built by Kienast Vogt Partner in 1996. The main design feature in the front is a large rainwater basin.

14. Seen from above it becomes clear how small the areaway for the Zurich office building of Basler & Partner actually is.

15. The concrete wall on the left is overgrown with wild vines, and on the right is the spontaneously seeded calcareous tufa wall. The well overflows after heavy rain.

experience of contrast, of nature's power and sensitivity. "It is not experience which is experienced, but nature—stones, plants, animals, diseases, health, temperature, electricity, and so on:" John Dewey explained this particular mode of experience in 1925. "Things interacting in certain ways are experience; they are what is experienced. Linked in certain other ways with another natural object—the human organism—they are *how* things are experienced as well. Experience thus reaches down into nature, it has depth. It also has breadth and to an indefinitely elastic extent. It stretches. That stretch constitutes inference."[24]

It was the same notion of contrasting the raw with the refined, the strategy of defamiliarization that led Dieter Kienast to give illustrative demonstration to an innovative integration of spontaneous growth processes in controlled urban garden

16. Seen from the conference room, the enormous well-head dominates the tiny courtyard for Basler & Partner in Zurich.
17. The growth of moss, lichen and algae runs counter to usual clichéd idea of nature in the city. The heavy carpet of plants detaches itself from time to time and the growth cycle starts again.

spaces coupled with the skillful consideration of ecological concerns, in this case rainwater management. In two of its smallest inner-city landscape architecture projects, namely the design of the small courtyard and confined area of outside space at the Basler & Partner engineering firm and the design of the interior courtyard of the office building of Swiss Re in Zurich, the landscape architect set the stages for an unusual, thought-provoking experience of urban nature (Fig. 13).

The most conspicuous elements of both projects are vertical walls of limestone tuff, which seem like installations by contemporary minimalist artists. Being permanently moist, not only do they improve the local microclimate, but over the years spontaneous vegetation has led to a living, changeable wet biotope on the porous wall areas. The simple concept of the spontaneously self-greening wet wall is formally reminiscent of minimalist art by an artist like Donald Judd, but conceptually also similar to the highly controversial fountain in Bern's Waisenhausplatz by the surrealist artist Meret Oppenheim, who died in 1985. There, a simple concrete column eight meters high has water trickling down it, transforming itself by permanent spontaneous growth, since 1983, into an ecologically valuable "hanging garden." However, the somewhat wild and scruffy image it presented offended widespread notions of cultivated natural beauty and caused a vivid public discussion about public art. This anarchical artwork is obviously a provocation to a society that prefers to keep everything under control, and so many citizens publicly asked for the immediate demolition of this "ugly" and "dirty" piece of art. But it is precisely the concept of a constantly evolving, growing urban garden that not only offers a new, a very direct, and above all an everyday experience of untamed urban nature but also stimulates discussion and reflection on one's own conception of ideal nature, the image of nature in one's own mind's eye.

The small courtyard of the Basler & Partner office building in downtown Zurich is filled with the sound of water trickling through the green wall, with the smell of lush spontaneous vegetation and cooling moisture evaporating from it (Figs. 14 and 15). For the engineers working in their offices and conference rooms every day, the wet wall they are looking at is almost like a wild living being, changing its green fur constantly, allowing a closer look into the true dynamics of uncontrolled, spontaneous natural growth. Especially for engineers, used to strictly controlling and meticulously planning their building projects, this limestone tuff wall in a way is also an intellectual challenge, a subtle note never to underestimate the dynamics of natural growth. For gardeners, on the other hand, used to designing beautiful images of nature, this wall is also a challenge as well as a provocation. It clearly questions the concept of ideal natural beauty. Again, it is the perception of the user that is transformed by these minimal, rather experimental urban interventions. In Zurich, as in many other thought-provoking projects by Dieter Kienast, architectural form and natural processes combine in close but at the same time relaxed symbiosis to create new gardens beyond traditional clichés of garden architecture. Nature in the city finds a new language, particular challenging for the Swiss society with its tendency to keep everything, especially the environment, clean and permanently under strict control (Figs. 16 and 17).

Compared to the strictly ecological projects of the 1970s to the 1990s, promoted by European garden architects like Urs Schwarz from Switzerland, Louis Le Roy from the Netherlands, and others, these contemporary projects do not try to sell an ideology, and their credibility does not depend on a design that tensely denies the human impulse to evidently shape the environment into a cultural landscape. Current research evaluates the projects by Kienast Vogt Partner as the invention of a new garden type, pointing the way toward a more consistent approach to designing vibrant inner-city gardens without constantly resorting—in a sense strictly diachronically—to the repeated static ideal images from the repertoire of classic garden art. The principles of process and openness, also developed by Umberto Eco in his groundbreaking book *Opera aperta* (The Open Work) from 1962, are the key concepts in current discussion on the future of landscape architecture and garden design in a society seemingly unaccustomed to processes but focused on finished objects. "The discontinuity of phenomena has called into question the possibility of a unified, definitive image of our universe," writes Umberto Eco. "Art suggests a way for us to see the world in which we live, and, by seeing it, accept it and integrate it into our sensibility. The open work assumes the task of giving us an image of discontinuity. It does not narrate it: it *is* it. It takes on a mediating role between the abstract categories of science and the living matter of our sensibility; it almost becomes a sort of transcendental scheme that allows us to comprehend new aspects of the world."[25]

Kienast did not force anyone to do without the finished product, but he was giving the spectators something that can grow, that they can grow on and experience nature in a new aesthetic way. His projects do not narrate the natural process. They *are* natural processes. Kienast did not deprive the audience of the finished picture, but offered them to experience the emerging picture. This is why even in discourse on an entirely different, specifically ecological sense of aesthetics the work of Dieter Kienast and its integrating synthetic force is acknowledged.[26] The dynamism of spontaneous vegetation in the design of open urban spaces, an aspect that was also a concern of Kienast's, has by now become one of the central themes of contemporary landscape architecture in Europe and has been realized in impressive dimensions, as, for example, in the new parks in Zurich-Oerlikon, parks that are not designed as finished objects but as permanent processes, taking place in concise formulated open spaces but incorporating the discontinuity of phenomena.

Dieter Kienast's plea for the garden as the last luxury in our times is one that until today most landscape architects have followed without contradiction. Yet his associated belief in an independent form of rich minimalism has frequently been the subject of controversial discussion and occasionally, for fear of ascetic cheerlessness, dismissed as a mistake by invoking the strongly decorative roots of garden design.[27] Kienast instead referred to the "luxury of the future," which was defined by the lyricist and essayist Hans Magnus Enzensberger in the mid-1990s: "The luxury of the future takes its leave of the superfluous and aspires to the necessary, of which it is to be feared that this will only be at the disposal of the few."[28] Enzensberger numbers fundamental prerequisites for living among the luxuries of the future, including time, consciously self-determined focus of attention, space for free movement, tranquillity, intact environment, and security. Today's society is greatly sapping these resources, and in Enzensberger's view, "Minimalism and doing without could prove to be just as rare, extravagant, and desirable as was once ostentatious wastefulness."[29] It was in this sense that Dieter Kienast, as a response to new cultural and social issues, pleaded against garrulousness in design and for creation of viable, freely available open space, which should stand out by the strength of its capability for enrichment (Fig. 18).

18. Dieter Kienast in Vicenza, 1996 (photo: Wolfram Müller)

The discussion on the garden as the ultimate luxury of our time has admittedly not just been in progress since Dieter Kienast's article "Sehnsucht nach dem Paradies" (Yearning for Paradise) published in 1990,[30] but he provided some decisive contributions, which still have not been sufficiently debated and, again and again, play a central role in discussion on the future of landscape architecture and garden design. In 1998 Kienast formulated his ten theses as a small theoretical basis for his work. In these theses he concentrated on questions about the contemporary relationship between chaos and order, landscape and city, nature and artifice, ecology and design as well as on questions concerning the role of garden art in our contemporary society and many other key aspects. We may wonder whether Kienast's positions with regard to the dramatic changes in today's society have not already passed their half life. This may be true of those of his propositions that are clearly orientated toward twentieth-century conceptions of clear boundaries between city and landscape, traditional, tending to be static and sometimes romantic. However, there is no reason not to accord a certain timelessness to his other propositions related to his belief in the modernity of the enduring, the return to simplicity, order in diversity, or restriction to the essential. The occurrence of minimalism and classical simplicity versus a kind of Baroque variety and complexity in European cultural history has been cyclical and is not just a phenomenon that has existed since the end of the twentieth century.

The positions in which Kienast declared his support for indistinctness, for the hybrid, for the fragmentary, for the transparent, for the unfinished, for what is ongoing, and for the seemingly chaotic are of surprising present relevance not only in view of the continuing state of flux in society. "The longer this precarious situation continues, the greater our tendency to cling to particular principles or roles models," concluded Kienast. He continued: "I find this state of flux particularly enticing as it offers the possibility of moving unencumbered and experimenting."[31] In his gardens the Swiss landscape architect succeeded in formulating a fine interaction between formal purism and the dynamics of natural growth and development. Even today, these kinds of contemporary garden creations offer both an almost meditative experience of poetic modern simplicity and the undisturbed perception of nature, unfolding its dynamic character. It would be dangerous though to consider this approach to garden architecture as Kienast's final conclusion. "So when you ask me about our viewpoint, it's important to realize that having an unequivocal position of one's own has given way to ambivalence, simultaneity, and ambiguity."[32]

NOTES

[1] Dieter Kienast, "10 Thesen zur Landschaftsarchitektur" (1998), in Professur für Landschaftsarchitektur ETH Zürich, ed., *Dieter Kienast - Die Poetik des Gartens. Über Ordnung und Chaos in der Landschaftsarchitektur* (Basel, Berlin, Boston: Birkhäuser Verlag für Architektur, 2002), 207-10.

[2] Dieter Kienast, in Udo Weilacher, *Between Landscape Architecture and Land Art* (Basel, Berlin, Boston: Birkhäuser Verlag für Architektur, 1996), 142.

[3] Stefanie Krebs, *Zur Lesbarkeit zeitgenössischer Landschaftsarchitektur. Verbindungen zur Philosophie der Dekonstruktion* (thesis, Fachbereich Landschaftsarchitektur und Umweltentwicklung der Universität Hannover, 2001), 90.

[4] Dieter Kienast, *Zwischen Arkadien und Restfläche* (Lucerne: Architekturgalerie Luzern, 1992).

[5] Kienast, "10 Thesen zur Landschaftsarchitektur"; *Dieter Kienast - Die Poetik des Gartens*, 207.

[6] See Udo Weilacher, *Visionary Gardens. The Modern Landscapes by Ernst Cramer* (Basel, Berlin, Boston: Birkhäuser Verlag für Architektur, 2001).

[7] Kienast, in Weilacher, *Between Landscape Architecture and Land Art*, 142.

[8] See Elizabeth B. Kassler, *Modern Gardens and the Landscape* (New York: The Museum of Modern Art, 1964).

[9] Hans Fischli, letter to Ernst Cramer dated 26 August 1959, Archiv für Schweizer Landschaftsarchitektur, Rapperswil, dossier 01.03.013.

[10] Manfred Schneckenburger, "Plastik als Handlungsform," *Kunstforum International* 34, no. 4 (1979): 20–31.

[11] Kienast, "Zwischen Poesie und Geschwätzigkeit"; *Dieter Kienast - Die Poetik des Gartens*, 145.

[12] See Dieter Kienast, "Vom Gestaltungsdiktat zum Naturdiktat—oder: Gärten gegen Menschen?" *Landschaft + Stadt* 3 (1981): 120–28.

[13] See Dieter Kienast, "Die spontane Vegetation der Stadt Kassel in Abhängigkeit von bau- und stadtstrukturellen Quartierstypen," *Urbs et Regio* 10 (1978).

[14] See Lucia Grosse-Baechle, "Eine Pflanze ist kein Stein. Strategien der Gestaltung mit der Dynamik von Pflanzen" (thesis, Fachbereich Landschaftsarchitektur und Umweltentwicklung der Universität Hannover, 2003).

[15] Kienast, "Vom Gestaltungsdiktat zum Naturdiktat."

[16] See Dieter Kienast, "Sehnsucht nach dem Paradies," *Hochparterre* 7 (1990): 49.

[17] Dieter Kienast, "Ökologie gegen Gestalt? Oder Natürlichkeit und Künstlichkeit als Programm" *SRL Schriftenreihe* 25 (1990): 103.

[18] Marc Treib, "The Hedge and the Void. The Landscapes of Dieter Kienast: An Overview over His Career," *Landscape Architecture Journal* (January 2003): 78-87.

[19] See Kienast, "10 Thesen zur Landschaftsarchitektur"; Kienast, *Die Poetik des Gartens*, 207.

[20] Kienast, in Weilacher, *Between Landscape Architecture and Land Art*, 154.

[21] Kienast, "Sehnsucht nach dem Paradies"; Kienast, *Die Poetik des Gartens*, 76.

[22] Hartmut Böhme, "Die Natur sprechen lassen," in Doris Cordis-Vollert, ed., *Nunatak Projekt. Schüberg. Die Natur sprechen lassen* (Hamburg: Sautter + Lackmann, 1989), 96–97.

[23] See Kunsthaus Bregenz, ed., *The Mediated Motion. Olafur Eliasson in Zusammenarbeit mit Günther Vogt Landschaftsarchitekt* (Bregenz: Verlag der Buchhandlung Walther König, 2001).

[24] John Dewey, *Experience and Nature* (Chicago: Open Court, 1925), 4.

[25] Umberto Eco, *Opera aperta* (Milano: Casa Ed. Valentino Bompiani, 1962), 90.

[26] See Herman Prigann and Strewlow Heike, eds., *Ecological Aesthetics* (Basel, Berlin, Boston: Birkhäuser Verlag für Architektur, 2004).

[27] Stefan Tischer, "Minimalismus als Irrweg," *Topos* 33 (2000): 68–72.

[28] See Hans Magnus Enzensberger, "Reminiszenzen an den Ueberfluss," *Der Spiegel* 51 (1996): 117.

[29] Ibid., 118.

[30] Kienast, "Sehnsucht nach dem Paradies."

[31] Kienast, in Weilacher.

[32] Ibid.

Contemporary Garden Aesthetics, Creations and Interpretations

Contemporary Garden Aesthetics, Creations and Interpretations

Contemporary Garden Aesthetics, Creations and Interpretations

Contemporary Garden Aesthetics, Creations and Interpretations

The "Garden of Seasons" by Bernard Lassus: Coming to Terms with Fleeting Encounters in a Decentered World

Michel Conan

A cultural conflict triggered the construction of Bernard Lassus's hanging gardens in 2001 and 2002.[1] The multinational Colas Corporation wanted to expand its headquarters and make the new building into a symbol of its buoyancy and engagement with modernity. The inhabitants of a neighboring multistoried dwelling opposed its construction because it would block their views over the trees of Boulogne-Billancourt. They wanted the commune to purchase the land on which Colas wished to expand and turn it into an enlargement of the municipal park with playground in between this land and their apartment building (Fig. 1). They maintained that a good city life depended on the development of planted areas and public amenities that allowed children to play in a natural environment in a city already very densely built up. Colas argued that its own developments would contribute to the increase of municipal revenue as long as it could expand in the city. These clashing arguments forced the city to intervene and mediate by imposing the transformation of the modernist building—highly inspired by the Corbusean admiration for cruise ships—into an artificial hill covered with suspended gardens. The corporation CEO, who also ran a foundation collecting works of art and organizing cultural events, wanted the lower garden terrace to be a work of art in its own right. He commissioned Pierre Riboulet, a neomodernist architect, as the building's designer[2] and Bernard Lassus as the garden's designer (Fig. 2).[3]

I shall first describe the whole project briefly, and then turn to the various ways in which the gardens are experienced before exploring the complex relationships between the forms of the project and the experiences to which they give rise, showing how the design strategy was related to the aesthetic experience of cultural conflicts.

Description of the Project

The expansion of the Colas Corporation is located in Boulogne-Billancourt between the Colas headquarters to the south, the Coubertin sport stadium to the north and its landscaped tennis courts to the east, and a large multistoried slab apartment building to the west.[4] The expansion is separated from this building by a municipal park and playground and a street running

1. Municipal garden between the Colas Corporation and the apartment building (Photo: Michel Conan, May 29, 2004).

along the apartment building; and it is separated from the headquarters by the small *rue Fanfan la Tulipe* at ground level, and linked to it by a light covered bridge reaching the second level of the extension. The building, designed by Riboulet, evokes the perfectly white transatlantic cruisers of the 1930s that fascinated Le Corbusier with their long horizontal gangways, geometric skyline, pointed bow, and large sun-bathing terraces (Fig. 3).[5] Balconies, evocative of transatlantic gangways, run along the office floors and reach the pointed bow of the building to the north. The largest terrace, on the street-entrance level, is located at an angle between the reception rooms and the municipal park and playground (Fig. 4). These architectural moves make the functional building into a poetic metaphor of progress, modernity, and affluence.

The landscape project concerned mostly the west façade in front of the municipal park and the apartment building, making all limits slightly ambiguous. Lassus persuaded the Colas Corporation to contribute to a slight enlargement of the municipal park and playground up to the foot of the building—somewhat lower than the lowest garden terrace—and in exchange, he gained the possibility of reshaping the box hedges at the entrance of the municipal park, to make them identical to the hedges he planted along the west façade gangways (Fig. 5). He also designed the extension of the municipal park in such a way that it gave depth to the park and screened the building. He also screened the visitors' entrance to the extension along the *rue Fanfan la Tulipe* with tall birch trees, lining a carefully designed planter enwrapped in a metallic casing, perforated by foliage-like holes that seem to echo the birch leaves' veil over the façade. Of course, the view of the building gained by employees entering by the second-floor bridge between the headquarters and the new extension is also screened by the birch tree foliage. Thus we can observe that all approaches to the building enshroud its stark geometric appearance in some light naturalistic veil (Fig. 6). The same waist-high box hedge that runs along the gangways enfolds the higher-floor terraces that seem to grow organically out of them and is open to view from most floors of the apartment building (Fig. 7). Prolonging the architectural cruise-ship metaphor, Lassus carpeted the paths along the gangways and on the terraces with a teak wood floor as would be found on the deck of a ship. He also wrapped the planters on the terraces in metallic plates—each side a different color borrowed from a neoplasticist paint palette[6] and decorated with groups of small round dots in neoplasticist colors repeated at regular intervals on the surface of the casings (Fig. 8).[7] The reflections of the masses and textures of the green vegetation and its planters burst into view and seem to invade all lobbies and offices that open out to them. Thus, even inside the building, the limits of the interior and the exterior that seemed to be clearly established by the modernist architecture become blurred and visually compromised by the reflections of the garden.

The lower terrace, at entrance level, is different (Fig. 9). It is closed to views from the outside by high hedges, and its deck floor is wide open, inviting free use by guests. This terrace is not visible from the entrance door. Only when approaching the entrance to the conference or the exhibition room would most visitors catch a first glimpse of a very colorful sculpture foregrounded against an open deck and a flowery bush in the background of the terrace. Upon entering this terrace, one discovers on the left two clipped trees in a box, a running water cascade that seems to issue from the white-building wall, and four artificial trees stemming out of a box hedge and set against a high perforated metal fence. This fence follows the irregular shape of a tall shrubbery hedge that profiles itself against the background of tall trees in the municipal park and

2. Photo of Bernard Lassus in the courtyard of his workshop with a red tulip tree and a blue hedge in 2002 (Photo Michel Conan, June 10, 2002).

playground (Fig. 10). The visitor's gaze is forced to circulate between four different garden elements, each calling attention to itself and preventing a comprehensive view of this otherwise small place. They are, first, the three planters filled with three layers of highly colorful enamel spheres; second, the water cascade; third, the blue metal hedge turning over two sides of the garden with its foreground of encased boxwood and artificial trees; and fourth, the shrubbery opposite the water cascade.

Experiencing the Whole Project

To understand how the project can be experienced one should adopt the point of view of its constituencies rather than the abstracting perspective of a critic visiting by special permission. Neighboring inhabitants, the staff members working in the extension, and visitors to the exhibition hall and the lower deck terrace experience the place in very different ways. For brevity's sake I shall review only briefly the perspectives of the first two groups, and concentrate the analysis on the aesthetic experiences of the third group.

3. The New Colas building seen from the top of the apartment building (Photo Courtesy of Eric Daniel-Lacombe).

4. Plan showing the four levels of planted terraces (Photo Michel Conan, May 29, 2004)

The inhabitants of the multistoried dwelling enjoy the view of the municipal park and playground and of the west façade that they discover by either walking into the park or looking down at it from their own building (Fig. 3). These two modes of engagement with the project merge into a holistic view of an enlarged garden at the foot of a cliff into which suspended paths and terraces have been carved. The unity of the suspended paths and the municipal park is made palpable by the identity of the box hedges on the earth and the suspended grounds (Fig. 5). Thus, from the tenants' point of view, the landscape project has brought some improvements to the park and metaphorically transformed the building into a distant garden background that offers an imaginary extension of the municipal garden. This metaphorical transformation does not impose itself as a new meaning upon the building, but rather introduces new horizons of understanding, allowing a choice between pure oblivion of the building and delight in fanciful appreciation of its gardens.[8]

The staff working in the building enjoy a completely different set of experiences. Most people experience the whole landscape project primarily from the interior of the building, either walking across the access bridge or along the interior passageways and the elevator, or sitting from time to time in a room opening onto one of the higher-floor garden terraces.

These views do not distract from the experience of a highly functional modernist building, but they introduce a different moment of sensual experience opening toward two very different imaginary horizons. For them, the building is suggestive of a very straightforward metaphor: it carries the development of the Colas Corporation in the way of progress, like a transatlantic cruise on a voyage toward an American future.

On the other hand, the moments of discovery of the refracted or reflected gardens and their evocative lights and colors open toward two diverging, imaginary horizons of interpretation. First, the dwarf-pine trees huddling together seem to offer an aerial view of a huge forest seen through a surrealistic window frame of box hedge. This experience completely deterritorializes the viewer and the building; it annihilates the built environment so there is no reciprocity of view between the multistoried apartment building and the Colas building in spite of the illusion created by photographic representations that seem to sustain the contrary. This experience invites flights of imagination into the world of nature in an unspecified way. It could, however, resonate as a criticism of the proud engagement of the corporation into the modernist ethos of active engagement with the world in the pursuit of "progress." Second, to the contrary, the reflections that paint the white walls of the passageways in colors borrowed by Lassus from the Dutch modernist architects can be seen as a reinforcement of the project proposed by the architect, a tribute to the idea that all human

5. Hedges in the municipal park and on the gangways and terraces, Lassus document in the Contemporary Landscape Design Collections (CLD) at Dumbarton Oaks
6. Detail of the façade seen from the municipal garden (Photo Michel Conan, May 29, 2004).

arts—including painting and engineering—can contribute to the modernist project of architecture. Yet many other readings can be made: the neoplasticist colors (Fig. 7) may be seen as an ironical distance to the elitist view of a pure white modernity defended by Le Corbusier, while Fernand Léger—Lassus' professor of painting at the School of Beaux Arts—advocated the introduction of color and respect for working-class taste.[9] However, they might also illustrate the capacity of the modernist

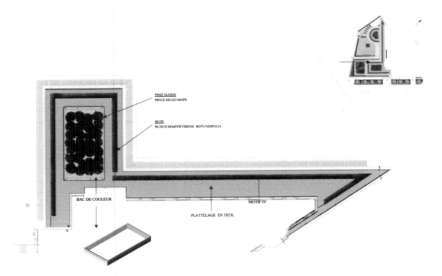

7. Rectangular Terrace on the 5th floor with plan and a detail of colored casings (Photo Michel Conan, June 10, 2002).

8. Deck and planter on the rectangular terrace (Photo Michel Conan, June 10, 2002).

project to lead toward a free appreciation of wild nature. Or else they might ironically underline the limited variety of colors and geometrical forms used by modern architecture as compared to the infinite variations in nature—be it dwarf pine trees or box hedges. This is to insist on the fundamental ambiguities introduced inside and upon the building and the property limits by the gardens (Fig. 6). These ambiguities, opening a fault into the metaphorical meanings of the building, contribute a fundamental aspect of the gardens to which I shall return.

The design of the lower garden terrace epitomizes Lassus' concern with the encounter with the other. The program specified that this terrace had to be left completely free of any obstacle. It was meant for casual encounters by high-ranking employees working in international subsidiaries, and key figures of the Parisian social circles with which the corporation engages. On the other hand, the city wanted it, as well as all other terraces, to be planted as a garden simply embosomed in the midst of a clump of trees, thus hiding it from view in the same way that the *bosquet* enclosures in Versailles were hidden from view from the windows of the palace.[10] This is a useful parallel, because following an interpretive approach proposed several years ago by Stephen Bann at a Dumbarton Oaks colloquium,[11] I want to argue that the Lassus' project invites a new questioning of the gardens at Versailles, and that the new understanding thus achieved, in turn, enables an appreciation for the new kind of aesthetic experience afforded by garden art that is introduced by this garden.

At Versailles, Le Nôtre designed the *Salle de Bal* as a large central deck facing a high water cascade in a green room separated from the surrounding woods by elaborated hedges and palisades (Fig. 11). Three hundred years later, in the first sketches he made for the lower terrace, Lassus decided that he would make the limit between the terrace and the municipal park and playground into a garden, as if it were a thicket through which the presence of a surrounding wood would be felt. He also designed a water cascade to evoke garden sounds, and a sculptural piece—the colored wood poles—to suggest metaphorically the presence of flowers. He wanted each of these features to catch attention and to invite multiple interpretations at the same time that he wanted the guests to experience a sense of being in a garden. He never intended to emulate the *Salle de Bal*, or *the Marais d'Eau* in Versailles (Figs. 11 &12). This parallel is introduced only to achieve a critical understanding of some relationships between landscape design and experience.

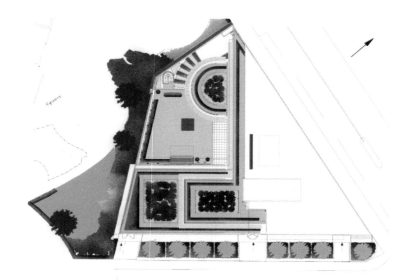

9. Plan showing the four terraces, the addition to the municipal garden, and the screening of the entrance on street Fanfan la Tulipe, Lassus document in the CLD at Dumbarton Oaks

Let us then ask what kind of experiences the green rooms could procure for courtiers at Versailles, on the occasion of staged events that took place there. Courtiers—each with a heightened sense of his or her own persona—would gather in green rooms like the *Salle de Bal*, or the *Marais d'Eau*, offering a representation of artificial nature. These rooms were surrounded by a palisade allowing the presence of the forest to be felt, and yet endowed with magical depth by the presence of cascades playing continuously. This scenery offered only the background to the real show that the king and the courtiers offered to one another, and such events provided them with superficial encounters with one another. Courtiers used to compete with one another for mutual attention. Garden feasts, however, were meant to bring them together into a shared reverence for the grandeur and generosity of the king. The surprising features of the garden were meant to captivate their attention. The *Marais d'Eau* with its artificial trees, birds, and oak trees made of painted metal that spit, spattered, and splashed water demonstrated the king's ability to grasp the essence of nature, to emulate it in an abstract manner in metal sculptures, and to surpass it by commanding the forces of water in unheard-of fashion. The garden features multiplied this Baroque display of power over nature. Their disposition in a completely balanced composition reinforced the shared awe in front of garden marvels and the sense of being part of a harmonious whole around the king.

Such encounters of glittering crowds at a princely court in the seventeenth century or in a cocktail party in the twentieth belong to the commonplace for their respective participants. They provide kaleidoscopic encounters with the other: a rapid succession of unconsummated experiences in a floating world as comically depicted by Molière in *L'impromptu de Versailles*.[12] Everyone is the judge and censor of all others even if the king's presence imposed compulsory civility and superficial agreement,

10. View of the lower terrace garden, flower parterre, clipped trees, fountain and hedge (Photo Michel Conan, June 10, 2002).

or smiling disagreement. The garden seems only to provide the background to these fleeting encounters, and yet its presence can transport them into a different realm.

I want to stress here the relationship between the experience procured by the event in the *salle verte,* and by the aesthetic engagement with the garden itself. The event procured a large number of superficial encounters between courtiers in which the figure of the king loomed large, but did not preclude failure to reach a sense of indebtedness and graceful submission to the king. In Dewey's words the social experience failed to reach closure.[13] Yet the garden background commanded the courtiers' attention. Extraordinary fountains, artificial birds and trees, and real swans and trees invited wonderment and moments of exchange between the courtiers (Fig. 12). Many engravings seem to record the contrast between courtiers engaged in fleeting interactions and others engaged in a careful examination of the landscape that seems to call for a slower pace of exchange (Fig. 13). Since each part metaphorically illustrated the power of the king over nature and contributed to the harmony of the whole, these aesthetic experiences allowed the courtiers to share a sense of unity around the figure of the king in a way that conversations did not. So there was a relationship between the experience of encounters in the green room and the exchanging of judgments about its landscaped setting. Yet only the experience of the landscape setting made aesthetic closure possible thanks to its formal and symbolic features. This analysis of courtiers' experience of the green rooms at Versailles suggests that the aesthetic experience of a landscape may trigger the same social encounters and cultural conflict as the casual interactions within it, and thus enable visitors to come to terms with this conflict and work it through. This is a potential of landscape design that Lassus develops intentionally.

The lower terrace of the Colas project is also meant to gather a highly eclectic group of people with a heightened sense of their own persona, prompt to pass judgment on the world from very different perspectives and yet brought together to achieve a sense of corporate or intellectual community. Lassus designed the lower terrace to engage them in the exploration of their differences of perspective and to allow them to reach a sense of unity that transcends the cultural differences between them. Differing from Versailles, however, he wanted to preclude any sense of an overarching order.

The Form of the Project for the Lower Terrace and Its Conundrums

Lassus pursued many interlocking goals that we have to examine as a whole. He wanted the lower garden terrace to appear larger than it was, the terrace to give a sense of passage between the real and the imaginary and between the building architecture and the municipal park wilderness. He also wanted designed features to invite a multiplicity of interpretations by all of its users while precluding the possibility of a final judgment bringing to an end all debates. Thus, it should be clear that Lassus brought into play a large number of personal artistic intentions at the same time that he paid attention to demands issued in the brief. The form of the artwork resulted from arbitrations between external and internal demands, only some of which were directly concerned with the experience of the place. I would like to show how much the artist and his history are present in this work.

The earliest sketch conserved at Dumbarton Oaks shows half-clipped trees in cylindrical boxes set in a room surrounded by a palisade with a fountain gushing out, and a sculpture of painted sticks somewhat like tall flowery reeds stemming out of a miniature parterre (Fig. 14). This is not the final project, and yet it shows the interplay of several artistic intentions.

The colored sticks (*Les batons colorés*)—as Lassus calls the centerpiece sculpture—represent a new development of a 1972 artwork.[14] Seen from a distance, the painted sticks placed in a bush of pink *orthensias* have the appearance of unknown flowers (Fig. 15). This work, exploring ways of creating an abstract sculpture that would convey the impression of a flowery shrub, had been part of an early exploration of the use of color to create visual passages between the artificial and the natural

11. *The Salle de Bal in Versailles,* by Perelle in Gilles Mortain, Plans et Profils, 1716 at Dumbarton Oaks
12. *The Marais d'Eau in Versailles,* by Perelle at Dumbarton Oaks

13. Some courtiers fleetingly meeting one another, and others engaged in contemplation of the Encelade fountain, by Perelle in Gilles Mortain at Dumbarton Oaks

world. Yet in the Colas project, it also contributes to a dialogue with the modernist architecture of the construction. It proposes a development, from plane into space of geometrical experiments by Gabriel Guevrekian in 1925 to create an abstract version of gardens.[15] Moreover, it forgoes the facile cultivation of flowers—accepted by Guevrekian—by replacing them with an abstract distribution of colors in space. The parterre is placed in a square box—a rendering of the mannerist parterre that parallels the reduction achieved by the Modulor of Corbusier of the four orders of Vignola to the golden section.[16] So the parterre seems to project the modernist architecture of the building into the middle of the deck at the same time that it claims the terrace as a garden. It is, however, impossible to decide whether this gesture is deferent or ironical. Lassus himself refrains from making a final choice on such issues. His commitment goes to an aesthetic of ambiguity.

We should not ignore, however, that this sculpture was placed to be seen from the CEO's dining room against the background of the hedge on the terrace. This hedge deserves close attention because it is, by itself, another abstract garden (Fig. 16). At first sight it looks like a flat surface, a paper cutout representing a linear cluster of small trees with a light airy foliage growing behind a platter filled with leafy undergrowth. It shows, in fact, a real volume occupied by a living plant that forms a low border, separated from the deck by a metal box, perforated with holes in the shape of an abstract variegated foliage; behind the low border there is another metallic fence, absolutely flat, representing a tree alignment through which appears the shade of the real trees in the municipal park. This can be seen as an abstraction of a pleached alley with its waist-high privet border.

In contrast to the flowers in the parterre in the midst of the deck, the privet border is made of vegetal material, but it takes third place in the visual interest of the linear garden to which it belongs. The eye is attracted first to the skyline formed by the trees, and second to the transparency between the tree trunks; the privet leaves and their foliated casing takes third position.

With this background in mind we may turn to a conundrum of visual experience proposed by this project. The three-dimensional sculpture of the colored sticks stands in stark contrast against the almost flat and dematerialized garden hedge behind it. It looks beyond reach while the sticks seem to invite grasping in the hand. This play upon two aspects of visual perception is a constant reference throughout Lassus's works since he started exploring it in painting in 1956. The primary observation that in everyday life the gaze provides us with a sense of tactile as well as visual experience for objects close at hand, and only a dematerialized visual experience for objects beyond reach, led to a design idea: creating spatial discontinuity by stressing a contrast between the tactile and the solely visual experiences of objects.[17]

This is clearly a conceptual difference, but the work of art is not meant to lead the viewer to ponder this conceptual difference—a didacticism foreign to Lassus's artistic intentions—but rather to maintain a critical control over sensorial effects achieved in the creation of forms. Since a concept of sensual difference has no form, a first step consists in producing an icon that may be remembered as a symbol for the concept. This symbol results from a first attempt at giving form to a sensual experience; it is not a work of art in Lassus's eyes, but a formal translation of a concept. As a young painter, Lassus spent several weeks attempting to translate into painting both a visual and a tactile experience of the same

14. Earliest sketch for the lower terrace, Lassus document in the CLD at Dumbarton Oaks

15. Artifcial Flowers by Bernard Lassus, *1972*, document courtesy of Bernard Lassus

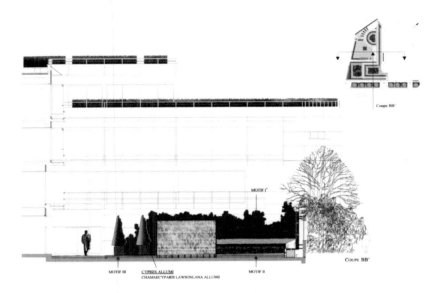

16. Section of the hedge between the lower terrace and the municipal gardens, Lassus document in the CLD at Dumbarton Oaks
17. The tactile and the visual glass painting by Bernard Lassus, document courtesy of Bernard Lassus

object—in the present illustration, a glass (Fig. 17). This iconic painting illustrates a design principle. We see on the left side the materiality of the color paste, evidenced by traces of the brush with fuzzy limits of the glass shape, as if it were softly held in the hand; a light blue and a red come to the fore, bearing visual testimony to the sense of depth that can be achieved by tactile discovery of an object. On the right-hand side there is only one plane, an ultramarine blue surface into which is inscribed the strict silhouette of a glass, an icy rendering of a dematerialized visual experience. Even on the same paper sheet they are in different spaces. Afterwards, he explored the possibilities this contrast offered in a number of paintings, sculptures, and landscape designs, each of them a development of the sensorial strategy adapted to a new environment. The Colas garden (Fig. 14) is such a development—the glass silhouette in a blue plane becomes an arbor drawing cut out of an ultramarine blue plate of metal—please note the absence of artificial trees at this moment of the design development—and the materiality of the red glass becomes the colored set of sticks.

A late glitch in the cooperation with the architect compelled Lassus to create a much higher metallic fence (Fig. 10).[18] This in turn led to new technical problems and a completely different design, in which the parterre of colored sticks in the middle of the deck disappeared and was replaced by boxes in which are planted three tiers of colorful enameled spheres that stand on the side of the deck, closer to the CEO's dining room (Fig. 18). Even though the forms are different, you may recognize immediately that they share in the same ambiguous relationship to modernist aesthetics, and the same tactile contrast with the metallic hedge that was accomplished by the colored sticks.[19] Although the flowers seem as much inviting to be grasped by the hand as the saucer on the table, the trees and the hedge do not. Flowers and trees belong to two different spaces calling into question the continuity of the floor space itself!

Let us move to the conundrum of nature and artifice. Lassus defends the idea that any limit separating two different places must be recognized as a space with its own identity to help visitors prepare for the difference between the two places (Fig. 16). Here, the hedge of the garden that separates the deck from the municipal garden had to achieve an identity because Lassus wanted the deck to stand for a garden, an artificialized nature, and the municipal park to stand for a large wood, a piece of untrammeled nature. Moreover the hedge was meant to contribute to a metaphorical transformation of the municipal park. Even though it was meant to prevent any physical passage between the deck and the municipal park, it had to be open to an

18. Tactile versus visual experiences from the CEO's dining room (Photo Michel Conan, May 29, 2004).

imaginary penetration (Fig. 19). The perforations in the metallic plate invite the gaze, but only the imagination can make sense of their darkness and link it with the trees that hover above the blue metallic hedge. To help the imagination travel between artifice and nature, the hedge itself proposes variations on the binary opposition of the two. It constitutes a visual passage that can be experienced as a passage between artifice and nature even if the idea of this opposition does not come to mind. Just as you may be moved by a portrait of Rembrandt without forming in your mind the idea of *chiaro obscuro* or by a garden party by Monet without thinking of the theory of complementary colors, Lassus aims at purely visual or plastic effects that convey a definite experience even in the absence of the concept of this experience. Yet Lassus also wants visitors to engage conceptually with the work of art. He wants it to be open to different modes of perception, refusing with Maurice Merleau-Ponty to draw a line between perception and understanding.[20] This leads his work on a razor's edge between abstraction and representation, introducing another conundrum. This is exemplified by the introduction of a miniature drawing of a flower seen from high above on top of the enamel spheres that form the abstract flower parterres (Fig. 20). He refuses mimesis because it invites an exclusive focus on a narrative that detracts from attention to the plastic features of a work of art; and he refuses meaningless abstraction because he wants a landscape or a garden to be a work of art that engages with the diversity of cultural ways of making sense of the world. Besides, the hedge also rests upon the opposition between inert artifice and living nature. The perfect geometry of the floor with its polished wood boards stands in stark contrast with the casings of the box and the trees

19. Perforations inviting the gaze through the hedge and an unknown species of tree (Photo Michel Conan, June 10, 2002).

that grow at its limit (Fig. 20).

Thus the terms of the contrasts he wants to explore are presented—like the musical theme in the introduction of a concert piece: inert/living materials, geometrical/organic forms. The casing of the box border proposes a first interlacing of the contrasting features; it is made of an inert material, but it presents the appearance of a natural hedge, however different from the metallic arbor behind it. It does not imitate or represent a hedge. Because of its flat and smooth surface, it offers only an abstract visual experience akin to the view of some distant hedge. In fact, in contradiction with natural forms, the relationship between the material leaf and the void around it is inverted. The leaves are suggested by perforated holes in the mass of the plate. Moreover, these leaves are purely fictional; they do not even look like leaves, and the upper limit of this abstract border bears the mark of the clipping scissors, a mark of artificiality. This seems even truer of the high abstract arbor that forms the last limit of the hedge before the trees at the municipal park. It displays the irregular opacity and the wild growth of a neglected palisade of arbor, and they share its color and flatness when seen at a great distance. Its variegated silhouette calls to mind the garden palisades growing wild in the eighteenth-century gardens recorded by Antoine Watteau (1684–1721). Why, then, should we call it an arbor? The workers who installed this heavy metallic fence did not hesitate to recognize them as arbors—even though their sheer weight should have dissuaded such interpretation—while other people hesitate. Should we see it as more natural than the wildly growing border of box shrubs in their escape from the garden discipline of shearing scissors? Or should we see the artificial trees emerging from this border as an even more naturalistic representation of nature? These trees (Fig. 21), in contrast to the arbor, or the low metallic border, really look like individual trees—or do they? If you approach them closely enough, you will readily identify an oak tree, because the metallic slab that stands for this tree is perforated by a spread of flat oak leaves. Yet no oak tree ever followed the shape of this tree or presented its leaves in such decorative manner (Figs. 20 and 21). This is an oak tree that owes as much to popular art as to cubism or Henri Matisse. It is an abstraction, not a representation. But more decidedly than the arbor, it is an abstraction of a definite tree species, and it leads to a question in front of the other two kinds of trees: to what species do they belong?

The imagination already has taken its flight, and we are ready to debate the identity of the two other kinds of trees. There is no doubt that they belong to different kinds since each of their leaves presents a set of variations around a different gestalt. A botanist will recognize one of them, because of the shape of its leaf, as a tulip-poplar tree,[21] known in France as the "Tulip tree of Virginia"—a tree first introduced in France at Rochefort and later reintroduced by Lassus in the Corderie Royale of Rochefort. Yet even a botanist will fail to identify beyond any doubt the third species of tree, simply because the shape of its leaves has been invented by Lassus (Fig. 21). So nobody can claim perfect understanding of the relationship of these flat representations to nature, and nobody who has been attracted to this hedge by the trees can escape discussing its meanings. The forms of the artwork are designed to raise conundrums that can be answered in different ways—almost mutually exclusive—without any possibility of claiming the absolute value of any cultural interpretation over the others.

This hedge constitutes a work of art by itself, and it triggers attention, stimulates the engagement of viewers in an effort for

20. Detail of the flower parterre showing the representation of a flower on the top of the enamel spheres (Photo Michel Conan, May 29, 2004).
21. Three different trees to play the game of the Seasons, Lassus document in the CLD at Dumbarton Oaks

CHENE   TULIPIER   QUEL ARBRE ?

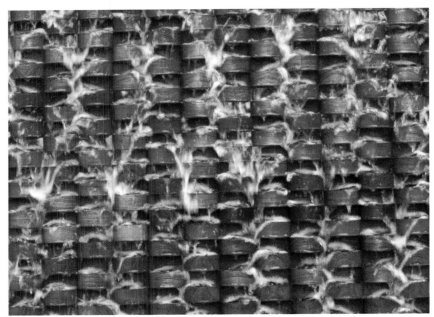

22. (left) Detail of cascading water (Photo Michel Conan, June 10, 2002).
23. (below) View of the Cascade the flowers and the deck (Photo Michel Conan, June 10, 2002).
24. (right) View of the lower terrace from the entrance (Photo Michel Conan, June 10, 2002).
25. (below right) Fault introduced into the arbor hedge (Photo Michel Conan, June 10, 2002).

PRINTEMPS   ETE   AUTOMNE   HIVER

26. An abstract Tulip-poplar tree at the four seasons, Lassus document in the CLD at Dumbarton Oaks

clarification, and draws attention as well to an opposition between nature and artifice that it deliberately blurs. In the liminal space it has materialized between nature in the municipal park and artifice in the garden, it opens a fault in perceptual as well as conceptual understanding, thus prompting imagination to make sense of the whole by recognizing the garden as artificial, the municipal as natural, and the hedge itself as anything it likes. The landscape approach of the liminal passage imposes the contrasting terms of reference, and the metaphorical understanding of the deck and the municipal park to all visitors who engage with this work, but it also leads them into the expression of diverging opinions about the hedge: is it abstract or figurative, naïve or ironical, modern or pop art, postmodern, botanical, or fictional? The diversity of cultural perspectives among the guests at a cocktail party can be brought into the open by the engagement with this work of art. It parallels the diversity of opinion and cultural attitudes brought by members of this club that may be discussed during their meetings and at cocktail receptions. Lassus wanted, however, the garden experience to reinforce the sense of being together in the garden, on the safe side of the great imaginary divide between nature and culture, and yet he wanted to maintain the ambiguity of form and meaning of the garden as a whole. He designed it as a fault.

The design of faults that allows the imagination to spring forward and to make poetical sense of the relationships between two neighboring places has been developed by Lassus in recent years.[22] The deliberate dissociation of a dematerialized and a tactile visual experience creates a fault between the two objects rather than an illusion of distance (Fig. 18). Just imagine yourself on a warm day in Geneva, drinking tea filtering through large cubes of ice out of a glass on a café terrace overlooking Mont Blanc in the distance. The iced tea gives you a visual and tactile experience of ice, the Mont Blanc a purely visual one. The ice feels cold, Mont Blanc does not;[23] it looks distant, but it is not possible to say how distant it is. It does not suggest an illusory distance like an accelerated perspective, but a sense of an unfathomable distance. Only your imagination can propose a more precise answer and make sense of a fault.

In the final version of the Colas gardens, the whole deck separates the flower parterre—giving rise to a tactile visual experience—from the metallic hedge with its colored trees—giving rise to a dematerialized visual experience. The whole deck becomes a fault, a void. Lassus was afraid that such an undefined space would be unpleasant, and he called upon the cascade to fill the garden deck with the gurgling sounds of tumbling water forming hundreds of miniscule cascades that keep changing course in an unpredictable manner (Fig. 22). It gives as much a musical as a visual density to the volume of air above the deck uniting the abstract flower parterre, the abstract tree hedge, the artificial cascade, and the minimal shrubbery opposite the cascade (Fig. 23).

Lassus was concerned, however, that it might procure too much of a sense of unity, and this sense of unity could impose an overarching meaning to each part in terms of formal contribution to a plastic composition, thus relegating any debate about the meaning of the artistic value of each part to the domain of aesthetic misunderstanding. He wanted, to the contrary, the three abstract works of art—the flower parterre, the cascade, and the tree hedge—to stimulate discussions, judgments, and arguments that would remain inconclusive, and he wanted each one to be acknowledged by some visitors as the main point of interest in the garden. Thus, he felt he had to destabilize the sense of unity he had constructed, to introduce a sense of imbalance that could allow the main features of the garden to remain perceptually independent of the whole. He needed the garden to remain a heterogeneous space to allow the expressions of cultural differences by its users at the same time that it procured a distinctive feeling of a unified ambiance where it is comfortable to be together and to enjoy each other's differences.

He placed the different elements so that they would pair with one another, thus creating different ways of experiencing the same space by focusing on the relationship between each

27. Earth covered with snow, document courtesy of Bernard Lassus
28. Earth covered with grass, document courtesy of Bernard Lassus

pair (Fig. 24). First, he introduced a shrubbery that is evocative of the municipal parks and gardens of Paris in the corner above the entrance to the parking, thus putting into question the radical distinction between the garden terrace and the municipal garden. Second, he placed the different elements so that they would pair with one another, thus creating different ways of experiencing the same space by focusing on the relationship between the abstract parterre and the shrubbery when entering the terrace, or on the relationship between the abstract parterre and either the cascade or the tree hedge, depending on the point of view adopted in the dining room or the reception rooms. Third, he created a visual imbalance in a fourth pairing between the fountain and the tree hedge. This demands a detailed explanation.

The tree hedge was designed, from the beginning, to turn on two sides of the garden and to enwrap the water cascades, thus transforming the white building wall into a cliff with a cascade that tumbles out of it—among trees at its foot. This transformation of the building into natural landscape and the visual similarities between the curtain of water and the metallic arbor prepared a semantic and sensual relationship between the fountain and the tree hedge as if they were meant to create a united landscape. When he decided to introduce the colored abstract trees along the municipal park he felt that the composition of this landscape demanded that at least one tree be placed along the building wall between the cascade and the corner of the building. This created the most important dilemma he faced during the development of the project. The whole formed by the two pieces would have offered a much better balance had the tree been added. His own visual culture prompted him to achieve balance. His fear was that this composition, however, would prevent the fluidity of the pairing relationships that he wanted to establish, and this led him to relinquish this move toward visual balance, and instead to tear open a hole in the abstract arbor against the wall at the very place where visual balance called for a tree (Fig. 25).

This dismembering of the place's unity that is created by visual or plastic composition of its elements, which he calls a *heterodite* approach of landscape design,[24] is always used in his work to enable a multicultural experience of place. The renouncement of composition results from a deliberate renouncement of the idea of cultural hegemony of one class over the other, one ethnic or religious group over the other, one profession over the other. It aims at creating an aesthetic experience in which people may experience the conflict of cultural differences and come to terms with this situation without denying or attempting to suppress the differences. At the same time, the sense of the garden's distinctive identity, as a place between functional modernist architecture and imaginary wilderness, is felt by all members of the garden party whatever their disagreements over the correct interpretation of different garden parts. The aesthetic experience achieves its closure when a visitor becomes fully aware that this sense of identity can be shared by all other visitors in spite of cultural differences in their modes of interpretation and appreciation.

Conclusion: A Sense of Duration

This analysis seems to have reached its final conclusion, even though I have not even mentioned the name of this garden: the Garden of the Game of Seasons (*Le Jardin du Jeu des Saisons*) (Fig. 26). In fact, I should have stressed that most visitors to this garden are members of a large group of people who come to this place, in different formations, several times a year. This is a place to be experienced through multiple visits and with different people belonging to a distinguished club. Lassus realized how much the garden experience could become a springboard for the development of a sense of unity within this club. He did not want the place to be experienced as an abstraction of a garden, a museum piece or an installation, but rather as a garden with a life of its own, and he feared that the fixity of the abstract flowers and tree hedges would not be lifted by the dialogue between the flowing cascades and the blooming shrubbery in the opposite corner. Gardens change with the seasons, and he simply decided to make four sets of each tree raised in front of the blue metal arbor and to give the CEO the possibility of replacing them as the seasons change or at will, as if playing with the seasons.[25] Thus it is not the stability of form, but the duration of a definite course of changes that procures an identity to the gardens. Recent developments of the project go further in this direction. Lassus was concerned that the changes would call attention to the tree hedge alone, thus promoting it to the role of central piece in the course of garden change. He proposed replacing the abstract parterre of flowers by either one of two abstracted garden pieces: one evocative of earth covered with snow (Fig. 27), the other of earth covered with grass (Fig. 28). These two sculptures will indicate clearly how a complex rhythm of change can be built in the garden with four differently colored sets of trees and three flower parterres. Thus, the form of the artwork results, like dance, from the transformation over time of spatial forms. It gives rise to a movement over a duration of several seasons or years that can be grasped by visitors only through an effort of memory.

In spite of the patron's role in ordering changes, the garden is designed to remain fundamentally ambiguous, and the more lifelike, the more ambiguous. It is meant to provide an aesthetic experience of the unity of life, a unity that can be shared by members of any society however different their sense of nature and culture.[26] This garden achieves its aesthetic purpose when it enables any of its users to work through the conflict between respect for the unity of man and universality of cultural disagreement, and to envision a human world able to withstand any cultural conflict in the defense of the unity of life.

NOTES

[1] The gardens were inaugurated on 10 June 2002.

[2] Pierre Riboulet (1928–2003) was a highly respected architect in France; he had received a doctoral degree for a dissertation on architecture in public housing under the direction of Nikos Poulantzas in 1979. He was a cofounder in 1958 of the Montrouge Architectural Workshop (l'Atelier d'Architecture de Montrouge) defending and pursuing Le Corbusier's intellectual heritage. He received the Grand Prix National d'Architecture in 1981, and was the Professor of Architecture at the prestigious École des Ponts et Chaussées from 1979 to 1996. He is known for his public housing projects and the national school of music at Evry, the children's library at Clamart, the libraries of Paris VIII, Cergy-Pontoise, and Toulouse Le Mirail universities, the municipal libraries of Limoges and Antibes, and the children's hospital "Robert Debré" in Paris.

[3] Bernard Lassus is an artist whose work has contributed to painting, sculpture, architecture, installation art, and landscape architecture since the end of the 1950s. In 1981 he gave a lecture devoted to "the minimal intervention" in landscape architecture, and he has often referred to his own work as minimalist. Yet this is somewhat a misnomer since minimalism is first and foremost the name of a short-lived movement in American art. In fact, we should not see his work at the beginning of this century as belonging to any art school or stylistic art movement. His call for a minimal intervention simply demanded a deep sense of respect for the historic layers of cultural transformation and appropriation of nature that any landscape is made of. This led him to a refusal of the imposition of forms expressive of a personal style on any site by a landscape designer. Method rather than form is the lynchpin of his works.

[4] The commune of Boulogne-Billancourt is located to the southwest of Paris with which it shares a limit. The Colas headquarters, 7 Place Clair, 92653 Boulogne-Billancourt, are not open to the general public, but the building and its hanging terraces can be seen from the street.

[5] In 1922 Le Corbusier started experimenting with the construction of roofed terraces that were meant to provide to the dwellers a vicarious experience of a voyage on the deck of a cruise ship allegorically leaving the Old Europe for the New World and its promises of a rationalized world. This theme that pervades a large part of his architecture has been continued by neomodernists even though it is doubtful that they thought of America as the goal of the voyage. The forms of the ship rather than the voyage itself became the references for the pursuit of a modernity without a goal.

[6] Neoplasticism is a Dutch movement that contributed to the early history of modernist painting and was active between 1920 and 1940. Founded by Piet Mondrian (1872–1944), it called for the use of a very limited palette of flat colors. Mondrian was interested in the doctrine of functionalism proposed by modernist architects, and he contributed to the creation of a group of Dutch artists with Theo van Doesburg, Bart van der Leck, and Gerrit Rietveld, who

created artworks spanning painting, sculpture, furniture, and architecture. Van Doesburg edited a periodical entitled *De Stijl* which gave coherence to the movement in which Mondrian published his formulation of the movement's aesthetic principles. They call for restricting colors to red, blue, yellow, white, gray, and black; composing with rectangles and straight lines; and achieving balance through contrasts and avoiding symmetry.

[7] The choice of the colors of the different side of each casing follows the neoplasticist principle and can be seen as a sign that Lassus wants to further reinforce the references to modernism present in the architectural design. Yet the round colored dots placed at regular intervals detract from neoplasticist principles, even though they follow primary colors. Moreover one of the terraces follows a half circle. The references to neoplasticism deliberately introduce successive levels of ambiguity.

[8] A few inhabitants of the facing apartment building even indulge in observing the cocktail parties on the lower deck terrace in front of the fountain, as if it gave them a vicarious access to this part of the hanging gardens that they cannot fully explore from a distance.

[9] Fernand Léger (1881–1955). In a small book, *The Functions of Painting* (*Fonctions de la peinture* [Paris: Gonthier, 1965]), he described the debate that opposed him to Le Corbusier in the mid-1920s. Le Corbusier advocated a pure white modernist architecture, and Léger pleaded for a greater attention to the sentimental attachment of the working classes to colorful objects and environments. So he proposed a cooperation to be developed between architects and painters to create a modern housing that would be rational and pleasing for workers at the same time. This offer did not receive an answer.

[10] It should be remembered that Dezallier d'Argenville in his famous treatise *La théorie et la pratique du jardinage* (Theory and Practice of Gardening, 1709–47) underlines in chapter 5 of the first part, devoted to "Woods and Bosquets," that "this chapter contains all the most beautiful and most pleasant features in a garden: the woods, and the bosquets that constitute their greatest ornaments."

[11] Stephen Bann, "Sensing the Stones: Bernard Lassus and the Ground of Landscape Design," in *Landscape Design and the Experience of Motion*, ed. Michel Conan, Dumbarton Oaks Colloquium Series in Landscape Architecture 24 (Washington, DC: Dumbarton Oaks, 2003), 53–74.

[12] Jean Baptiste Poquelin, dit Molière (1622–73). *L'impromptu de Versailles,* a one-act comedy by Molière, was performed first at Versailles on 14 October 1663.

[13] John Dewey, *Art as Experience* (New York: Perigee Books, 1980; first published 1934), 35–57.

[14] This work was presented at the Salon des Réalités Nouvelles at Vincennes (near Paris) in France in 1972 under the title "Artificial Flowers." It proposed a new development for abstract painting.

[15] Gabriel Guevrekian is one of the very few modern artists who attempted a renewal of garden art in the 1920s. For a presentation of his work, see Dorothée Imbert, *The Modernist Garden in France* (New Haven, CT: Yale University Press, 1993).

[16] Le Corbusier (Charles Edouard Jeanneret), *The Modulor: A Harmonious Measure to the Human Scale Universally Applicable to Architecture and Mechanics and Modulor 2 (Let the User Speak Next),* 2 vols. (Basel: Birkhäuser, 2000) (facsimile of the 1954 Faber and Faber first English language edition).

[17] These concepts were presented to an English audience first by Stephen Bann in 1970, and much later in a book by Lassus published by the University of Pennsylvania Press in 1998. Stephen Bann, *Experimental Painting, Construction, Abstraction, Destruction, Reduction* (London: Studio Vista, 1970), 47–49; Bernard Lassus, *The Landscape Approach,* with introductions by Peter Jacobs and Robert B. Riley, and afterword by Stephen Bann (Philadelphia: University of Pennsylvania Press, 1998), 67–70.

[18] This was not an easy cooperation. Riboulet was very sick, and lots of technical problems were left for Lassus to solve. He was greatly helped by Eric Daniel-Lacombe, the architect with whom he has recently developed several of his projects.

[19] This confirms the judgment of Stephen Bann, who already in 1970 included Lassus among the artists he discussed in his book on experimental painting where he defined the experimental painter as "committed to a particular *path* of controlled activity, of which the works he produces remain as evidence." Bann, *Experimental Painting,* 7. He insisted that this was a revolutionary direction in the arts that demanded "that the new propositions should themselves be linked, and that the individual work may in this way relate to a program." Bann, *Experimental Painting,* 8.

[20] "We do not reduce the signification of a word, or even the signification of the perceived world, to a sum of 'bodily sensations,' but we say that the body, insofar as it indulges in 'conducts' is this strange object that uses its own parts as a symbolic system of the world through which, consequently, we can 'dwell' in this world, 'understand' it and find significations for it." Maurice Merleau-Ponty, *Phénoménologie de la perception* (Paris: Gallimard, 1997; first published 1945), 273–74, translation by the author.

[21] "Yellow-poplar (*Liriodendron tulipifera*), also called tulip tree, tulip poplar, white poplar, and whitewood, is one of the most attractive and tallest of eastern hardwoods. It belongs to the family of Magnoliacae." Source: U.S. Forest Service, Department of Agriculture, http://wildwnc.org/trees/Liriodendron_tulipifera.html.

[22] See "The Theory of Faults" (1989) in Lassus, *The Landscape Approach,* 62–64.

[23] We may note that this introduces a modification to Merleau-Ponty's theory of perception. Instead of accepting that "senses communicate between one another thus giving access to the inner structure of the thing itself," Lassus proposes that this only applies within the range that can be reached by the body, while beyond the visual appearance of the world is open to broad interpretation by the imagination. Merleau-Ponty, *Phénoménologie de la perception,* 265, translation by the author.

[24] This design approach is presented in English in two texts in Lassus, *The Landscape Approach,* "The Heterodite" (1985), 53, and "The Landscape Entity" (1987), 954–56.

[25] Lassus has created several games as artworks. Most of them were published in a small book (Bernard Lassus, *Jeux* [Paris: Édition Galilée, 1978]). Each of these works demands an active participation of the audience and leads all participants into the invention of a final product that results from a jointly developed sense of the experience. Thus each participant is free to decide the nature and the form of his or her own contribution, and yet shares in the joint development with the other participants in the game. In that respect each game results in the creation of a moment of intense intersubjectivity that

results in a temporary interworld. In recent years Lassus has developed his ideas about games in the context of landscape creation. The colored facades of public housing in Lorraine or the game of the garden at Barbirey (*le Jeu du Jardin de Barbirey)* are the most obvious antecedents to the *Jardin du Jeu des Saisons*. In all of these cases the objects to be played with have been created by Lassus—whereas in the preceding ones they were created by the audience—but the players—here the CEO—are left free to decide how they will use them, and what sense they will make out of the game.

[26] The game of the seasons is open ended: the CEO can decide to play it as he pleases, and the members of the club whom he gathers for periodical meetings are free to provide any interpretation they like. These differences are necessary for a collective sense of the capacity to communicate in spite of cultural differences that emerge. In fact, all the games created by Lassus are designed to enable a group to experience the capacity to create a collective work and to make sense of an apparently undefined situation. They are aestheticized moments of ordinary life that allow—whenever successful—an aesthetic closure in the sense proposed by Dewey.

Contemporary Garden Aesthetics, Creations and Interpretations

Contemporary Garden Aesthetics, Creations and Interpretations

Contemporary Garden Aesthetics, Creations and Interpretations

Contemporary Garden Aesthetics, Creations and Interpretations

Echoes of Paradise: Feernando Chacel's Gardens in the Coastal Plain of Jacarepaguà

Peter Jacobs

The "New World" Paradise of Amazonia

When the Spanish friar Gaspar de Carvajal first encountered the Amazon River in 1542 as part of an expedition determined to discover rare species and the fabled city of El Dorado, he observed: "It came on with such a fury and with so great an onrush that it was enough to fill one with the greatest fear to look at it, let alone to go through it … and it was so wide from bank to bank from here on that it seemed as though we were launched out upon a vast sea."[1] Visions of profit-making ventures have threatened indigenous cultures and their natural habitat since the early period of European colonization in the sixteenth century. Hundreds of native cultures and species of wildlife live in an interdependent world where the delicate balance between man and nature is both fragile and difficult to comprehend.[2]

Brazil is a paradigm of the New World—a paradise "discovered" by European explorers who saw in the abundance of nature the echoes of paradise lost. The vision was, of course, very much Eurocentric insofar as the New World was as accomplished as the Old. Civilizations such as those of the Maya, the Aztec, and the Inca developed expertise in architecture, agriculture, and astronomy of unparallel sophistication. Smaller tribes and societies mastered the complex ecology of the rain forests, savannah, and coastal *restinga,* developing sustainable strategies in support of modest and relatively mobile human settlements. Indigenous peoples were almost as diverse as the flora and fauna of the mighty rivers, coastal plains, and mountains of Brazil. The very local specificity of people and plants could be seen in the rich patina of the native color and form, a power of place captured by Margaret Mee in her sensitive portraits of the flora of Brazil.[3]

Yet the lessons that might be learned from indigenous cultures were lost in the utilitarian lens through which the New World was viewed,[4] a cornucopia of marketable products that continue to be harvested at clearly unsustainable rates.[5] Even the name Brazil is nothing other than that accorded a precious wood, *Caesalpina echinata,* whose bark was the color of burning embers (*le bois de braise*).[6] Its beauty and function in the complex ecosystems of the forest were of little concern to the marketplaces of the world. Today this attitude extends to the conversion of the forest for agriculture products destined for

1. The cost of construction and land in Rio locates the middle and upper economic classes on the thin plateau that borders the beaches. The less affluent inhabit the slopes of the Santo Antonio and Providencia mountains.

international markets, to the search for genetic materials and the traditional knowledge required to produce pharmaceuticals,[7] and to the settlement of coasts that harbor urban agglomerations among the largest in the world.

Between the *Favelas* and the Sea

São Sebastião de Rio de Janeiro, founded in 1565, lies within the sandy coastal beaches, lagoons, and *restinga* that border the Atlantic Ocean. Mountains weave their way along the coast where headlands reach into the sea at critical points, constraining the evolving pattern of human settlement. The picturesque mountain peaks and famous beaches of Copacabana and Ipanima frame the urban region, providing a natural setting among the most spectacular anywhere in the world.

Rio is a typical, although intense, example of the cohabitation of nature and human settlement. Squatter settlements perch on the hills overlooking the thin strip of intensely developed coastal beaches that outline Rio de Janeiro as lace on a formal dress, where the wealthy are caught between the *favelas* and the sea. The cost of construction and land in Rio locates the middle and upper economic classes on the thin plateau that borders the beaches. The less affluent inhabit the slopes of the Santo Antonio and Providencia mountains (Fig. 1). The outstretched arms of an immense statue of Christ perched above the city embrace both populations below, linked as well by the drama of Carnival,[8] the sun and salt spray of the sea, and the music and spectacles of the night.

In Rio, as in other large urban areas in Brazil, continuing migration from the countryside has introduced a complex pattern of life styles and diverse traditions into a compressed urban context where new and unimagined patterns of city life emerge.[9] Not the least of these patterns is the patchwork quilt of official and unofficial housing in the city of Rio de Janeiro.

By 1933, informal housing settlements, the *favelas*, represented twenty percent of the total housing in Rio.[10] The dynamic of these phenomena was captured by Oscar Niemeyer, who observed that "misery always existed and was always overlooked, but never as today when our brothers the *favalados* regard the city as a enemy camp of luxury and corruption"[11] (Fig. 2).

Today there are as many as 613 *favelas* in the greater metropolitan region, and the spreading footprint threatens the 3,300 hectares of urban forest in the Tijuca National Park, a UNESCO Heritage Site and one of the largest such urban forests in the world. Simultaneously, many of the abandoned coffee plantations in the adjacent forests of the Tijuca are occupied by squatter settlements.

The Jacarapaguà Coastal Plain

Mountain ranges frame a vast triangle of land to the west of Rio de Janeiro, the Jacarepaguà coastal plain, where the forests of the Tijuca were exploited for charcoal and lumber from the very beginning of colonization in the 1560s. Tijuca is the word for wetlands or marsh, the name the Tupi Indians gave to the flat stretch of coastal land that include the natural coastal complex of beach, *restinga,* and lagoon.[12] Land that was cleared served as animal pasture, and coffee was cultivated from 1760 onwards, reducing the forest matrix to those areas that were inaccessible or that bordered water bodies. The need to ensure water quality generated conservation and protective status for the Tijuca and Paineiras forests in 1861, and the first attempts at reforestation occurred shortly thereafter. By 1941 the region had achieved legal planning status and until the 1960s was sheltered from the urban shadow of Rio by mountain headlands that descended to the sea, effectively cutting off any viable link with the urban strip of settlement that bordered Rio's coastal beaches. The Jacarepaguà coastal zone is framed by major conservation lands in the municipality of Rio, including the urban forest of the Tijuca National Park and Pedra Branca Provincial Park. (Fig. 3).

2. A view of the Rocinha Favella from the summit of the community to the Sao Conrado beach. The Jacarepaguà coastal plain lies beyond the Joa mountain to the right of the photo.

Historically, concern with the conservation of the biologically rich countryside, coupled with urban development in the Jacarepaguà coastal plain, has stimulated a number of innovative landscape and urban planning projects. These include an early master plan for the region by Lucio Costa, a demonstration garden by Roberto Burle Marx, and more recently, the restoration of the degraded landscapes of the Barra da Tijuca by Fernando Chacel.

Lucio Costa's Regional Plan for Urban Growth

In 1969 the Minister of Transport of the Federal District commissioned Lucio Costa to develop a master plan for the entire region within the triangle defined by the Tijuca and Pedra Branca massifs and the Jacarepaguà coastal plain.[13]

Costa was concerned that the system of coastal viaducts and tunnels under the Joa mountain peak, providing access to the costal beaches of the Barra da Tijuca, would serve as a southern gateway to an indiscriminate, even predatory, approach to urban growth (Fig. 4). He knew that the occupation of the coastal region would be irreversible, and that there was an obvious need to conserve the remaining fragile landscapes of forest, river, and beach ridge in the region.

Costa's plan is complex, recognizing the landscape constraints of the mountain ridges, the fragility of the coastal flora and fauna, and the intricacy of the lagoons and waterways of the plain below the foothills. His approach was both evolutionary

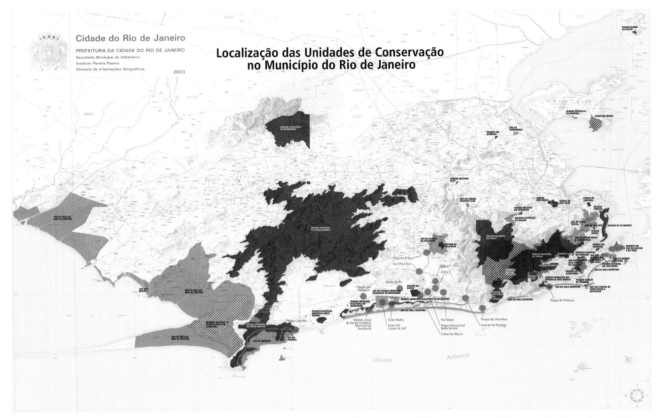

3. The Jacarepaguà coastal zone is framed by major conservation lands in the Municipality of Rio, including the 3,300 hectares in the urban forests of the Tijuca National Park and the Pedra Branca Provincial Park.

and structural. He was at pains to reconstitute the urban history of the region to better project future growth and development. He understood that a plan was both a physical representation and a development strategy that could guide urban growth, but certainly not dictate it. Thus his plan emphasized urban infrastructure that he associated with a set of principles that would guide appropriate patterns of human settlement and landscape conservation. One of the key provisions of his plan was the proposal to conserve the sandy coastal ridge, developed many years later by Fernando Chacel as the Marapendi Municipal Ecological Park.[14]

Burle Marx's Botanical Garden

Roberto Burle Marx shared Costa's concerns, particularly with respect to the loss of nature, nowhere more so than in the urban fringe of Rio de Janeiro. Burle Marx needs little introduction to those aware of the modern development of landscape architecture, and even less to those who have studied his enormous influence in Brazil and Latin America. Burle Marx was a pioneer in developing many of the formative principles of modern landscape architecture:[15] "The parallel between the achievement of Burle Marx and that of Modern Brazilian architecture is so close that, with due allowance for the difference in scope and scale, they can almost be described in the same terms: emotional spontaneity, striving for integration with the circumstances of land and climate, and re-assessment of the plastic language and of the means of expression, all under a growing intellectual discipline."[16]

As early as the 1930s Roberto Burle Marx witnessed the rapidly vanishing, and now extinct, *Pavonia alnifolia* in the state of Rio de Janeiro as well as other impacts of growth and development along the Jacarapeguà coastal plain. In conjunction with Henrique Lahmeyer de Mello Barreto and José Candido de Mello Carvalho, Burle Marx proposed to develop a demonstration garden dedicated to preserving the beauty and vitality of the coastal flora and fauna (Fig. 5).[17]

He choose a flat site with rock outcroppings in the Jacarapaguà region, close to the coastal lagoon of Marapendi. The rational

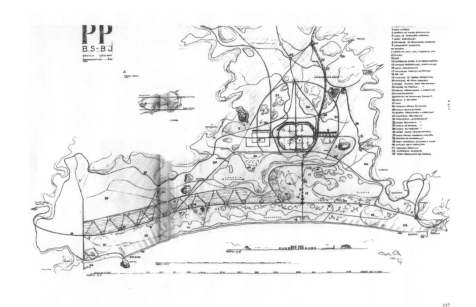

4. Lucia Costa's plan recognized that viaducts and tunnels built in 1969 under the Joa Mountain peak would redefine urban development in the region, threatening the natural heritage of the coast.

for the choice of setting was his desire to illustrate the continuity of the flora and fauna that ranged from the beach and lagoon to the *restinga* and then to the foothills of the mountains that defined the Tijuca and Jacarapaguà triangle mentioned previously. His proposal was to be situated on a site of some 25,000 square meters, organized as a series of clusters of plant associations that reflected the general biotic communities of the former Federal District.

The programmatic commitment to illustrating the mosaic of plants that can be found in the various climatic and landscape settings that stretch from the coasts to the foothills of the mountains that surround Rio is almost hidden behind the formal framework of the plan, immediately recognizable as a work of Burle Marx's. As Fernando Chacel observed, "He painted with plants creating focal points, hierarchies and a multiplicity of uses at different scales of landscape intervention, creating harmonious and balanced microcosms … and left us with the extraordinary polychromes of his parks and gardens where the friendly shadows and the blooming expositions of his trees perpetuate his relationship with the landscape".[18]

Burle Marx, with his friends the biologists Henrique Lahmeyer de Mello Barreto, José Candido de Mello Carvalho, Luiz Emygdio de Mello Filho, and Grazeila Barroso ventured far and wide on plant expeditions, discovering a vast array of flora native to the Amazon and other ecosystems of Brazil.[19] These were carefully planted and propagated in nurseries, including Marx's own at the Sitio Santo Antonio da Bica, where he carried out scientific and artistic experiments all his life. The Thermal Park at Araxa, designed in 1947, was one of the first projects organized according to phyto-geographic regions, using local rock plants, cactus, and lichens. It was here that Burle Marx learned to observe the ecology of plants in their original environment before using them in gardens and other urban sites.[20] Rossana Vaccarino notes that the return to the forest and the

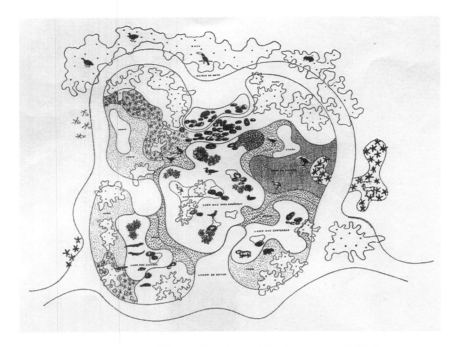

5. An early garden proposal by Burle Marx, Mello Barreto, and Mello Carvalho demonstrates the plant associations of the Jacarepaguà coastal plain.
6. The Bromeliad garden and stairway in Gleba E, designed by Chacel and Mello Filho, with cacti from the *restinga* landscape in the foreground.

appreciation of indigenous cultures was the core of *brasilidade*, the national essence of Brazil, and of the avant-garde modernist movement represented by Burle Marx's discovery and celebration of Brazilian flora: "Native vegetation thus acquired both cultural and didactic value for Burle Marx, representing a national legacy and symbolizing national pride."[21]

Two aspects of this vision are of particular importance: the commitment to a rigorous scientific methodology in support of the disposition and presentation of the plant materials in question, and an understanding that the ecosystems to be illustrated would be inspired by nature but could not be an exact copy. These principles have been embraced and, in fact, developed by Fernando Chacel in the course of his career, particularly in the series of projects associated with the restoration of the shorelines that border the Lagoa da Tijuca.

Fernando Chacel's Strategy for Coastal Restoration

If Roberto Burle Marx concentrated on the artistic project of expressing the genius loci of Brazil, Fernando Chacel has spent considerable time and energy in repairing the ravages of industrialization and urbanization that developed as a result of modernization. Although many of their concerns are similar, their approaches and strategies differ. Roberto Burle Marx was a committed botanist who fiercely advocated the use of the rich palate of native vegetation in all his landscape design projects. He was, however, first and foremost an artist. His landscape designs focused attention on the beauty of the world of plants, and through his art stimulated an interest in the conservation and use of the native flora of Brazil.

Fernando Chacel's love of the native plant material of Brazil is no less than that of Marx (Fig. 6). His designs subtly highlight a rich array of flowering plants that draw attention to the relationships between plant communities and the continuum

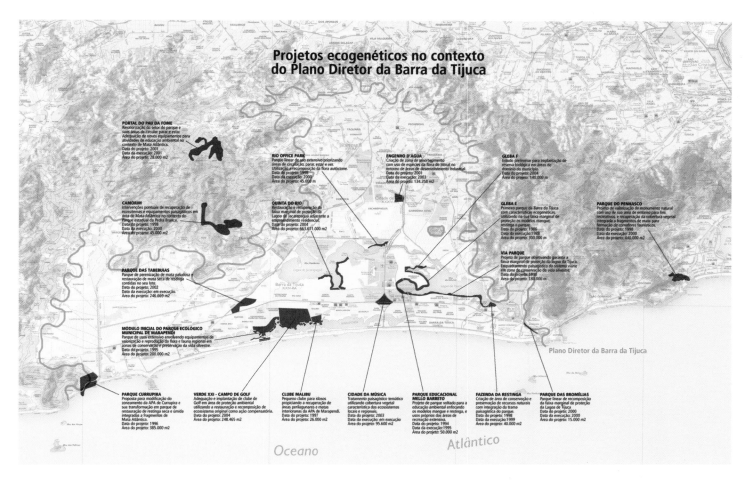

7. The plan locates ecogenesis projects in the Jacarepaguà region, including those that comprise the thirteen kilometers of the coastal belt protection zone.

and interdependence of the ecosystems to which they belong. In the Jacarepaguà coastal plain these include linkages between the lagoon, mangrove, and *restinga,* and most important, to the city. He has achieved many of his projects by forming partnerships with botanists, geomorphologists, engineers, and architects united in the mission of reconstituting the landscapes of Brazil lost through greed and neglect.

     His career has been something of a *parcours d'accident*. In the early 1950s he played the accordion in a band featured in local music halls while he was studying architecture. He was introduced to landscape architecture while working in the studio of Burle Marx, where he produced gouache paintings of the master's plans for an exhibit in Paris. While building a reputation as a landscape designer, he began to realize that the landscape was much more than a source for visual display, and his career changed course in 1963, when he started to work on the restoration of dam sites being constructed by the Central Electrique du São Paulo (CESP). He and his partners, the biologist Luis Emygdio de Mello Filho and the architect Almir de Lima Machado, formed the firm *A Paisagem* and were the first to deal with issues of landscape and environment at this scale. Chacel later succeeded Mello Filho as director of the Parks and Gardens Department of the City of Rio.

     By 1986, the democratic structure of the country had reasserted itself, although the loss of forests and other unique

8. Initial phases of the recuperation, preparation, and planting of the lagoon margin protection zone in Gleba E.

9. A group of *Ananas bracteatus* and the restored mangrove across the water, with the Gavea Sugar-loaf mountain formation in the distance.

landscape structures continued at an alarming rate. Where pure conservation measures failed, as was so often the case, the opportunity to mitigate the impacts of development stimulated his imagination. He began to devise aesthetic strategies that would contribute to nature conservation without imposing unnecessary restrictions on the urban users of parks and green spaces. Chacel quickly embraced the domain of landscape planning that built on his accumulated experience in landscape restoration, working with multidisciplinary teams and his significant experience within the rapidly expanding urban environments of São Paulo and Rio. Landscape solutions might ideally seek to re-create an ecosystem as compensation for development impacts, a process he called "ecogenesis."

Ecogenesis involves human intervention in the landscape; it is a manmade process that utilizes the plant associations and individuals of original ecosystems to restore neglected or devastated landscapes to biological health. The idea of ecogenesis accepts human intervention in the design of natural process, adapted to the social and environmental context, to augment and to substitute for those aspects of the natural setting that have been disturbed or destroyed. Conservation cannot be geared to a world free of human presence. Chacel acknowledges that the attitudes of developers, entrepreneurs, and inhabitants will not be transformed overnight. His projects seek to implant an admiration for nature enlisting the sheer beauty of tropical plants. He creates these environments in places where only traces of historic ecosystems are still visible, knowing that he cannot reestablish those that have evolved over thousands of years and have been used by all manner of living species, including small human groups, who have vanished from the surroundings of Rio de Janeiro. These ecosystems of substitution, even if somewhat different from those that have been lost, are intended to transmit to future generations the environmental value and the complex web of social and natural associations that were found in the original. As such, they form an important part of the infrastructure of a new cultural landscape and garden aesthetic.

Fernando Chacel's Design Strategy

The Barra da Tijuca is the living laboratory where Fernando Chacel has explored the potential and perhaps the limits of the idea of ecogenesis. The cycle of initial settlement of the Tijuca region by farmers, coffee growers, fishermen, and foresters; the opening of the territory in the late 1960s through new transportation infrastructure; the devastation of many of the coastal ecosystems through uncontrolled and even rapacious urban development—all provided Chacel with the ideal context to test his ideas. Notwithstanding

10. Clusters of *Acrostichum aureum* border the recuperated mangrove across the water, with the Barra da Tijuca skyline in the background.

a growing awareness of the loss of original and indigenous coastal ecosystems, the challenge is overwhelming.

Urban development has erased the natural cover of the coastal ranges of Rio, contributing to the destruction of the mangroves that maintained the chain of life that grew along the river banks and lagoons. The rehabilitation of the mangroves is thus an essential aspect of any program of landscape restoration. It is, however, sustainable only under two conditions. The flora that surrounds the mangrove on higher ground, the *restinga,* has to be rehabilitated to protect the mangrove and allow the mangrove to reestablish itself, and both the *restinga* and the mangrove have to be protected from inappropriate use. Chacel's strategy is three pronged. First, he establishes the conditions for the mutual support of strips of *restingas* and mangroves; second, he negotiates the conditions under which houses, offices, and roads are built; and third, he designs access paths that invite people to stroll and view the *restinga* settings while admiring the mangroves that remain largely out of reach.

The scope of the shoreline restoration projects and the conservation and recreation parks proposed by Chacel and his partner, Sidney Linharaes, in cooperation with the municipal authorities and the development community is impressive. More than thirteen kilometers of otherwise devastated shoreline has been planned as mangrove and *restinga* landscapes (Fig. 7) in the Tijuca, Camorim, and Marapendi lagoons. The projects make use of, while simultaneously protecting and conserving, local flora, mountain foothills, and water bodies.[22]

The most intensely developed project is situated on a peninsula that juts into the Lagoa da Tijuca. Gleba E will eventually support some 20,000 residents. Until recently, the peninsula was virtually denuded of vegetative cover even though it occupies a site with glorious vistas to well-known natural monuments such as the Sugar Loaf formations of Panela and Itanhanga as well as the Tijuca massif (Fig. 8). Given the future planned population for the peninsula, the potential of reestablishing a viable lagoon-margin protection belt as an extensive park with an ecological focus could complement the more intensively organized areas of parkland, plazas, and squares that are planned to support the residential communities (Fig. 9). This layering of the physical frames of nature, to which we will return, "would be the precursors of a landscape continuum capable

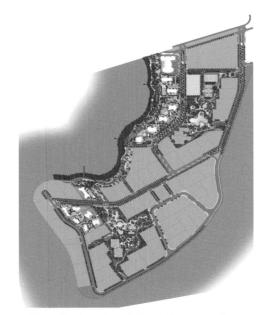

11. Chacel's plan for Gleba E illustrates the narrow, thirty meter mangrove fringe; the major parks on the peninsula; and the urban squares adjacent to the apartment complexes.

of providing aesthetic qualities and an amenable climate to the venture, as well as biotic compensation for the inevitable impacts caused by the implementation of the proposed development project"[23] (Fig. 10).

Immediately adjacent to the peninsula, a public park dedicated to the memory of Professor Mello Barreto forms part of the coastal protection belt that was once covered by a substantial mangrove before squatters occupied the land. Once the relatively few squatter families were relocated, the reconstitution of the previously viable mangrove shoreline could be initiated.[24] Destroyed by repeated landfills and deforestation, neither the soil nor the land profile was appropriate for the educational park that was planned. Rubble had to be removed and habitats established that would allow the lost plant communities to be reintroduced and to support themselves.

Another coastal park, Parque Fazenda da Restinga, features the typical *restinga* vegetation of the region. A wide variety of planting strategies animates the paths that flow through the park, skirting the *restinga* forest and shrub lands, leading eventually to a nine-meter-high observation tower that looks out to the Gavea Sugar Loaf formation, and over the adjacent protective belt of mangrove forest. Notwithstanding the introduction of new planting zones in the area, "the rustic environment of the park was maintained so as to allow the visitor to experience the richness of the local flora."[25]

A divided highway, Via Parque, with a broad heavily planted median strip, was located at some distance from the shoreline in such a way as to ensure protection for the native vegetation and landforms while providing for a linear park. In much the same spirit, the Rio Office Park was planned and organized both to accommodate significant office space and to contribute to the overall strategy of protecting and enhancing the health of the shoreline ecosystems. This particular project created a protected area, adjacent to the intensively used office park, whose width and other measures conformed to the regulations required for permanent protected areas. The shoreline was treated as a wildlife preservation zone that features vegetation associated with the original *restinga* of the region.[26]

Finally, the Marapendi Municipal Ecological Park created in 1978 and then organized around a zoning plan in 1995 is the single most important conservation unit in the Barra da Tijuca, enclosing an area of some six million square meters. An elaborate master plan for this area, proposed by Fernando Chacel and his collaborators, is based on a number of innovative conservation principles.[27] These are designed to ensure the "maintenance of native vegetation remnants of the park's primitive ecosystems plus the reintroduction of typical plant associations from these segments of the Atlantic forest domain" that will have important repercussions in the realm of urban landscape protection and restoration.

Each of these projects forms part of an integrated strategy of conservation and rehabilitation of the coastal mangrove and the *restinga* landscape that had previously inspired Lucio Costa and Burle Marx. Fernando Chacel's strategy of restoring shoreline and park landscapes adds a promising cultural dimension to the continuing need to manage this landscape, and to that a new "garden" aesthetic that may well emerge from it (Fig. 11).

Aesthetic Aspects of the Coastal Gardens

Seventy years ago John Dewey spoke of the consequences of globalization on our understanding of art. He observed "the mobility of trade and of populations, due to the economic system has weakened or destroyed the connection between works of art and the genius loci of which they were once the natural expression. As works of art have lost their indigenous status, they have acquired a new one—that of being specimens of fine art and nothing else." Dewey goes on to say "objects that were in the past valid and significant because of their place in the life of a community now function in isolation from the conditions of their origin. By that fact they are also set apart from common experience, and serve as insignia of taste and certificates of special culture."[28]

The construction of modern national identity in Brazil, of *brasilidade,* in which the avant-garde is coupled with the cultural and natural diversity of place, was, however, the very opposite of those conditions Dewey feared. The collage of experiences derived from diverse cultural and natural settings provided the background against which Burle Marx and

12. Parkland in Gleba E with the Gavea profile in the background
13. An urban public space adjacent to the apartment complexes, in Gleba E

latter Fernando Chacel expressed their art. "These cultures teach us to see and respond to the world in a variety of ways. Art is simply an intensification of this process."[29]

In articulating how, or whether, Chacel's coastal gardens provide a framework for new aesthetic experience, the task is "to bring to light the cultural background that makes his work both within reach of public appreciation and yet genuinely innovative."[30] Specifically, two seemingly disparate cultural issues inform the projects proposed by Chacel: the perceived and very real losses in the beauty and diversity of the native flora, fauna, and human cultures of Brazil, and the intractable social stresses that urbanization exerts on the equitable provision of social and economic services in the development of human settlement. Both are typical of the large and contemporary urban conglomerations in Brazil, where the shifting relationship between these two forces dulls the senses to the destruction of the land. Paradoxically perhaps, a commitment to *brasilidade*

14. Orderly frames that structure messy ecosystems: textures, volumes, and patterns of light and shadow along a pathway through the Mello Barreto nature park

15. A stairway and path lined with bromeliads and *Syagrus romanzoffiana* palms

simultaneously stimulates a vibrant culture of music and art expressive of the hopes and aspirations of a confident people. Chacel's work embraces the latter, although it is clearly aware of and informed by the former. It is informed, perhaps, by a vision of a "New World" paradise and the realities of contemporary human settlements of wildly varying quality.

The attitudes of the development community toward urban growth add an additional, altogether critical, component to this mix. Initially, the property owner and developer, Carlos Fernando de Carvalho, thought of the proposed housing complex in relatively traditional terms, high-density residential towers surrounded by gardens of imported plant materials organized in somewhat traditional, picturesque designs. The fact that the peninsula had been virtually denuded of vegetative cover coupled with governmental concerns with landscape restoration that grew out of the environmental impact studies required by the new national legal regime resulted in the rejection of this traditional development model and the mandate to develop a serious scientific strategy directed toward restoring the coastal belt zone. Over the course of a number of years, not only did Carvalho begin to embrace the strategy of ecogenesis, he began to understand that he was building and should be marketing a new urban lifestyle and not just offering an isolated apartment space to the highest bidder.

Fernando Chacel's design intent is to structure the layers of nature from plaza, to parkland, to *restinga* and mangrove, moving from the social to the wild and back again. In this context ecogenesis can be understood as a contemporary design strategy rather than some nostalgic desire to return to a virginal state of nature (Fig. 12). Although this new garden experience recalls the forest and the natural settings of cultures long since lost in the mythology of Amazonia and the Mata Atlantica, it does so in the context of emerging contemporary issues of pressing concern to urban Brazil. The projects invite the active participation of new urban residents whose experience at the edge of, and surrounded by, these gardens literally stretch "out of sight."

The emerging aesthetic is informed by the physical frames of the projects proposed by Fernando Chacel, their shared meanings and contribution to past memories and future visions, and the curious and somewhat ambiguous relationship of the natural and the artificial in the outcome of the projects themselves (Fig. 13).

Physical Frames

16. A pebble path lined with a ground layer of *Ipomoes pes-caprae* and bromeliades

The projects proposed by Fernando Chacel stretch for some thirteen kilometers along the Jacarapaguà coastal complex. The spatial strategy is linear and continuous rather than concentrated and punctual. The scale of the network is much larger than the typical project, extending well beyond the range of activity that any one individual is likely to experience at any one time. Repeated visits, over a rather extended time span, most probably would incorporate discontinuous and disconnected sites that are unlikely to be experienced in any predictable, spatial sequence. Access to the network of greenways is constrained, as well, by public and private ownership and will occasion visits for different purposes in different social contexts that are equally difficult to predict. Issues of "passing through" a sequence of environments, strategies whereby these experiences are linked one to the other, and how they are framed in space and time provide us a rich mixture of aesthetic issues to contemplate.

The network of open green spaces proposed by Chacel consists of small areas of relatively untouched remnants of coastal flora; coastland that has been restored and rehabilitated, consistent with the ideas of ecogenesis; parkways and parkland that support residential and commercial activities; and plazas and squares that invite more intensive community-based social interaction.

Joan Nassauer suggests that messy ecosystems require orderly frames. The experience of viewing and moving through areas formed with respect to ecological quality and integrity (Fig. 14): "... is not a straightforward problem of attending to scientific knowledge of ecosystem relationships or an artistic problem of expressing ecological function, but a public landscape problem of addressing cultural expectations that only tangentially relate to ecological function or high art. It requires the translation of ecological patterns into cultural language. It requires placing unfamiliar and frequently undesirable forms inside familiar, attractive packages."[31] Further, in the urban context "we must design to frame ecological function within a recognizable system of form,"[32] as residents expect to see the hand of human intention within the settled landscape (Fig. 15).

The orderly frame is one such sign of human presence, a signal that there is both purpose and intent associated with the "wild" gardens that border the lagoons and waterways of the coastal complex. Signs of caring for the landscape are another strategy in support of the comfortable reception of messy nature within a settled landscape. These signs can be as modest as bird feeders, a group of exercise equipment in a clearing, or the obvious grouping of flowering plants at a conspicuous location where paths may cross (Fig. 16).

A major part of Fernando Chacel's approach to design is built upon the infinite variation of planting displays. While Burle Marx highlights formal invention in a way that is recognizable as an artistic signature, Chacel's formal designs in the coastal plain are modest and somewhat inconspicuous. Paths lead from the densely built residential sectors with their bustling activity to secluded clearings within the *restinga,* only tangentially approaching the mangrove. Moving from one park setting to another, the framing strategy of the paths serves to structure the different experiences throughout the rehabilitated landscape projects. The focus is on the unique form, structure, and beauty of the plants rather than on a formal design vocabulary, fusing the various landscape conditions into common experiences. There is a deep sense of modesty in the art of focusing the attention of the user on the beauty of nature while rendering the frame invisible.

Yet one wonders if the network of reconstituted shorelines of mangrove and *restinga* and the new park lands and plazas that form the infrastructure of the residential and mixed land-use development in the Lagoa de Tijuca basin simply mask the destruction that preceded them, or are there other ways in which the shared meanings of these three natures might be understood within the contemporary setting of Rio de Janeiro?[33]

Shared Meanings: Memories and Memorials

"A place owes its character to the experiences it affords to those who spend time there—to the sights, sounds, and indeed smells that constitute its specific ambience. And these, in turn, depend on the kinds of activities in which its inhabitants engage. It is from this relational context of people's engagement in the world, in the business of dwelling, that each place draws its unique significance. Thus, whereas with space, meanings are attached to the world, with landscape they are gathered from it."[34] In this sense the landscape is a story, and by living in it and viscerally experiencing it, the landscape becomes part of us and we part of it.

Perhaps the strongest support for the popular appropriation of the gardens that Chacel proposes is the insistent use of the flora with which everyone can identify. The gardens devoted to bromeliads, fruit trees, *restinga,* and coastal forests are powerful aids to the collective memories of those that will inhabit this region. Plants are as much scripts as they are memorials, the individual trees of the mangrove forest not unlike the names carved into the polished black granite of the Vietnam War Memorial. They form a matrix of sensual and sensorial settings; they recall history and restore memories of the genius loci of a place.[35]

Experience of and within the landscape is sensorial—feeling the landscape through the feet, and evoking memories through our sense of smell. *Restinga* and mangrove parks are located in densely populated environments supporting very diverse activities. All sorts of people roam through the *restinga,* and their experiences of a vicarious wilderness become part of their daily life. These experiences then become ritualized, resulting in the popular appropriation of the aesthetic experiences that the parks provide (Fig. 17).

This experience can, as well, be based on new approaches to the virtual world of nature. Diana Domingues, for instance, has grounded her art in the cultural roots of Brazil. Her project INSN(H)AKES is an interactive project that uses new digital and auditory technologies to convey the language of serpentine signals and native human ritual in which both myth and materiality, the spirited and the spiritual, combine into a new synthesis. Her experience living with the Kuikuru Indians in the Mato Grosso were instructive of the ease with which the human condition can be transformed into that of the animal, or in this case a snake. The project uses web cameras, computing interfaces, hypertexts connected to the web with television, and telecommand

17. Plants serve as markers and memorials amid the intense urbanization of Brazil, as illustrated by a grove of *Schinus terebinthfolius* in the parkland of Gleba E.

devices to experience the perspective of the reptile by "crawling and seeing the elements of the world through their viewpoint."[36]

"Experience is the on-going world of nature culturally inhabited. It is not therefore primarily either subjective or unshaped, a manifold of blooming buzzing precepts. It is shaped and shaping, primarily cultural and therefore interactive."[37] As Fernando Chacel recalls, "I know Barra da Tijuca and the Jacarepagua Coastal plain in their unsophisticated state. Sea dunes, lagoons and marshes, gallery forest arching over rivers—these formed the basis of a relief dotted with natural monuments, where forests stretched between the watercourses, and slopes were covered by dense vegetation. These memories from my childhood and my youth, of times gone by, were lost over time. But they are hidden away somewhere in my memory."[38]

John Dewey insists that "culture is the product of prolonged and cumulative interaction with environment" and cites the boyhood memory of Ralph Waldo Emerson, who noted, "Crossing a bare common, in snow puddles, at twilight, under a clouded sky, without having in my thought any occurrence of special good fortune, I have enjoyed a perfect exhilaration. I am glad to the brink of fear."[39] Clearly, Fernando Chacel has similar and equally strong emotional ties to the rich variety of plant life in the region that engages those that walk through the gardens he proposes.

The question remains as to whether or not the structure and form of plant materials within the protective belt of mangrove and *restinga,* organized with respect to the principles of ecogenesis, and framed so as to signal both care and human intention, can evoke the same or similar reactions rooted in the memory and meanings of the regional landscape of Rio de Janeiro, and to the distant time and visions of Amazonia. My sense is that they can and that they do, and in so doing add an intriguing component to the aesthetic impact of the coastal complex.

18. The centerpiece of the Carnival is the Samba parade where the sensual and the artificial fuse our ideas of nature and culture.

Of Nature and the Artificial

Do the physical frames and shared meanings associated with the network of landscape projects proposed by Chacel conform to our idea of wilderness, a landscape, or a garden—that is, to which of the three natures do they belong? If ecogenesis views the strict reproduction of nature as an impossible mission, the issue of what is nature and what is artificial becomes an active variable of the aesthetic equations that inform our experience of the coastal complex.

Consider, once again, the images of the bromeliad that Margaret Mee painted and Leme Elton described as "miniature universes—pure mystery—where thousands of life forms are in orbit ... their own private worlds, with lakes, beaches and swamps, where beings are born, grow up and die without ever leaving their hosts."[40] Mee sought out and produced faithful portraits of nature in situ, presented artfully and with scientific precision. There was no attempt to modify what was seen as the very viable and wonderful workings of nature; rather the mission was to communicate these wonders in support of scientific research and cultural development, contributing thereby to the movement of *brasilidade*.

Contrast this with the work of George Gessert, who develops hybrids of iris, daylilies, streptocarpuses, nasturtiums, and poppies as a form of art, for the pleasure of working with plants and because "hybrids are various, astonishing, and wonderful in themselves."[41] He suggests that breeding can even bring back into gardens and cities some of the visual qualities of wildness. Gessert notes that there is an aesthetic to the economic production of these plants, where doubles and ruffles sell well, and therefore predominate. Other aesthetics arise, however, when the plants are bred to learn more about them, or to explore the integrity of their form. These hybrid plants are then exhibited in galleries and may later be placed in the wild, perhaps even in areas similar to those along the coastal gardens of Barra da Tijuca.

Is the hybrid iris artificial? When they are introduced in the wild, does wilderness become landscape or garden? Can the entire coastal protection zone that was designed and furnished through human agency for a continuous length of thirteen kilometers be considered as a work of art, even subject to copyright as intellectual property? If art is experience, and the coastal gardens support this experience, if not nurture them, then surely the response must be positive.

Further, wild gardens are fragile and persist only with human care, including those that are designed to approximate "natural conditions." And care is one of the critical clues of the physical frames and cultural signs required to maintain human interest and experience in "messy ecosystems."

"The landscape is never complete: neither built or un-built, it is perpetually under construction." This is why the conventional dichotomy between the natural and the artificial, or man made components of the landscape is so problematic. This is particularly so in Brazil where Roberto da Matta speaks of the predatory extraction of nature on the one hand and nature as inhabited by the marvelous and the magical on the other; where nature is entwined in culture and culture in nature.[42] Thus the Carnival is celebrated in a spirit that is as visceral as it is social, melding joy and seduction with visions of the Garden of Eden (Fig. 18).

Prospect

The emerging garden aesthetic associated with formal dimensions of landscapes and gardens that are designed to grow in patterns that are not fully fixed in space or in time require spatial frames that support our sense of human agency and even familiarity with the changing garden scene. The aesthetic is no longer one that relates to and builds upon a scene, but rather on conditions in the landscape.

Meanings associated with these conditions in Brazil are derived from the cultural context of urbanization in the New World, with its associated joys and vigor as much as its environmental impacts and social inequities. The spatial frames of residential development, of parks and plazas, help to establish the context for messy gardens at the edge of lagoons. The choice, structure, and form of the plant materials are designed to recall the flora of the region that, in many cases, is no longer present.

What then of the future? Can the gardens of the Jacarapaguà coastal plain be sustained? As Joan Nassauer cautions, "For new forms of ecologically rich landscapes to be sustained, the forms must be recognized and perpetuated by people in everyday situations, maintaining the landscape and creating their own landscapes."[43]

Sustainability requires more than conservation or even restoration—it requires human creativity and the magic of art to provide meaningful and publicly valued landscapes. "Burle Marx described the garden as the place to display, conserve, and perpetuate the existence of native species otherwise threatened in the wild. The natural environment, in turn, would be a source of inspiration, a large reference, readable and meaningful to people through direct experience in the details of the designed garden. Ecology for him was the means of analyzing plants in their native habitat; art was the means for creative reconfiguration and gardening the art of constantly editing a composition through years of supervision."[44] An art that requires "constant editing" requires as well a deep sense of appropriation by those who agree to participate in the long-term health of the garden. The aesthetic that emerges is one that is rooted not so much in a physical condition but in the changing cultural vision of this condition. There is an open-ended nature to culture.

There is, as well, an open-ended nature to nature—a system that is neither closed nor enclosed. Fernando Chacel recognizes that the projects he has initiated along the Jacarapaguà coastal plain, or in the Barra da Tijuca forest, incorporate elements that he cannot anticipate, forms that he can aspire to achieve but cannot completely control, conditions that he can attempt to replicate and forms that he can imagine. Like the ink spots on rice paper, the results are not fully predictable. In his words, "*Il y a un geste, mais pas un style.*"

How, then, does one develop an aesthetic that is based, not on the landscape as a "picture seen from one vantage point," but on a language of forms that stretch "out of sight," of ecological structures and natural indigenous plant associations that are rarely experienced in the urban context of Brazil? The gardens of the Jacarapaguà coastal complex respond to this implied challenge, partly through orderly frames that structure messy ecosystems, partly because the shared meaning and memory of plant materials is so thoroughly engrained in the Brazilian culture, and partly because the mix of cultures and natures is integral to the national pride of an increasingly urban Brazil.

They do so by creating a new liminal zone, a narrow stretch of self-sustaining natural life within a vital zone of bustling urban activity. This new garden is not simply about the forms that we give to nature, but rather about the conditions under which we dwell and acquire experiences *in* nature. If, as Dewey insisted, culture is the product of prolonged and cumulative interaction with environment, then the new coastal gardens may well generate new forms of urban culture.

Residents, visitors, and gardeners will respond to the display and abundance of plant materials in different ways. Those from the countryside may recognize the plants that remind them of home; those from the city, the plants that were never proximate; and those from distant regions of Brazil, the signature of a new land. Although reception may vary with the circumstances of those who inhabit Glebe E, the linkage between the natural ecosystems of the region and the natural setting of the urban paths and parks is common to all. Shared experiences give rise to shared interpretations and eventually to shared values that support new cultural attitudes and positions, to a new aesthetic rooted in the people and places of Rio, and to a new *brasilidade*.

NOTES

[1] Brazil's Amazonian Region; Adventure Travel Society brochure, Englewood, Colorado, January 1993.

[2] See *Amazonia at the Crossroads*, ed. Anthony Hall (London: Institute of Latin American Studies, University of London, 2000).

[3] Elton Leme, Postface, in Margaret Mee, *Bromélias Brasileiras* (São Paulo: Instituto de Botanica de São Paulo, 1992), 156.

[4] Posey notes that it was not until the seventeenth century that indigenous people were believed to have souls. See Darrell Addison Posey, "Biodiversity, Genetic Resources and Indigenous Peoples in Amazonia," in Hall, *Amazonia at the Crossroads,* 189.

[5] The Amazon region of Brazil is approximately the size of western Europe, and the area cleared, by 1997, was the size of France. Every minute 3.2 hectares are lost. Philip Fearnside, "Deforestation Impacts, Environmental Services and the International Community," in Hall, *Amazonia at the Crossroads,* 20.

[6] Jacques Leenhardt, "Le retour à l'origine: genius loci, le cas de Roberto Burle Marx," in *Le jardin planétaire* (Paris: Éditions de l'Aube, 1997), 50.

[7] Up to 40 percent of the cost of $200 million to bring a new drug to market can be saved through biodiversity patents and traditional local knowledge available in the Amazon. Posey, "Biodiversity, Genetic Resources and Indigenous Peoples in Amazonia," 189.

[8] Alma Guillermoprieto, *Samba* (New York: Vintage Books, 1990). Guillermoprieto describes the social and spiritual energies, the rituals and the rhythms of the samba schools in the *favelas* of Rio, and the unrestrained joy of the *cariocas* in the face of poverty, violence and racism.

[9] Paul Rambal, *In the Cities and the Jungles of Brazil* (New York: Henry Holt, 1993), 182–99. Short sketches describe the presence of magic, African folklore, guiding spirits, *orixà*, and the kissing saint that animate urban life in Rio.

[10] G. Nunes, *Rio: métropole de 300 favelas* (Petropolis: Vozes, 1976).

[11] Rambal, *In the Cities and Jungles of Brazil*, 63.

[12] The *restinga* landscape is characterized by herbaceous vegetation, bushes, and trees typical of the meridian coast and the north of Brazil, including beach vegetation and dunes and fore dune grasses that extend to the lagoon shoreline mangroves.

[13] Lucio Costa, *Barra 1969, registro de uma vivência* (São Paulo: Empresa das Artes, 1995), 344–54. "Plano piloto para a urbanizacao da baixada compreendida entre a Barra da Tijuca, o Pontal de Senambetiba e Jacarepaguà."

[14] Fernando Chacel, *Paisagismo e ecogênese* (Rio de Janeiro: Fraiha, 2001), 121–29.

[15] Silvio Soares Macedo suggests four key design concepts that informed Burle Marx's work: "the use of native tropical vegetation as a structural element of design, the rupture of symmetrical patterns in the conception of open spaces, the colorful treatment of pavements, and the use of free forms in water feature." Silvio Soares Macedo, "Roberto Burle Marx and the Founding of Modern Brazilian Landscape," in *Roberto Burle Marx: Landscape Reflected,* ed Rossana Vaccarino, Landscape Views 3 (Princeton, NJ, and Cambridge, MA: Princeton University Press and the Harvard University Graduate School of Design, 1998).

[16] Quoted in Lucia Maria S. A. Costa, "Burle Marx e o paisagismo no Brasil contemporâneo," *Revista Municipal de Engenharia* (December/January 1999): 32.

[17] Roberto Burle Marx, Henrique Lahmeyer de Mello Barreto, and José Candido de Mello Carvalho, "Groupo biologico des lagoas litaraneas do Distrito Federal; Janeiro–Março, 1949," *Revista Municipal de Engenharia* (December/January 1999): 9–10.

[18] Fernando Chacel, speech in honor of Roberto Burle Marx, Institute of Architects of Brazil, Rio de Janeiro, 16 December 1994.

[19] Ibid.

[20] Anita Berrizbetia, *Roberto Burle Marx in Caracas: Parque del Este, 1956–1961* (Philadelphia: University of Pennsylvania Press, 2005), 19.

[21] Rossana Viccarino, Introduction, in *Roberto Burle Marx: Landscapes Reflected* (New York: Princeton University Press), 11.

[22] The 13 kilometers of shoreline are protected by the state of Rio de Janeiro as a Protected Environmental Zone defined by Federal Law no. 9.985, 18 July 2000, which corresponds to the flexible protection of ecosystems within which a certain amount of urbanization is permitted.

[23] Chacel, *Paisagismo e ecogênese,* 50.

[24] Ibid., 67.

[25] Ibid., 90.

[26] Ibid., 109.

[27] Ibid., 125, 126. The plans and construction drawings of the first 200,000 square meters have already been developed in great detail.

[28] John Dewey, *Art as Experience* (New York: G. P. Putnam's Sons, 1980), 9.

[29] Thomas M. Alexander, *John Dewey's Theory of Art Experience and Nature: The Horizons of Feeling* (Albany: State University of New York Press, 1987), 189.

[30] Michel Conan, "Fragments of a Poetic of Gardens," *Landscape Journal*, no. 1 (2006): 11, 1-21

[31] Joan Nassauer, "Messy Ecosystems, Orderly Frames," *Landscape Journal* 14, no. 2 (1995): 161.

[32] Ibid., 162.

[33] Peter Jacobs, "Folklore and Forest Fragments," *Landscape Journal* 23, no. 2 (2004): 85–101.

[34] Tim Ingold, "The Temporality of the Landscape: Conceptions of Time and Ancient Society," *World Archeology* 25, no. 2 (1993): 155.

[35] Peter Jacobs, "Playing with Time," *Studies in the History of Gardens and the Designed Landscape* 20, no. 4 (2006): 325–39.

[36] Ruy Pauletti, "Transdisciplinarity and Cyberculture," in Catalog INS(H)NAKES, April 2001, Universidade de Caxias do Sul.

[37] Alexander, *John Dewey's Theory of Art Experience and Nature,* 270.

[38] Chacel, *Paisagismo e ecogênese,* 25.

[39] Dewey, *Art as Experience,* 29.

[40] Leme, Postface, 156.

[41] George Gessert, "On Exhibiting Hybrids," Art + Technology Supplement of *CIRCA* 90: S 8–9.

[42] Roberto da Matta, "Autour de la representation de la nature," in *Les sentiments de la nature,* ed. Dominique Bourg (Paris: Éditions de la Découverte, 1993).

[43] Nassauer, "Messy Ecosystems, Orderly Frames," 169.

[44] Vaccarino, ibid., 8.

Contemporary Garden Aesthetics, Creations and Interpretations

Contemporary Garden Aesthetics, Creations and Interpretations

Contemporary Garden Aesthetics, Creations and Interpretations

Contemporary Garden Aesthetics, Creations and Interpretations

Walk through the Crossing: The Draw at Sugar House Park, Salt Lake City

Xin Wu

The Draw at Sugar House is a sunken pedestrian corridor, almost a secret passage along the stream bed of Parley's Creek, which was the original point of entry for the first Mormon settlers to the valley of present-day Salt Lake City.[1]

In July 1847, the pioneers arrived in view of the Great Salt Lake after a grueling exodus. The vanguard encountered a rattlesnake while searching for a gateway into the verdant basin. He reported: "I crawled [... on my hands and knees] through this thicket ... admonished by the rattle of a snake [which lay coiled up a little under my nose ... but as he gave me the friendly warning,] I thanked him and retreated."[2] A safe passage was then discovered. The settlers entered the valley and established their first encampments along Parley's Creek. Struggling against a harsh environment, they survived the early days by eating roots of the wild sego lily. The community sustained, and the sego lily became the state flower of Utah. Nearly 160 years later, urban development has erased many historic ravines; the world of settlers fades into the remote past. Although monuments were built, the legacy of the Mormons' covenant with nature remains an unanswered question.[3]

The Draw: A Linear Garden

Images of the rattlesnake and the sego lily reemerge in a new public garden along Parley's Creek designed by artist Patricia Johanson in 2003. The garden is named the Draw at Sugar House. Its primary goal is to connect two zones of the Parley's Creek Valley that are set apart by an expressway. On the mountain side, Parley's Creek flows across Sugar House Park (Fig. 1). On the city side, a stretch of the creek, known as Hidden Hollow, is turned into a wilderness reservation. Both part of the history, the park and Hidden Hollow, are incorporated in a monumental conservation plan of the whole Parley's Creek Valley, and the Draw at Sugar House is the linchpin of the plan.[4] Johanson's new garden not only links the two sides of the expressway and the three branches of the trail system; it also recaptures the unity between Wasatch Mountain, Parley's Creek Valley, and the Great Salt Lake, all of which constitute a living world that the pioneers wrestled, adapted, transformed, and dwelt in.

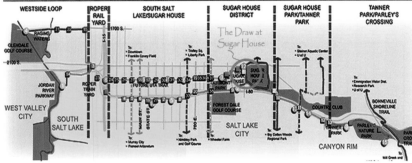

1. Upper—site of the Draw at Sugar House; lower—location of the Draw in relation to the Parley's Creek Valley conservation project and its trial system connecting the Wasatch Mountain to the Great Salt Lake.

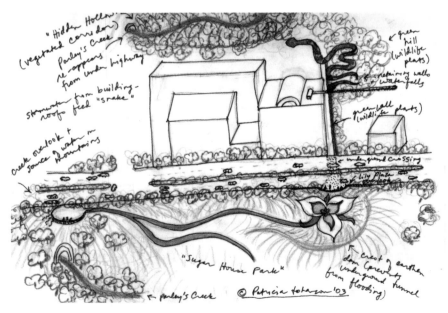

2. Sketch of the plan of the Draw at Sugar House, by Patricia Johanson 2003 (Courtesy of the artist).

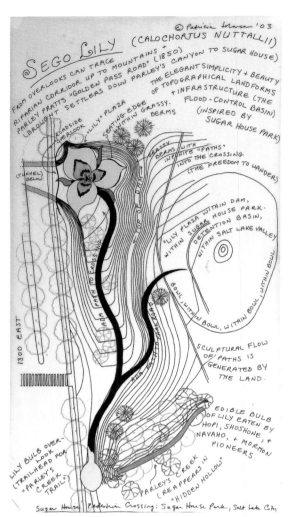

3. Sketch of the sculpture of Sego Lily, by Patricia Johanson 2003 (Courtesy of the artist).

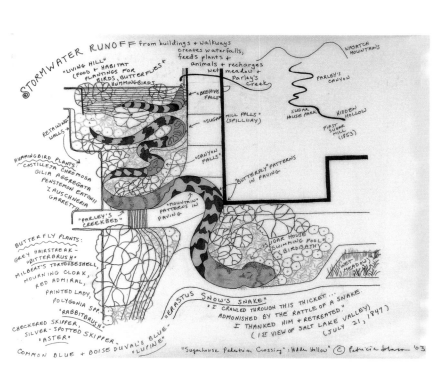

4. Sketch of the sculpture of Rattle Snake, by Patricia Johanson 2003 (Courtesy of the artist).

5. Computer drawing of the master plan of the Draw at Sugar House, by G. Brown Design.

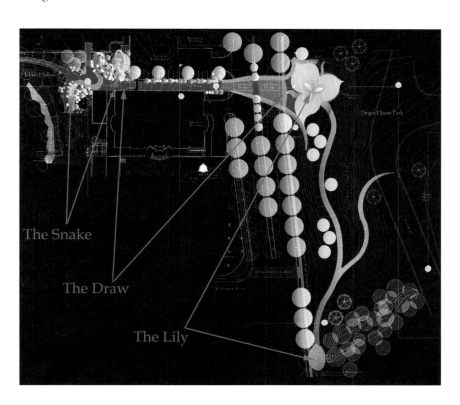

Linear Configuration

This design was the winning scheme of a national competition.[5] Johanson's proposal features two giant sculptures, the "Sego Lily" in the park and the "Rattlesnake" along Hidden Hollow. In a sketch, Parley's Creek appears distinctively on both sides (Fig. 2). The Lily unwinds between the road and an earthen dam. The creek passes beneath its root bulb, like an endless life force nurturing the plant. A leaf branches out and arches toward the mountain. As the Lily grows, its green stem runs through the parkland and flowers at the top (Fig. 3). The Snake looms from the other side of the expressway. Its body, with red and yellow patches, waggles among foliage and crawls into the wilderness of Hidden Hollow. Its triangular head probes vigilantly while it inches its way toward the creek for the life-giving water source (Fig. 4).

The representations of the Lily and the Snake are undoubtedly figurative and colorful, offering striking visual images. Although Johanson's drawings might call to mind the cliché of employing form as sign of meaning, any such comparison would be naïve given the fact that none of the sculptures appear on site. The sculptures are so mammoth that their full figures are invisible to visitors on the ground; in addition, the figures are camouflaged and fragmented through deliberate design (the details will be discussed later). The sculptures can be experienced only piecemeal through bodily engagement with their materiality. In other words, the forms of the sculptures remain a secret existence that is only hinted at by visual cues. Polar apart from formalism, the forms of the Lily and the Snake do not inscribe meaning but signify the possibilities of being meaningful. Furthermore, the forms are not imposed upon but derived from the geomorphological characters of the site—the winding course of Parley's Creek casts the shape of the Snake, while the topography of the valley is projected into the enclosure embracing the Lily. Thus, the scale of the figures is in fact the scale of landscape, and the possible meaningfulness of the figures dwells beyond their forms.

Johanson's aesthetics is a functional one, and her design a fusion of practical and artistic dimensions. Despite the brilliant sculptures, the real intention of the design is to meet the primary challenge of the infrastructural requirements of an accessible pedestrian crossing between two zones of different disposition and topography—Sugar House Park and Hidden Hollow (Fig. 5). To Johanson, the Draw, a sunken pedestrian corridor between the Lily and the Snake, is the core of her design, and both sculptural forms are there to fulfill a safe crossing. Functional, rather than decorative, use of the images of the Snake and the Lily can be further comprehended through comparison with the "Snake and Butterflies" footbridge by Bernard Lassus. Images of snake and butterflies are integrated by Lassus into the railing of a footbridge that is meant as an easy highway crossing and a reminder of the parkland. The fable materials are used here specifically for a partly functional purpose—as a necessity for encouraging children to use the footbridge for the sake of a tongue-in-cheek experience of flight, since "the metallic butterflies fly more easily than the rock" (Fig. 6).[6] Even though Johanson's approach is far less direct than that of Lassus, both designs take functional concerns as the departure points of art creation.

Combining civil engineering with art, the Draw becomes the nucleus of the configuration of a continuous passage. It joins seamlessly the two sculptures—the lily flower bends into the underpath, while the snake body intersects the walkway. Meanwhile, the straight profile of the Draw contrasts with the organic contours of the sculptures, highlighting three distinctive segments. As a whole, the three characteristic segments integrate into an interlocking linear garden, which fulfills in straightforward fashion the need of a passage. Were we more familiar with the artist's career, we would realize that the emphasis on linearity and linkage in the garden is not, however, merely a practical response, but Johanson's signature design strategy evolved over thirty years.

6. "Snake and Butterflies" Footbridge by Bernard Lassus 1981 (Courtesy of the artist).

Artistic Venture of Lines

The Draw at Sugar House can be better understood with reference to the "line garden" concept that Johanson put forth in 1969.[7] Her line gardens are meant to perform minimal intervention by directing human attention and curiosity to specific sites; and the linear paths are not avenues to designed viewpoints but eye-

7. *William Rush*, by Patricia Johanson 1966. Left—the sculpture after its original installation, courtesy of the artist; right—the sculpture in summer 2003, photograph by Xin Wu.

8. An image of Chatsworth with paths colored by Patricia Johanson 1966. (Courtesy of the artist).

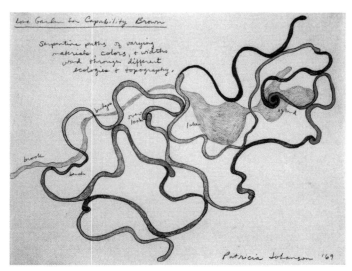

9. *Line Garden for Capability Brown*. Sketch by Patricia Johanson 1969, as one of her drawings for the *House & Garden* commission (Courtesy of the artist).

and foot-catchers pointing to the infinite natural world beyond. Johanson's obsession with lines in garden design bore its seeds from her earlier line paintings and sculptures, and her disappointment with the petty conceit of historic garden styles. She grew interested in color and light as a student at Bennington College, an art school influenced by John Dewey's theory of art and experience.[8] Attention to aesthetic experience beyond the visual was already evidenced in her first notable work, *Color Room,* created in 1960. In the following years, she explored paintings, whose pictorial component was distilled into a single monochrome line or a band of color. Discovering how the visual presence of a colored line alters with the interaction of spectators led her to ever larger canvases. When galleries were not big enough for her paintings, she moved outdoors for more spectacular linear creations. Her first attempt, *William Rush,* a 200-foot-long installation, was built in 1966 (Fig. 7).[9] Ever since then, every visit to this sculpture has amazed the artist, as if a kaleidoscope would open to a myriad of worlds beyond artistic invention. The sculpture captivates the eyes at first glance, attracts the gaze to details that would be ignored otherwise, and then redirects the attention to the surroundings. Moreover, the sculpture becomes habitat for living beings and carrier of inherent site information. In a sense, the work of art spurs discovery of natural lives and forces and at the same time derives a new existence for itself.

Following all these artistic ventures, her 1969 proposals envisioned the line gardens as a new genre that would encourage visitors' engagement with nature beyond the design, as opposed to the "classical perfection" of formal gardens that were meant to serve the monolithic goals of the designer.[10] On a photograph of the Chatsworth estate landscaped by Capability Brown, Johanson colored a number of serpentine paths (Fig. 8). Instead of allowing the paths to mark the ownership of the domain as the source of its manmade unity, her paths endeavor to remind visitors of the diversity of nature, and to lure them to experience the world of nature as a work of art. One of her line garden proposals is dedicated to Capability Brown (Fig. 9). Colorful wavy lines intertwine against a blank background, incorporating paths, bridges, an overlook, a large beach area, and an island in a lake. A sinuous river implies that the site is a delta. The text in the sketch reveals that the gaze of visitors on site is to be turned beyond the serpentine paths to the diverse site ecology and topography. Johanson asserts in a surprising way that "the most important aspects of my landscapes and the key to their success lie in the parts I do *not* design."[11] In other words, the focus in her garden locates in the void of the sketch where a living world unfolds under real site conditions. Experience of the undesigned is the goal of her garden designs, and the content of her garden rests upon the range and extent of visitors' engagement with nature. Every visitor would experience differently, and each would compose in their mind a specific garden of his or her own as a professional would in design. As the famous Capability Brown gained the nickname from his ability to reveal features of a site, Johanson's garden encourages visitors alike to explore their capability of discovering. As the title of the scheme indicates, this sketch proposes a "Line Garden *for* Capability Brown," rather than in the manner *of* Brown.

Design beyond the Visual

Johanson has been rejecting the notion of "art as object" and insisting to "design beyond the visual"—that is, to create conditions for serendipitous experience.[12] Her garden entices visitors to venture into the site for individual exploration. Such a garden calls forth an interaction with the natural world that unfolds in time and space. Our earlier depiction of the Draw at Sugar House, however, accredited only the graphic representation. If we see the garden merely through its artistic forms, we miss its true impact lying in experience beyond visual perception. Examination needs to be carried further to reveal the mechanism through which the design paves the way for particular experiences. Johanson's design has been honored with the Utah Governor's Grand Achievement Award of 2004, but the construction is yet to be completed. That the discussion has to be based on what exists on paper rather than in reality might raise the question whether this kind of approximation of experience is a genuine experience. Nonetheless, Dewey's demarcation of aesthetic experience and experiences in general reminds us that aesthetic experience differs by necessity from "what is experienced."[13] On the other hand, the contemporaneous effect of a work in progress is exciting, as it brings the idea of the "contemporary garden" right up to date and allows a discussion of the artist's attention for future experiences of the place. In that respect the design drawings demonstrate better the intention of artist to propose to different user groups new aesthetic experiences than does an observation of an existing garden where the public would engage in new experiences beyond the vision of designer. Hence I shall not report real life experiences, but the intended agency of the design. I shall first examine how the artwork attracts visitors into a sculptured garden and leads them to immersion in nature, and then analyze what transforms such immersion into *an* experience with aesthetic significance; and finally, what is the aesthetic experience of this garden.

From Experience to Immersion

Johanson claims that "once visitors take their first step into my gardens, there is a physical pause and the dialogue becomes internal."[14] Her description underscores that the interaction between the mind, the artwork, and the site takes place in multilayer. Visitors' attention is first attracted by the design, then lured away from its artistic elements and projected toward the artless site beyond.

The Agency of Artwork
The agency of artwork unveils in three tiers: the visual, the bodily, and the sensual.

    The Visual
Unlike many works of land art, such as Spiral Jetty—comparable in size—in the nearby Great Salt Lake, in Johanson's garden the full figures of the Sego Lily and Rattlesnake evade immediate grasp. The colorfulness of the artwork is arresting upon visitors' arrival, yet the ground is modeled in an undulating fashion so that any overviews of the two sculptural forms are blocked intentionally (Fig. 10). Views of the sculptural forms are maintained on the ground level, and careful designs and planting are carried out to ensure visual obstructions. Although the distinctive sculptures attract

10. Perspective drawing of the garden, by G. Brown Design.

attention, the planting stages obstacles for the visual perception. The garden thus imposes a slow pace of discovery, and a sense of wonder to be superseded while walking through.

The visual obstructions stimulate curiosity while the linear design encourages exploration. Although the artwork cannot be seen in full, visual cues are designed to make its presence conspicuous. Both the Lily and the Snake are made of colorful materials, which catch the sight and impel visitors to pursue the existence of a hidden figure. Yet the design itself does not provide focus points within its spatial confines; any attempt at figuring out the patterns would induce the gaze beyond the paths into the surroundings.

Such visual arrangement fosters tension between the artwork and its site. The figurative sculptures elude direct visual perception, and their forms dissolve into the natural background. The wrestling between the ambiguity of full patterns and the conspicuousness of their fragments makes the artwork a vehicle for discovery. The paths flow smoothly on the surface of the undulating ground, opening infinite possibilities for "the freedom to wander."[15] Visitors are not only invited to look beyond the confines of the sculptures but also compelled to wander to gain a larger view of them. Paradoxically, the linear paths provide invitations for *following up* as well as powerful drives of *walking away* from them.

The Bodily

Whereas the sculptures cannot be seen fully, they are experienced bodily. Johanson's design amalgamates art with function. She ensures that the departure point of perception in her gardens goes beyond merely the visual by making most parts of the artwork utilitarian elements.[16] The lily root forms the trail head and an outlook; the stem and leaf become trails; the flower turns into a plaza; and the snake transforms into retaining walls, waterfalls, paths, and ponds. Instead of seeing the sculptures, visitors engage bodily with their materiality while walking through the garden. Thus the visitors become inside explorers rather than outside observers, and memories of the artwork rest upon discrete bodily engagements rather than homogenous visual appreciation as seen in the presentation drawings.

The agency of the artwork could be direct, even radical. At some points, visitors are driven physically away from the design and left alone to make sense of the environment. Sloping down Hidden Hollow, the snake head becomes a birdbath at the end. The visitors are virtually pushed out of the path, and displaced from the artificial to the wilderness. A similar situation is staged on the lily leaf path. After branching out of the main stem, the path descends smoothly toward the Sugar House Pond. As the leaf reaches its tip, the path narrows and disappears on the driveway. Contrast between the green concrete and the asphalt surface marks unmistakably a visual end of a path that seems to be heading to an interesting point. Visitors are lost all of a sudden. As they resume their views toward the pond, the eyes are compelled to look beyond the park and to discover the distant Wasatch Mountain and Parley's Canyon (Fig. 11). By undergoing such abrupt physical halt, the path confronts visitors directly with the natural world.

The Sensual

Apparently all these visual and bodily experiences on site do not match the visual presentations. Like camouflage in the natural world, presentations of Johanson's gardens in drawings precisely conceal the real intention of her design. Confrontation with the natural world results from the visitors' efforts to make sense of a design that escapes full comprehension. Although the sculptural figures remain invisible and accessible only through imaginary reconstruction, their constitutive elements invite close inspection. In the Draw at Sugar House, the fact that visual appreciation is impeded while bodily engagement is enhanced sets

11. View of the landscape across the Sugar House pond from location of the Lily leaf path. Photograph by Xin WU 2004.

the stage for an experience that is deemed to be sensual. Symbolic, metaphoric, or metonymic details unleash imagination and impel interpretation.

The Snake is charged with symbolic patterns of natural or cultural implications (Fig. 12). Wiggling down the hill toward the remnant valley of Hidden Hollow, the surface of its body changes from rattle rings, to abstract patterns echoing butterflies and insects, to mountainous pavements, to patches of snake skin. Like native artwork, these designed patterns suggest living beings, as well as landscape within the body of the Snake that is itself a symbol of the history of the site. Arrangements of the water features are also symbolic. The three waterfalls, "Canyon Falls," "Sugar Mill Falls," and "Beehive Falls," may bring back memories of the first settlers into Sugar House and their use of Parley's Creek for agricultural and industrial functions; while the two ponds, "Parley's Creek Bed" and "Sugar House Swimming Pool," may recall various transformations that had befallen the watercourse.

The design relates to the site through metaphors that spring from sensation. Visitors descend along the lily stem path to reach the flower plaza enclosed by high dams (Fig. 13). A text on the design drawing refers to this feature as a microcosm echoing the topography of the locale:

> LILY PLAZA WITHIN DAM, WITHIN SUGAR HOUSE PARK-DETENTION BASIN, WITHIN SALT
> LAKE VALLEY/BOWL, WITHIN BOWL, WITHIN BOWL, WITHIN BOWL.

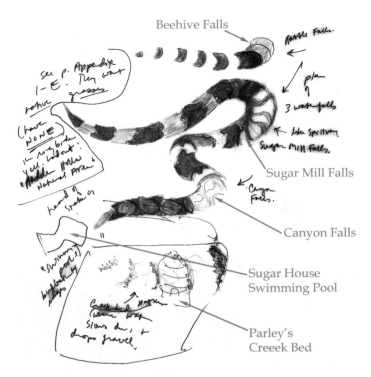

Beehive Falls

Sugar Mill Falls

Canyon Falls

Sugar House
Swimming Pool

Parley's
Creeek Bed

12. Sketch of the Snake, by Patricia Johanson 2003 (Courtesy of the artist).

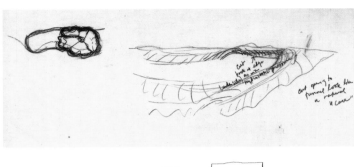

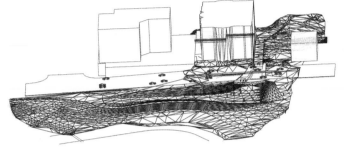

13. Studies for the flood-control dam around the Lily flower plaza. Upper—sketch by Patricia Johanson 2003, courtesy of the artist; lower—computer modeling of the designed topography, by G. Brown Design.

14. View of a natural canyon land in the Wasatch Mountain. Photograph by Xin Wu 2004.

15. Perspective drawing of the sunken walkway, by G. Brown Design.

Inside the underpath, the restricted feeling of a tunnel is replaced by a vivid ambience of a canyon. Natural light and vegetation spill down from the open medians.[17] Exiting from the underpath, the sunken walkway is punctuated by sculptural vertical gardens in the retaining wall. Narrow skyline, diffusing light, seeping water, slant side rocks, strong colors, rich plants, and animal habitats—all these are the exhilarating natural atmosphere that the design endeavors to introduce (Fig. 14). Johanson does not, however, intend to imitate a canyon, but rather to create an abstract artwork that would trigger an experience akin to that of walking through a canyon, an experience that is sensual and evocative. Stratigraphy of coal and fossil formations is included, together with root patterns, to convey the feeling of being underground. These details allude to the geology and history of the valley where the Mormons had a mining industry and sugar beet cultivation (Fig. 15). A walk from the plaza through the underpath to the sunken Draw summons up the dramatic feeling of exiting into a valley from a canyon. Thus the function of the garden as a passage harks back to the historical ravines that once occupied this site and memory of the journey of the Mormons.

Acting like a catalyst, the artwork brings attention to the landscape and presents visitors with fragmented details overlaid with ambiguous meanings. The image of the riparian corridor of Parley's Creek up to Wasatch Mountain surfaces in metonymic manner at several locations: from the lily root overlook, from the roadside overlook, and from the overpath at the west end of the Draw (Fig. 16). Each of these viewpoints frames in a particular way a visitor's retrieval of the links between the artistic form, the natural surrounding, and the cultural memory. Approaching the Snake, visitors can follow its body down to the creek bed, where they would find themselves all at once deeply entranced by and ensconced in the sheltered wilderness of Hidden Hollow. Even though the mountain and the canyon are not visible anymore, the serpentine form of the Snake and the watercourse of Parley's Creek would strike a chord in the mind and recollect the previous images of Parley's Creek streaming down Wasatch Mountain (Fig. 17).

I must stress, however, that none of the fore-mentioned details are displayed in literal manners. The water features, the stratigraphic patterns, the earthen berm and the distant landscape—all these are physical presences of the garden itself. Johanson opposes any graphic or textual signs in her gardens. Her art explores the possibilities of creating multilayered abstraction that would provoke improvisational sensual experiences and initiate unbound play of imagination. Thus, a walk through the garden will as well be a journey occurring within visitors' minds.

The Agency of Natural Life

Besides the agency of artwork, there is the agency of natural life. Sixty-two plant species are proposed to provide food and habitat for small animals.[18] Functional structures, such as retaining walls and the structural support incorporate niches, cubicles, perches, and nesting shelves prepared for wildlife. The vivid atmosphere of a living world takes visitors mentally away from the artwork into intimate observations. Inspired by the myriad of worlds and the ceaseless transformation of human artifacts into natural habitats, Johanson makes fostering plant and animal lives a core of her art (Fig. 18). She believes that attention to the minutiae is the starting point of all sorts of indefinite yet significant experiences. Similarly, Dewey remarked that our experience of any object expands beyond the acknowledgment of its physical boundaries. He illustrates the point by quoting the following verses by Tennyson:

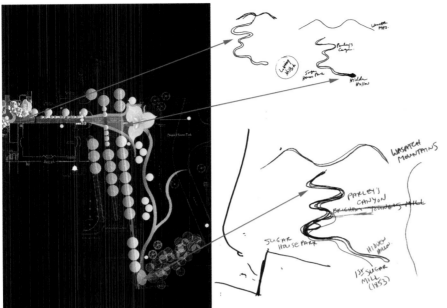

16. Locations in the garden where view of Parley's Creek up to the Wasatch Mountain emerges. Left—plan of the garden; right—sketch of the landscape image by Patricia Johanson 2003, courtesy of the artist.

17. View of Parley's Creek up in the Wasatch Mountain, from the site of the garden. (Photograph by Xin WU 2004).

Experience is an arch wherethro'
Gleams that untravell'd world, whose margin fades
Forever and forever when I move.[19]

Moreover, Dewey's commentary seems to provide an explanation for Johanson's work:

> We are never wholly free from the sense of something that lies beyond. Within the limited world directly seen, there is a tree with a rock at its foot; we fasten our sight upon the rock, and then upon the moss on the rock, perhaps we then take a microscope to view some tiny lichen. But whether the scope of vision be vast or minute, we experience it as a part of a larger whole and inclusive whole, a part that now focuses our experience.[20]

In Johanson's gardens, discovery of the encroachments of natural life upon the artwork, as well as the perceptual echoes between the designed forms and the surroundings, beguiles the visitors to immerse in nature with full power of the imagination.

Meaning Making versus Didacticism

The path splits at the end of the Draw. At this point of the crossing, one can either head to the street back to the city or linger along the Snake into the wilderness of Hidden Hollow. It would not be occasional that pedestrians who pass the Draw for practical reasons abandon themselves to the invitation of the garden, and fall into contemplation. Different reflections of the place might emerge, stressing either cultural memories of the Mormon settlers or the broader horizon of a natural world that preceded the settlement history. Johanson's design strategy should be contrasted with the didactic intent of the celebrated "This Is the Place" Monument, where specific narratives are conveyed by texts and images (Fig. 19).

To the contrary, the Draw at Sugar House triggers flights of imagination beyond the connotation of expressive signs; it discourages ceremonial visits and dismisses any compulsory relationship between the visitors, the artwork, and the site. The meaning of this place is not a content that was inscribed into the landscape fabric—an idea imposed upon its form—but an understanding to be achieved through experiencing the place. All designed details, as well as views of Parley's Creek from Wasatch Mountain, are open to interpretations. This garden is not a didactic memorial, but a place where specific memory of the past is facilitated in its material forms and its links to the surroundings.

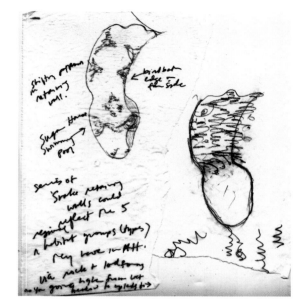

18. Sketch of the Snake head birdbath, by Patricia Johanson 2003 (Courtesy of the artist).

To the visitors, the invisible, yet ever-presenting, existence of the giant sculptures is like the unknown mountains and waters to their ancestors when they migrated. This garden does not commemorate history as fact, but celebrates it as a experience by inviting visitors to encounter the very environment as the Mormons did. A walk through the crossing, retracing the ancestors' footsteps, experiencing the enduring landscape, then attunes the mind of the visitors with the spirit of the settlers. A local historian wrote about the landscape of Parley's Creek Valley:

> Oh, the freeways have made their mark and filled in much of the [valley] hollow, but basically, the [valley] hollow, or this part of it, is still the same land that [the settlers] they followed on their way from the canyon into the city west of here.[21]

Walking and jogging are popular outdoor pastimes in Salt Lake City. To many, the history of the city fuses in the natural world and was embedded in trails and passages throughout the place. Physically walking through the landscape opens the door to both nature and history. A flight of birds, a stretch of stream, or a glance to the majestic peaks will suffice for waking up the memory (Fig. 20).

Both art forms of the Lily and the Snake are evocative. Yet the figures are not only obstructed on site but disintegrate into details that are symbolic signs signifying discrete messages. The details are graphic, but the landscapes they kindle are imaginary. Paradoxically, although the invisible sculpture is figurative, both the visible details within it and the visualized landscape beyond it are nonfigurative and abstract. The details are abstract in terms of their forms; the landscape is abstract in terms of its meaning. Each design feature proceeds from various sources about the site, such as historic records, natural scenery, ecological links, functional concerns, and art creations, so that they each provide an entry point to interpretation. Moreover, the design deliberately switches the attention from one detail to another, so that the sources in each feature become interlaced. The overlaying and enmeshing of different interpretative frameworks make the garden the embodiment of an entangling web of potential meaning rather than a given linear narrative.

The Draw at Sugar House capitalizes aesthetics of fragments and ambiguities. The fragmented details may touch off deep-seated emotions, engage visitors into sensual experiences that trigger flights of imagination associated with individual

19. Upper—view of the "This is the Place" monument; lower—image of the Mormon migration engraved in the monument (Photographs by Xin Wu 2004).

memories, sensitivities, interests, and concerns, and eventually lead visitors into an internal struggle of making sense of their own experiences. Each of these shifts proceeding from a fragment of artwork invites one or several possible frames of interpretation. Thus each moment of experience gives rise to a personal engagement in the objects and events observed in nature and in their understanding. We can say that "the objects and events are as much a part of experience as we are ourselves."[22] The complex design strategy de-centers the attention from the artwork and weaves a multiplicity of relationships through fragmentation. Thus any visitor is entitled to immerse in this garden and to develop individual interpretation of moments of experiences that shuttle between nature and culture.

There is no fixed boundary for this garden; its spatial confine expands into the landscape. The existence of the artwork holds the ever-shifting edge between a wild nature and a designed landscape. Johanson calls her gardens "the garden of art" and believes that humans and the living world are the two *inter*dependent sides of nature. Gardens are extraordinary situations that intensify the encounter of the two sides, and landscape emerges when the person is immersed in nature.[23] Landscape then is neither the intact natural scenery nor the artwork, but the mental construction of a view that visitors achieve through their encounters with the artwork and the natural world. It is intrinsic and depends on the cultural framework adapted for the interpretation. For instance, the snake trail can be read as a historic symbol, a sign of the topography, an art creation, an ecological habitat, or a stormwater runoff; and Wasatch

20. View of the Hidden Hollow, part of the Parley's Creek streambed, where remnants from the early settlements can still be found (Photograph by Xin Wu 2004).

Mountain can be seen as a scenic resort, a monumental landmark, or an unconquerable obstacle. All these comprehensions have truth value. The landscape one would capture through this garden, therefore, is circumstance and individuality related. Such perceptions of landscape bear the mark of fragmentation at the detail level of the design itself.

From Immersion to Closure

Yet immersion in nature and construction of landscape are only a part of the experience; they do not ensure *an* aesthetic experience. *An* experience is not an immediate perception, but a holistic process with a beginning and an end, and a temporality of its own. Such a process bespeaks confrontation and struggle with deeply felt conflicts or tensions.[24] In short, *an* aesthetic experience comes into being as an integrated whole when a closure of the experienced inner tension is obtained through a temporal process. The wholeness of experience implies that, to achieve *an* aesthetic experience, visitors have to not only be the composers of the discrete symbols, but also engage in active meaning making that takes root in the cultural framework from which interpretation derives. The closure of *an* experience depends on how the symbolic fragmentation is perceived and how the fragmented perceptions are integrated.

Johanson takes her own experiences of the landscape as the departure point of design. But differently from Dewey, she does not expect visitors to rediscover her experiences and wishes every visitor to achieve personal experience beyond the design anticipation. Moreover, she endorses that nature is far more complex than any human creation, deserves far more attention and meditation, and is far more powerful in evoking sensual resonance. Her art aims at setting the course of a quest for unlocking a question that is framed by the design yet has to be defined by the visitors. The work of art gives rise to both a sense of curiosity about nature and the belief that such curiosity can be satisfied through experiencing, rather than inducing, the contemplation of a transcendental mystery. This dimension of Johanson's work contrasts significantly with American landscape paintings of the mid-nineteenth century—a form of painting essentially based in New England (as is Johanson herself), and then expanded to cover spectacular sites in the West.

The incalculable possibilities of perception and interpretation created by the design, however, do not suggest that the significance of the artwork dissolves in fragmentation, and that the experience could not achieve its closure. Aesthetic experience is not bound within a definite time frame; it develops through a process of doings and undergoings. This may take place in one or several units, it may result into a purely intimate experience, or it may lead to the construction of a new domain of intersubjectivity. The emphasis placed on fragmented visual perceptions arouses the visitors' curiosity, while discovery of the whole place is triggered by the fragmentary, yet not so exclusive, site presence of the Lily and the Snake, which could be pictured only in the mind through imagination. So any effort at making sense of the whole of the fragmented experiences leads to a shift from spontaneous observation to reconstructive configuration of the two sculptures and of the sunken passage in between. Visitors' understanding of the relationships of all the elements will frame their perception of the garden and the landscape as a whole. This understanding in turn carries deep implications for their experience of the place as a whole.

The juxtaposition of stories of the sego lily and the rattlesnake encapsulates a dilemma in the reliance between human beings and the natural world. From the viewpoint of nature, the sego lily, by providing the edible bulbs, helped the settlers to survive the severity of environment, while the rattlesnake defended wild nature from the interference of humankind. From the viewpoint of culture, the settlers sustained by conquering the environment in the story of sego lily, and by protecting the wildlife in the story of rattlesnake. How should we value the triumphs, as well as the sacrifices? Should humans plunder the resources of the environment to fulfill their needs of progress as implied by the story of the sego lily? Or should humans acknowledge the rights of all natural beings to their own territory and retreat from interference with them as implied by the story of the rattlesnake? Such a cultural dilemma is not only the conflict of consumption versus conservation, but also of nurture versus nature. The Draw at Sugar House, however, does not simply juxtapose the images of sego lily with rattlesnake; it integrates them in a poetic yet functional way. The achievement of civil engineering enables visitors to experience the existence of a linkage between the two sides of a dilemma.[25] As Dewey would agree, this work of art does not state meaning, but expresses it for people who engage actively and share mutual interests.[26]

This dilemma, encapsulated in the stories of sego lily and rattlesnake, frames the experiences of immersion in nature and of landscape appreciation. Visitors will certainly reach multicultural interpretations; however, none will fail to experience the Draw as a passage and the sculptures as allusion of mysterious signs waiting to be decoded. The unsettled meaning of the design then makes it possible to envisage a kind of undifferentiated potentiality for creating meaning, with individual being regarded, not as "the possessor of particular meanings," but as their "fabricator."[27] In this light, the significance of the Draw at Sugar House lays not so much in the visitors' knowledge of the history of the place, but in their sensitivity to experiences of the landscapes and their fabrication of the meaning of such experiences through "continuous and cumulative interaction" with the world, including, of course, the society where they live. *An* experience so fabricated is culturally reflexive and socially communicable; it is both individual and collective.

Such *an* experience is contemporary, since it concerns the conflict of our time. To approach the epiphany of art form and the illumination of landscape in the mind's eye, one needs to reach both outwards to the natural world and inwards to the cultural frames of seeing nature. A walk through the garden therefore becomes both the passage and linkage to a living world and our inner self. It does not bring knowledge of, but rather fosters sensitivity to, the past, the present, and the future. Thus, the functional aesthetics of a pedestrian crossing re-orients historical commemoration of its place.

Conclusion

Building upon the everyday need of a safe crossing, Johanson enmeshes function with art and entices pedestrians into reflection of nature by an aesthetics of fragments and ambiguities that directs them to landscape. The visitors' perspective would be framed, but not constrained, by the dilemma incorporated in the figures of the Sego Lily and the Rattlesnake. Thus their heightened sense of a continuity of self and nature entails the development of an inner sense of the conflict between the welfare of human beings and natural beings. This conflict is not so much registered to the mind for rational examination, as presented to the sense in the place. It calls for an arduous resolution that surpasses individual choice. The garden itself, however, proposes a symbol for a successful quest. The Draw, a functional civil engineering structure with historical allusion to the transformations of the place, connects two sides of the road. It makes the garden both a passage between the Lily and the Snake, a symbol of the possibility of a mutual relationship, and a passage between the park and the city, a symbol of a possibility for a larger dialogue. Far removed from didacticism, this symbol is ambiguous and open to interpretations.

So this garden of art, as well as a work of civil engineering, provides a symbol of the hope that can be placed in mutual definition of a new cultural perspective toward nature. The experience of achieving closure is a very simple idea. The Draw invites its users to come and go as they please between the city and the park, and to develop a new concept of relationships between humans and nature. The design approach produces two striking yet mutually conflicting results: first, the inscription of the design obscures the presence of figurative elements, and leads the visitors from exploration of details to immersion in nature; second, the puzzlement stirred by these incomplete experiences leads to the discovery of the symbolism encapsulated in the figurative design, and opens the way to a collective interpretation of meaning.

This is a prolonged crossing. The lengthening of the journey by this garden of art is a necessity for the transformation from daily routines of road crossing into an aesthetic experience that traverses the natural and human worlds.[28] Walking through the crossing, the art and the experience emerge into one another; they are both the framer of the journey and at the same time framed by it. Visitors are invited to refresh their understanding of a landscape that is alive. The discussion of aesthetic experiences forces the community to reexamine its view of nature. This entails possible reconstructions that would foster a new culture. Thus, aesthetics can not be divorced from ethical pursuit. Although Johanson's landscape approach is educational in this sense, her approach shuns any foregone conclusion. The design does not propose an ideal model of relationship between the human society and the natural world,[29] but reawakens each visitor's attention to conflicting views about them. Johanson's gardens help their visitors to envisage a new mode of their life together as a community within nature. These gardens then provide a fundamental approach to artwork in our heterogeneous society, as the art offers a linkage between individuals, and a passage toward the construction of a new ethic group connected by shared relationships with nature.

To end, let us return to Dewey: "The closure of the experience is both an ending and beginning point. It is a closing together which holds within it the opening of the world."[30] The prolonged crossing at the Draw at Sugar House then corresponds to the painful reconstruction of contemporary culture. It bespeaks the challenge that, to fulfill the linkage and passage, we need first to walk through the crossing. And more so: the garden of art as a path to the renewal of culture.

NOTES

[1] Most visitors to Salt Lake City take it for granted that Emigration Canyon, where the "This Is the Place" monument stands, was the original point of entrance for the Mormons. Patricia Johanson, the designer of the garden that we are going to discuss, however, points out that the location of the monument does not match the fact that the Mormons first entered the valley from Parley's Canyon to the south. As an artist, her sensitivity to history, its truth and representation, leads to an innovative approach in her design of the Draw at Sugar House.

[2] Erastus Snow Journal Excerpts, 21 July 1847. Three days later, on 24 July, Brigham Young made the famous announcement "It is enough, this is the right place, drive on," at a canyon north of the location recorded by Snow. The announcement terminated the Mormon migration west and launched the history of Salt Lake City. To commemorate the arrival of the Mormons, the canyon was named "Emigration Canyon" and "This Is the Place" Monument was established at its exit, to mark the historic moment rather than the historic fact.

[3] The location of our project Parley's Canyon, for example, is the last remaining stream bed in Salt Lake City. A detailed account of the history of this canyon listed the transformation it went through since the arrival of the Mormons in 1846, which includes railroad, mining, damming, highway, etc. A local historian commented, "It will take many years for the healing power of nature to take over the devastation caused by humans, but it can and will happen so that future generations will be able to see the entrance into our lovely valley as the pioneers saw it." See Florence C. Youngberg, *Parley's Hollow: Gateway to the Great Salt Lake Valley* (Salt Lake City: Agreka Books, 1998), 112–15.

[4] The conversation project was initiated and promoted by local groups. It concerns the area in the upper part of the Parley's Hollow just west of the mouth of the canyon. A beautiful natural scene and remnants of the settlers are seen while strolling down the walkways. The whole plan bears an estimated cost of $8 million. For many years, the Canyon Rim Citizens Association has been the main driving force behind the project, in the hope that "more people will become aware of those noble people who struggled so valiantly to come to this beautiful valley and help the dessert 'blossom as a rose.'" Information on the conservation project and the Draw at Sugar House, is available on the homepage of PRATT, a nonprofit organization working to create the Parley's Creek Corridor Trail. See also Florence C. Youngberg, *Parley's Historic Nature Park* (pamphlet published by Talon Printing, undated).

[5] Patricia Johanson teamed up with G. Brown Design to submit the winning proposal for the Draw at Sugar House. Five teams competed. The design competition was sponsored by Salt Lake City and funded through the New Public Works Initiative of the National Endowment for the Arts. The site is in the planned Parley's Historic Nature Park. The program required that the Draw will connect Sugar House Park, Hidden Hollow, and the Sugar House business district, and that it will be an integral part of the Parley's Rails and Trails Coalition's efforts to link the Bonneville Shoreline Trail on the east with the Jordan River Parkway Trail eight miles to the west.

[6] Refer to text and drawings about the design in Bernard Lassus, *The Landscape Approach* (Philadelphia: University of Pennsylvania Press, 1998), 119–20.

[7] The marriage of Johanson's art with garden initiated from the *House & Garden* Commission in 1969, when she produced 150 proposals of imaginary gardens. Many of her later projects were refinements and adoptions of those ideas in real-site conditions. She proposed seven new garden genres through these drawings. "Gardens by the mile … the line garden" is the first of these seven genres.

[8] Bennington College was established in 1932 as a women's college. In an interview the president stated: "Bennington is a progressive college. It follows the educational philosophy of John Dewey and William James. The college's experience seems to us to demonstrate the validity of this philosophy. This means, then, that our method differs from that of most colleges." From "Bennington President Edward Fels Airs Views on Task of Education," *The Williams Record,* 30 September 1959. By the time Patricia Johanson attended the college in 1958–62, Bennington was a hotbed for American modern art of the 1950s and 1960s. Many American contemporary artists and sculptors, including Jackson Pollack, David Smith, Kenneth Norland, and Barnett Newman, were given Bennington's support and recognition during early or crucial periods in their development, well in advance of their public acceptance.

[9] In a recent interview (January 2005) Johanson recalled: "I moved outdoors because my paintings were becoming too large for presentation in any gallery. I thought *William Rush* would just be a larger painting, but then I was really surprised. Here is the world, the pine trees, life interacting with a work of art. It was an amazing thing to me. Then I became engaged in a dialogue [between art and nature]."

[10] Johanson concluded in her companying essay for the line garden: "By immersing the person in the real world and by developing an interwoven art of multiple concerns, rather than the monolithic goals of a single designer, the ideal of 'classical perfection' is replaced by the ideal of cooperation and flux." "GARDENS BY THE MILE ... THE LINE GARDEN," *House & Garden Commission,* 1969, unpublished manuscript.

[11] Patricia Johanson, "Beyond Choreography: Shifting Experiences in Uncivilized Gardens," in *Landscape Design and the Experience of Motion,* ed. Michel Conan (Washington, DC: Dumbarton Oaks Research Library and Collection, 2003), 75–102.

[12] The idea of "design beyond visual" was mentioned in various papers by Johanson, for example, in a speech, "Designing beyond the Visual: Life, Death, and Trade-offs in the Garden of Art" (College Art Association, New York City, 24 February 2000), unpublished manuscript.

[13] The term of "experience" is used here in light of Dewey's theory in *Art as Experience.* For Dewey, *an* experience of aesthetic significance is demarcated in the general stream of experience of other experiences. "Such an experience is a whole and carries with it its own individualizing quality and self-sufficiency." See John Dewey, chapter 3, "Having an Experience," in *Art as Experience* (New York: Perigee Books, 1980), 35–58.

[14] Johanson, "Beyond Choreography," in *Landscape Design and the Experience of Motion,* 75.

[15] A note on the design drawing by Johanson reads: "GRASSY BERMS WITH INFINITE 'PATHS' INTO THE CROSSING (THE FREEDOM TO WANDER)."

[16] Civil engineering and infrastructural need are the major concern in many of the artist's designs. Johanson was born to an engineer father, and she admired very much engineers who create "meaningful forms" (interview with the artist).

[17] Since the very beginning, the interior of the Draw has been the primary concern of the design. Johanson's notebook for this project begins with these words: "Design (1) Interior of Tunnel—give them the canyon colors + forms of the red—yellow—purple rock. Desert wash—varying the color." She also

noted the "Spring line" in canyons at Zion Park, registering the different plants such as the columbine, the shooting star, and the monkey-flower for which this park is famous.

[18] Parley's Creek Valley is frequented by birds and other species. More than 110 varieties of birds and some 81 species of plants have been observed.

[19] Dewey, *Art as Experience,* 193.

[20] Ibid., 193–94.

[21] Youngberg, *Parley's Historic Nature Park,* unpaginated.

[22] Experience is the fusion of the subject and the object. "When we are fully immersed in experience, its components so interpenetrate one another that we lose all sense of separation between self, object, and event." See Philip Jackson, *John Dewey and the Lessons of Art* (New Haven, CT: Yale University Press, 1998), 3.

[23] Johanson wrote, for example, in her essay "GARDENS BY THE MILE ... THE LINE GARDEN": "Line Gardens aim at creating a dialogue between man and nature, by providing an orientation to the world, while preserving it intact. Art and landscape become interwoven structures that give the world form and shape and focus—making the whole world available to the person, without disturbing anything that is already there." From *House & Garden Essays,* 1969, unpublished manuscript.

[24] *An* experience is achieved when the experiencing process runs its course to fulfillment. "Then and then only is it integrated within and demarcated in the general stream of experience from other experiences." Such *an* experience "is so rounded out that its close is a consummation and not a cessation" (Dewey, *Art as Experience,* 35).

[25] The idea of an integrated whole is central to this design. From the very beginning, the concept of an integrated passage transversing the two terrains was the central concern of the design. A line in the designer's notebook reads: "(4) Need 1 large form (overall) so the whole (sculpture) encompasses the dam, crossings, tunnel, etc—then the 'journey' occurs within."

[26] Dewey, *Art as Experience,* 85.

[27] Stephen Bann's comments on Roland Barthes's words on the rise of structuralism, in *The True Vine: On Visual Representation and the Western Tradition* (Cambridge: Cambridge University Press, 1989), 2.

[28] Dewey writes that "culture is the product not of men put forth in a void or just upon themselves, but of prolonged and cumulative interaction with environment" (*Art as Experience,* 28). Similarly, Johanson's comments on the "prolonged crossing": "For anything powerful enough to remain in the memory the dialogue will continue in transformations and permutations" (e-mail to author after reading this paper, 6 March 2005).

[29] For example, ecological relations that should be evaluated everywhere as Ian McHarg demanded of landscape architecture.

[30] Dewey, *Art as Experience,* 41.

Contemporary Garden Aesthetics, Creations and Interpretations

Contemporary Garden Aesthetics, Creations and Interpretations

Contemporary Garden Aesthetics, Creations and Interpretations

Contemporary Garden Aesthetics, Creations and Interpretations

The Garden at Portrack Designed and Created by Charles Jencks (1986–2004): Entrapment and Release

Michael Spens

This paper investigates the extent to which a major contemporary garden, that at Portrack in south western Scotland, created by the designer and architectural historian and critic Charles Jencks has been able to extend the realm of experience in landscape and garden art by developing a range of new definitions and responses to contemporary existential issues, as bearing upon new cultural and social preoccupations within society. The possibility of exploring this garden within its own temporality has to acknowledge that a garden as such, like a work of art, does possess its own temporality and, indeed, as the philosopher John Dewey would claim, can offer a sequential process, having a beginning and an end. The extent to which Portrack, for instance, participates in a shared language of gardens and indeed of nature itself, is clearly important to identify. To what extent, in this process, does Jencks develop new cultural forms of expression within the field, allowing for the interaction and transfer of these ideas with and to others, so fostering new cultural forms in the twenty-first century?

It has been fortuitous that Portrack lies so close to Ian Hamilton Finlay's superb garden at Little Sparta, formidably created by its mentor for over forty years. It provides a useful counterfoil to Portrack, since at a human and perceptual level Finlay has focused on many of the issues with which Jencks has inevitably become engaged at Portrack, but the two gardens and their creators have little in common in their approach to certain fundamental issues concerning nature and its ramifications today that preoccupy humanity universally. But there is, notwithstanding this, considerable value in addressing the comparison of the two, although Little Sparta will not be subject here to the same degree of analysis as Portrack.

At Portrack (Fig. 1) Charles Jencks has used the more rapid implementation of his garden to offer a fresh interpretation of humanity's place in nature, and more so, in the cosmos, as we now know it. One can divide nature, as John Dixon Hunt recently reminded us, into three parts.[1] Jencks is not the first astute observer to recognize that thereby lies the possibility of entrapment, for garden designers possessing the best of intentions for the creation of a better world can fail to break out. If one can, as is suggested, divide nature into three, the first part has to be "wilderness," the "wild," as "uncivilized" in any form from the period of Neolithic hunter-gatherers onwards. The second part is, of course, the productive landscape as exploited by man over at least a millennium. In the third part can be found the "sanctuary" gardens, increasingly of need to humanity today, yet having antecedents that run back at least to the Middle Ages. Here, even in the post-Darwinian epoch today, human enquiry about the nature of the universe itself mingles uncertainly with humanity's love of nature in the abstract. Never has conservationism been so strong as today. However, it was only with the development, over a relatively short space of time, of the Italian Renaissance garden that the perfect model for the three natures became explicit:[2] this can be best experienced at the Villa Lante, Bagnaia, near Viterbo (Vignola, c. 1564).(Fig. 2) Here the gradual gradient, emphasized by the flow of water cascading down a rill, marks the gradual transition from the first state, the wild, to the elegance of the formal, Baroque garden that forms a serenely omnipotent climax.

To preempt entrapment at Portrack, Jencks relies on a process of reaching for what he refers to as "Zero Nature," via an inversion of the order in which these three natures might be expected to be presented by the garden designer, and in this way he arguably skillfully sidesteps precedent. Jencks presents a new iconography (Fig. 3, Fig. 4, Fig. 5) constructed on the ground with a combination of inert matter and sculpture. At another level, this discourse is presented by means of a selection of letters, phrases, a rebus, and unfolding DNA

1. Portrack: Clare's Gate, Entrance to DNA Garden.

codes. Where the garden here seems at its most successful is in the major, sculptural landforms that Charles Jencks and his late wife, Maggie (formerly Keswick) had constructed, from sand, gravel, topsoil, and turf, resulting in sharply edged curves, and free for the most part of any planting other than carefully maintained grass lawn "cladding." These landforms do seem to provide the template governing much of the perceivable profile of the garden. Certainly these are not "wild" features. They are cosmological, but also cosmetic, both in design and in presentation.

To quote Jencks, "the Garden of Cosmic Speculation" (See Fig. 5) and (Fig. 6), as it is aptly named, "is a landscape of waves, twists and folds, a landscape pattern designed to relate us to nature through new metaphors presented to the senses. It is

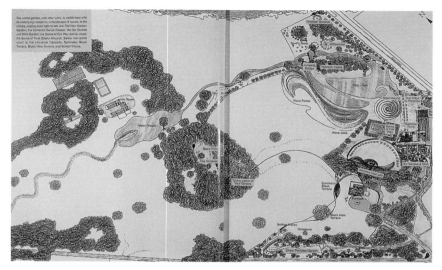

2. Villa Lante, Bagnaia, Italy (Vignola 1566)

3. Portrack: the Ground Layout. The house is on the bottom right, the "jumping bridge at top right; the universe cascade is (east) above the house on the plan.

4. Portrack: in the hill sequence, the view is to the mound over water features.

5. Portrack: an early sketch of the Garden's main axis and ensuing viewpoints.

6. Portrack: the view across water from the Snake Mound.
7. Portrack: the Symmetry Break terrace with view to distant landscape panorama.

partly based on the new sciences of complexity developed with the aid of the computer over the last twenty years—strange attractors that organize such things as the flow of water, the movement of soil, and the patterns of weather. DNA underlies all life and comes in several states, supercoiled or congested and unfolded beautifully in the double helix."[3]

Jencks points out the ways in which, in his experience, the study of nature was shifting. Such sciences as cosmology saw a dialogue opening up. Scientists meditating on nature found significant advances in thinking about the universe, which had become what he describes as a multiverse with a thirteen billion–year history. Accordingly, the Garden of Cosmic Speculation provides three partial hints of truth, as well as other pleasures. Jencks introduces certain key scientific elements into the garden. The first is the omnivalent spiral, as seen to be found in minute DNA molecules that form the basis of everything. The sciences of complexity are symbolized by the introduction of visible spirals into the garden. The underlying metaphorical foundation of the garden is literally a landscape of waves. There are some ten key zones or elements perceptibly at play throughout the garden, as shown in the plan: (Fig. 6) and (Fig. 7, Fig. 8):

The New Kitchen Garden, The Common Sense Garden, The Sixth Sense and DNA Garden; The Sense of Fair Play (tennis court): The Sense of Twist (Snake Mound). Below the tennis court is The Universe Cascade, Symmetry Break Terrace, Black Hole Terrace, and Soliton Waves. (Fig. 9)

The Common Sense Garden is replete with what Jencks entitles "The Ambiguous Words of Nature." Here Jencks resorts to contrasting a planned form of disorientation, in the Nonsense Garden, deploying a series of verbal parodies of Scottish philosophy of the time of the Enlightenment.

The garden is best first approached through the enclosed space that itself is entitled the Garden of the Sixth Sense. This appears as a conventional garden at first, but the visitor soon realizes that there are a number of word riddles, which form the basis for a new garden game that exhibits a set of word plays, known as "ambigrammi." These words are so designed that they can be read in two ways, right side upwards and facing downwards, and carved on walls or pavings. This is an intellectual play on the concept of symmetry and, in fact, becomes an introduction to word play operating to a greater or lesser degree throughout the complex of Portrack as a whole. The visitor with experience of gardens will be impressed by the high degree of planting and craftsmanship deployed throughout this enclosure. The significance of the long undulating wall here can be read experientially on two levels, that of the aesthetic quality, and that of the meaning within the cosmological search for reality which Portrack pursues. (Figs. 10, 11).

Moving from this formal enclosure, one reaches the Snail Mound, with the Snake Mound to its west. The mounds provide a dramatic and contrasting experience, which is amplified by each one's proximity to the water features. The experience for the visitor here is one of some release and wonderment, after the sense of entrapment of the Garden of the Sixth Sense. These are appropriately also tangible in that the visitor can, and is encouraged to, walk up and over and around these curving grass terraces. The Snail Mound is circular. From its upper levels one is also aware of the secondary garden features to the east, such as the Fractal Terrace, the Gaia Atom sculptures, the

8. Portrack: the Black Hole Terrace, radiating black cuts through the landscape.
9. Portrack: the DNA Structure as modeled in the DNA Garden.

10. Portrack: the Fractal Terrace.
11. Portrack: "Ultimate Particles (red) as grouped in 'families.'"

simulation of "Hell," and close by the formulation of "Two Ways to Paradise." Moving northward, one reaches the Willow Twist and the Devil's Teeth to return via the Jumping Bridge (Fig. 12)past the Snake Mound, to suddenly reach by surprise encounter, in its semicircular space, the dramatic elevation of the Universe Cascade, something of a tour de force, placed to take advantage of a steep and forbidding gradient (Figs.13, 14). Other elements of this landscape of waves, moving westward, via the Quark Walk reveal what is virtually a small "lochan," called the Water Dragon, from which one can traverse southward toward the House of Portrack itself (Fig. 4), via a number of diverse features again, such as The Black Pond, The Nonsense, and a timely enough transition named Taking Leave of Your Senses. One then reaches the Symmetry Break Terrace (See Fig. 7), the Black Hole Terrace, and rising up a steep lawn, the preserved octagon building, close to which is the Linear Paradise Garden (See Fig. 3).

As Jencks clearly states in consideration of the state of mind of the visitor, "It seems better in the first instance if [visitors] come on these installations in the right frame of mind, interpreting and feeling the garden according to their mood, and the few clues provided, not as if they had to pass an exam in astro-physics. Since in garden art, as others, there is always more active significance than intended, and since perception is best as an active, projective affair, the intended meanings can be secondary or left to be uncovered later."[4]

Portrack undoubtedly lends itself, as a whole, to offering the visitor a series of experiences that are cumulative in terms of perception, acting on a single level of purely aesthetic awareness, and depending upon the proactive nature of the visitor. Behind these spectacular and often inspiring "events" the visitor subsequently can develop a curiosity about the very same realities of the universe that have persisted to preoccupy humanity for centuries, and find their expression in garden terms.

12. Portrack: the "Jumping Bridge." The bridge jumps over two streams and dives into the ground, made from "fractals that tilt into each other."
13. Portrack: the "Universe Cascade."
14. Portrack: base of the "Universe Cascade."

Landscape historians, of course, will find that certain key parameters that purport here to form acceptable precedent for Portrack in landscape and garden history may, in fact, be in breach of longstanding codes and conventions. We might wonder at the disposal of parallax to the bin, ever since the Renaissance considered it to be a workable and readily comprehensible convention of scale. Then there is the wholesale abandonment of the tradition of "picturesque" composition in such a way. At Portrack, there is offered the development of an aesthetic critique of landscape that combines a linear experience having a beginning and ending but reacts experientially to a found, newly formulated text comprising the "existential issues of the contemporary art world."[5]

It is useful here to remind ourselves of the degree to which prominent artists of the late 1970s, in particular Richard Serra and Robert Smithson,[6] sought to disassociate their works from categorization by earlier precedent as "picturesque," seeking to remain outside. Richard Serra claimed emphatically that his sculpture *Clara-Clara* was concerned with the effect of parallax, the progress around the work of the spectator, and of formal disjunction. Robert Smithson came to abhor the picturesque depiction of Spiral Jetty, usually presented by aerial photography, as a clear distortion of a fundamentally

15. Portrack: Shute, Wiltshire, England. Geoffrey Jellicoe's cascade that forms the center piece of the garden

"grounded" experience. Smithson indeed had a clearly "sustainable" prescription.[7] It was also a challenge "to the prevailing high-modernist aesthetic" then dominant. There is some affinity between Portrack's "mounds" and Smithson's subsequent Broken Circle/Spiral Hill constructed for Sonsbeck 1971 in Holland. The Portrack "mounds" and landforms have subsequently themselves generated a series of commissions in their own right. But Smithson in his time had already embarked upon an exploration of the alignment of the earth's movement in the solar system, a more "grounded" investigation than the myriad of Jencksian speculation on the entire cosmos.

One might also revisit here, in the context of cosmic exploration within the context of the garden or landscape, the unbuilt proposals of Geoffrey Jellicoe (1967) for the Medieval monastery, subsequently cathedral town, of Armagh in Northern Ireland (Fig. 15). This location was, for 700 years, the center of a Christian-Celtic civilization that, for a time, seriously rivalled Rome. Jellicoe proposed here "gardens of cosmic contemplation." In the late eighteenth century an archbishop had provided a precedent there in establishing an observatory, following the rotation of the planets. Jellicoe's scheme provided five compartmentalized

gardens of contemplation, south-facing, and each having sheltering walls. The curvature of the cathedral hill allowed a slight variation in the orientation of each compartment. The intention was to express in the context of a garden the actual movement of the planets: the first enclosure (at top) is called "morning," the third "noon," and the fifth "evening" (at bottom). The times relate to the early Christian canonical hours of "sext" (9 A.M.) "terce" (noon), and "nones" (3 P.M.), which Jellicoe had found actually incised on stone, in a manner Ian Hamilton Finlay would have appreciated, on a slab in neighboring Louth. The five gardens seem to change in nature as the sun moves around planet earth. Jellicoe made the point, of course, that it is man who is actually in rotation.

The garden at Ian Hamilton Finlay's Little Sparta is discussed briefly below, but it is relevant at this juncture to consider this artist's own insertion of the sundial in varying forms there, so as he sees it conjoining poetry and philosophy. Some five widely differing sundials carry text of poignant or searing timelessness in its meaning. But they also serve to remind the visitor of humanity's vulnerability, and not only to planetary or climatic intervention. Indeed, one might say that the recent and dramatic effect of hurricane disasters serves notice that it is the manifestations of climatic change, as quoted rightly by Charles Jencks from James

16. Ian Hamilton Finlay, Little Sparta, Scotland (from 1966–2006.) Stones with "Ripple" legend from dictionary, carved (Acknowledgement to Udo Weilacher).

Lovelock, and recent thinking on Gaia[8] that must concern designers of landscape and gardens in this century at least as much, if not more so, than any cosmic speculation in the wider field. Cosmic enquiry has, however, a long engagement with garden design. Three models stand significantly like beacons in the garden here: the first is of the universe, the second of Gaia, and the third of the atom. Jencks is at pains to describe the universe as a symphony, its laws as harmonies. One example in the garden is the point where a reflected sculpted element in water "mirrors" according to Jencks available photographs of subatomic explosions in an accelerator. What is more essential here, seen from such margins, is the major work constructed as a centerpiece. This is the Universe Cascade. At the level of pure aesthetics, the visitor can only find this structure both pleasing and stimulating to the mind.

Using the precedent of Vignola's cascade at the Villa Lante, Jencks proceeds with considerable ingenuity to create a zigzagging, but nonetheless symmetrical, cascade as a formal centrepiece to the entire *mise-en-scene*.

Jencks has made, over a protracted period, a long study of the advance of science, new knowledge of the composition of matter, structural analysis of natural form and process, to the point at which a number of issues have demanded clarification. In terms of garden design, it is the application of text, together with "model" sculptures, that reveals its author's ambitions, namely to show the essence of the universe in microcosm. The Universe Cascade seems to offer a probity that enlarges the inherent narrative potential of much of the remainder of the Portrack complex.

Fundamental questions here consider the perceived success, or not, of the Portrack garden. Is it only a reinvention of landscape art and tradition, rather than a break with it? There are traditional spaces. Yet this garden occurs during a period of rapid change in society, science, and technology. Do the labyrinthine fractal, surprising, and ultimately questioning forms and their sculptures as positioned really actually relate to the surrounding hills and also simultaneously to recent discoveries in cosmology as Jencks claims? This aspect seems unproven, in comparison with the same landscape interaction with the wilder surroundings experienced, for instance, at Finlay's Little Sparta. Such issues need to be clarified in terms of the relationship between the forms of the artworks incorporated and crucially the information and experience thus communicated to the visitor. (Fig.16)

17. Frontispiece to a 1722 Bible (Edinburgh). Landscape of the Enlightenment.

Definitions are critical in any theoretical study as a basis for the advancement of theory. Does a sense of nature really exist, in contemporary terms or in its traditional meaning at Portrack? For every designer there is a perceptible sense of nature, of what it entails. For example, Geoffrey Jellicoe was acutely aware of "sense of nature," and this was more often than not, it must be said, an intuitive process, guided by a sense of classical mythology. So in his later projects he turned to allegory. He did not attempt, in his generation, to grasp the secrets of the cosmos, but used allegorical sequences to give a wider meaning. In the Kennedy Memorial at Runnymede, England, he laid all the emphasis on the route through nature through a wicker gate, through a darkening wood, twisting and turning up a winding path to the memorial stone itself, more a construct of the sublime than of the picturesque, appropriately to the subject of a presidential assassination. At Portrack, Jencks draws upon a sense of nature through allegory in a different way. But the visitor has to draw this out, among the clues and riddles provided.

Concepts of the sublime, as the eighteenth-century Anglo-Irish thinker Edmund Burke recognized, serve to correlate beauty with a sense of foreboding (Fig. 17, Fig. 18) and may usefully involve, as normative, the background field for disaster and catastrophe, or at least provide its foreboding. In the twenty-first century we find that the "sublime" is a continuing visual and literary device in spatial and filmic composition (as with Bernard Lassus's Crazannes quarries). In the twentieth century there came a greater awareness of the extent to which concepts of the sublime, the picturesque, and especially the evocation of beauty could be brought to bear upon manifestations of garden art. The sublime and the picturesque may not have been welcome ingredients at Portrack, but nonetheless they can be said to be identifiable, however subconsciously in the ultimate field of view. They occur incidentally, but the visitor will find the presence of both concepts, together with, given the tragic background of family mortality, a profound sense of foreboding, a sense of nature that seems implicit and not fully dispensed with by means of the sense of wonderment that the presentation of a cosmic speculation represents.

Representations

The garden at Portrack, created by Charles and Maggie Jencks, is in reality about nothing if it is not about the representation of scientific and cosmological advances and the extent to which they have altered our universe-view of the cosmos. Therefore there is in the narrative sense a clear subtext of intellectual verification and so hence an urgent quest for probity that lies under the proliferation of apparently discordant features. Nature's "secrets" are indeed drawn out. It is necessary to consider what new aesthetic experiences this garden provides as viewed against the continuum of garden history. Primarily, we must look to the extent to which the thematic exploration of the scientific basis of the cosmos can provide new meaning, in experiential terms to the expanding field of garden design. It is necessary to review the episodic expression here of these phenomena in material terms, as perceived in an aesthetic dimension. The various constructed elements and landforms dispersed around Portrack form a sequential temporality, however episodic they may appear. How meaningful then is the experience as it confronts the visitor?

Here, looking at the episodic trail that is offered, there is a deliberate codification through the use of metaphor. Jencks laid claim to create a new form of landscape design, one based essentially on the wave forms uniting the atom to the galaxy. The impediment to this episodic voyage of discovery is that increasingly, as Jencks has admitted such are not "inherently natural forms." And this is immediately apparent to the questing visitor.

Here at Portrack we find that Jencks is in determined pursuit of this new codification with a comprehensive reiteration of precisely those astrologies of the late twentieth century that continue now to drive contemporary philosophy across ever newer boundaries. These new preoccupations seek, as we have seen, to correlate advances in the science

18. 1722 Bible: 'The Creation of the Sun, Moon and Stars on the First Day.'

of biology, such as the role of DNA and indeed beyond that of cosmology, seeking to resolve the persistent questions governing the birth of the universe. It can be seen that a fundamental definition arose about whether garden design as a process had really progressed at Portrack, or whether there was no actual sequence, but instead a series of unrelated, episodic events experienced or indeed contrived by Jencks, and upon which he focuses. The elements and formulations created at Portrack have collectively exhibited an authenticity through this episodic sequence, which defines the whole temporality of the work.

Sourcing Portrack

Jencks has explored the standard model of quantum physics, and in the garden there are symbolic models of various forms of atoms, for example, the deuterium atom, related to a model of Gaia. This model reveals the essential neutron, the proton, and various quarks. Jencks had studied the fractal theory of the mathematician Benoit Mandelbrot.[9] This fractal theory became, for Jencks, instrumental in garden design. So he now moved forward from a quest purely to find metaphors in terms of a landscape field of waves. A superb undulating wall was created through the merging of several wave forms. A further study led to the realization in landscape form of a self-denying form of symmetry, named by Jencks the Symmetry Break Terrace, (See Fig. 7) representing the history of the universe as four breaks in symmetry. Jencks then became engaged as has been mentioned above, in his own definitive project related to the universe, which has become the central built element of the garden at Portrack. As we have seen, in sequence the Universe Cascade followed on naturally from the work on the Symmetry Break Terrace. Although on the one hand it was grounded in quantum theory, on the other it skillfully draws upon historical precedent for the idea of the cascade in garden design. This was a composition of concrete steps, plus massive rocks forklifted into place. By any standards, the Universe Cascade is a dramatic garden structure. The scientific basis for the design seems to lend consistency and credibility to the project. Also, unlike other more speculative configurations at Portrack, the Universe Cascade offers probity. It is too easy to see the various other schemes within the gardens as mere illustrations of ideas, or speculative games, without this tour de force.(Fig. 14).

Yet the knowledge base for Portrack has been assiduously researched and compiled by Jencks since 1990. He has placed a much greater reliance than anyone before, in garden design, upon the rapidly evolving corpus of scientific research into matter, and so has significantly extended the scope for representation in future garden design. He claims, with telling foresight, that "living nature, and inanimate matter both evolve through shifts, phase changes, and catastrophes as well as continuous variation."

Discriminations

One can say that the twentieth-century work of Geoffrey Jellicoe always sought and found a fundamental definition about whether a garden was really progressive in sequence rather than (as we find now at Portrack) a whole series of unrelated, episodic "events." In such a way, for Jellicoe, a reliable teleology emerged. But at Portrack, for example, a significant set of garden events is achieved with great craftsmanship and proficiency but also a garden apart: the Garden of Sixth Sense and the DNA Garden are closely aligned on low ground to the northeast of the complex, almost in the shadow of the Snake Mound and, in the evening, of the mysterious Snail Mound. Ambiguous Words of Nature are inserted here and evidently a series of riddles concerning "symmetry," played out by the visual rotation of such letters to mirror "the symmetries in the universe." The adjacent Snake Wall itself contains inscribed walls and doors. Within the Garden of the Sixth Sense, an elaborate game is available to be played out, a kind of party game, sequential in words from the Renaissance toward the future itself. This garden, and its game, seem to exist within the long perspective of games and puzzles long been part of the repertoire of the garden designer, since before the Renaissance. A series of finely crafted metal gates represent waves of energy in their design, but in practical terms fend off the continually invasive rabbit population.

Little Sparta

We now briefly draw comparison of Portrack with its famous neighboring garden, Little Sparta by Ian Hamilton Finlay. A remarkable set of circumstances, entirely fortuitous, bring two such major gardens of the later twentieth century into realization in such proximity. Little Sparta (Fig. 16) has been the culmination of almost forty years of deeply researched contemplation and continuous activity by Finlay, frequently with his own bare hands. The garden now occupies a similar extent of ground to Portrack, but here mostly won from bare moorland; it lay treeless at the start for the most part, in distinct contrast to Portrack, and open to the searing prevailing winds from the Atlantic on the southwest. Ponds and a small lochan were dug out and in due course provided a focus for Finlay's wizardry. One farm building was converted into a temple dedicated to Apollo. As Finlay grew in confidence, and became aware of his skill with plants, his resort to his own interpretation of society through the images and language of classicism developed. Fundamentally, Finlay has always sought to provide at Little Sparta (Stoneypath as originally known) a sense of sanctuary, and indeed the most common reaction from visitors is that it is a small "paradise." What is critical about Little Sparta too is that like paradise it has grown through adversity in terms of circumstances created externally to hinder, even to close down Finlay's venture. But his poetic approach to developing the whole garden overcame all adversity. There is a superficial similarity between Little Sparta and Portrack in one area, namely, the reliance upon textual messages or words to convey ideas, at least in Portrack's Garden of the Sixth Sense. But the true meaning of the words and phrases inserted all over Little Sparta is both philosophical and poetic, rather than that of a riddle or intellectual game, as at Portrack. One must add that both are entirely legitimate in garden art: but at Little Sparta the device is central, whereas at Portrack it is peripheral to the meaning and experience of the gardens as a whole, offering clues rather than answers.

At Little Sparta we are brought into a deep meditation, using the juxtaposition of word, text, and object. So we must view Finlay's Little Sparta as indeed a deliberate creation of "paradise." Unlike Portrack, tragedy is not that of a few individuals, but, for Ian Hamilton Finlay, the plight of humanity itself. In the forty years since 1966, Finlay has come to create a superb paradise. By slow and gradual development, a fulfilment has been reached. Little Sparta, of course, located so close by makes a powerful contrast to Portrack. Jencks has imputed a much greater reliance here upon the knowledge base of science. Jencks firmly claims that living nature and inanimate matter are both seen to evolve through shifts, phase changes, and catastrophes combined with a continuous variation. He would say that "particles have indeed been the primary reality." The cosmic discoveries made by Newton in the eighteenth century took general understanding well beyond previously established norms (Fig. 18). More importantly for our current examination, these qualified and gave meaning to examples of the sublime, as perpetrated by Edmund Burke. As the theorist Andrew Wilton recently claimed, "Science itself had an aesthetic dimension, and aesthetics might legitimately be put to the service of scientific enquiry"[10] (Fig. 17). Indeed, we are drawn back inexorably to a reappraisal of the sublime, at Portrack, in the Symmetry Break Terrace and the Universe Cascade. As Kant would say, the findings have to rely upon the reactions of individuals, requiring a transcendental scale for reference: at Portrack, then, we are not looking for the sublime other than via our own intellectual analysis of what, incidentally, we find there, any more than was its creator, Charles Jencks.

One could postulate that the garden at Portrack reflects perhaps more than anything an escape from aesthetics and philosophy into pure science, which is seen to provide therefore the theoretical basis for its evolution. Given the background of tragic bereavement that underlay much of the thinking, it must be recognized that, whatever the stated intentions, Maggie Jencks' remarkable personality has loomed over all that has transpired since her death from courageously battled cancer in 1996. Therefore the garden at Portrack, which also includes so much of her own thinking, represents a celebration of her life through nature itself. However, the ensuing embrace of science at Portrack perhaps might be recognized as quite separately deriving from a defensive representation of the human subconscious, embellished in reality perhaps by a fleeting return of the repressed, even depressed, state of mind of its creator. If there is to be a reconciliation as such, between stated intentions and feelings, it might only be achieved here in just this experiential context of a garden, allowing for its temporality, and a clear sequence of

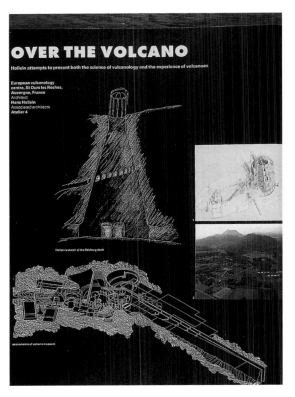

19. Igualada Cemetery, Catalonia, Spain (1991) by Enric Miralles & Carmen Pinos; view down the recessed tomb court.
20. Vulcanology Museum, Clermont-Ferrand, France (2002) by Hans Hollein. The Entry into "the bowels of the earth."

events as portrayed. There can be seen here available for the taking a new opening, not a closure, for those closest to the personal contemplation of a real, not a metaphysical or mythical tragedy. Inevitably Jencks, mindful of this fundamental loss, sees his work as essentially now standing not within but outside the long sequence of garden history. For both Charles Jencks and Ian Hamilton Finlay, each garden represents some victory over adversity. For Finlay, Little Sparta contains still an embattled, defensive mood, as if paradise was always under threat in the experience of humanity. For Jencks, the imponderables of the cosmos still threaten and continue to moderate any sense of wonderment.

Both gardens can be seen to be representations of a presumed world and, as gardens must, to seek after that greater perfection. They are not mutually exclusive, but pursue different agendas. One could safely say that during the period from 1975 up to the close of the last century, just as in the closing years of the eighteenth century, concepts of the sublime, and their common philosophical and ideological basis, were deliberately downgraded and devalued. For Portrack, neither an aesthetic nor any philosophical concept seems to be prevalent, nor do such concepts have any relevance in the cosmological reappraisals of the twenty-first century. And yet, certainly in essence, both could be in play, and in aesthetic terms at least, experientially both can be found here.

I would like to draw briefly upon three clear examples of what is meant by the contemporary sublime. Most recently, Enric Miralles (and Carmen Pinos) achieved a quite similar and dramatic expression of the sublime, and nothing less, in their Igualada Cemetery (1991) (Fig. 19). Here the materiality of the stonework in the former quarry gives along the routes for the visiting mourners an inescapable quality of an open life cycle, which Miralles wished not to see closed. It was as if Miralles was reaching back through life, not death, to prehistory in creating a garden without closure. A second example within this genre is the recent Museum of Vulcanology by Hans Hollein (2002) near Clermont Ferrand in eastern France (Fig. 20). Hollein paid

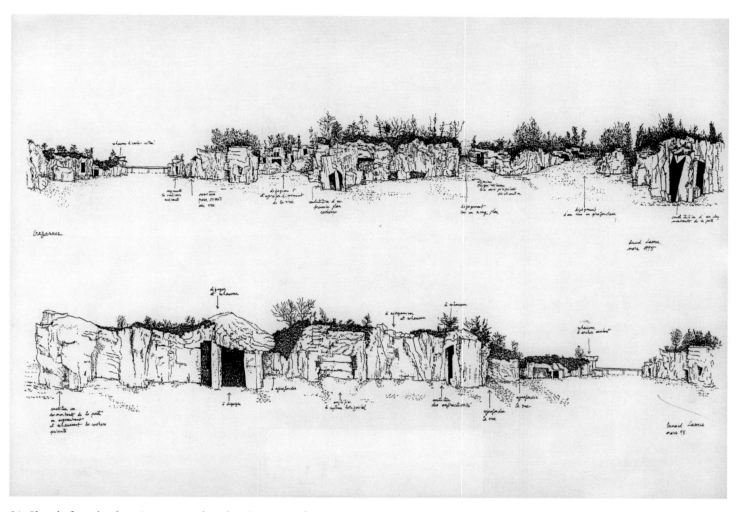

21. Sketch for a landscaping proposal at the Quarries of Crazannes, France. March 1995, by Bernard Lassus (Contemporary Landscape Design Collection, Dumbarton Oaks).

due reverence to the wild, volcanic environment, celebrating in built-landscape terms the traditional qualities of the sublime. The architecture was subsumed wholly to the landscape. The cone indicates the entrance to the "underworld." A spiralling pathway leads the visitor downwards into the "bowels of the earth" via an existing 30,000-year-old crater with walls of volcanic lava. Farther down there is a large, volcanic garden, containing in a humid state giant ferns from New Zealand. This garden forms a fulcrum to the whole subterranean world, as presented here. But again, there is no experience of closure.

My third example here is the landscape created by Bernard Lassus in the Crazannes area in France (2002) between Saintes and Rochefort, in an area characterized by manmade stone quarries (Fig. 21). Here also it is in a total awareness and focus on nature that the scheme is fulfilled. Lassus has considered the materiality of the landscape as vital to its continuity of meaning. Among the many characteristics shared by all three examples here (which I would classify together as landscapes of the sublime) and one that is carefully pointed out by Lassus is the quality of *Stimmung*. Here it is the landscape ambience that becomes critical. Michel Conan quotes Simmel here: "It is with our entire being that we stand before a landscape, be it natural or artistic. And the act that creates it for us simultaneously one of sight and of painting."[11]

There remains now, on the matter of Portrack, a fundamental question to be resolved. At Portrack, Jencks is reaching forward rather than back in time, in searching for a greater certitude, if not perfection. The assiduous application of theories of the sublime, which can assist in resolving this apparent dilemma, is not possible, because the sublime is itself rendered largely void, and the universe ultimately remains an imponderable speculation. In the twenty-first century, at Portrack, the concept of *Stimmung* and the related idea of the sublime, in aesthetic and perceptual terms, are ruled out. Whatever the embellishments of the picturesque in contemporary form as "picturesque games," such remain perceptible only in the mind of the visitor. The reality of the universe, as pursued by Jencks, effectively forecloses such definitions. Here lies, for the unwary visitor, the likelihood of entrapment, with no apparent release. The introduction, thematically, of scientific phenomena into the realm of garden design poses new challenges, but also substantial risks. Portrack demonstrates that an important range of experiences can be introduced, within rather than outside the realm of garden art, but that in the end, as Jencks himself says, "visitors can and must come upon these installations in the right frame of mind, interpreting and feeling the garden according to their mood."

Across the hills nearby at Little Sparta, (Fig. 16), Ian Hamilton Finlay has not fallen into the trap of closure even though he seeks beauty in emulating paradise. His own philosophy appears not to have any scientific basis for his presumption, other than to incorporate the politics of survival with a succinct wariness of historical precedent, and above all a continuing predication of the essence of humanity itself. So, returning now to Portrack, one is on much safer ground if, as has been suggested earlier, one were to explore, say, the specifics of the highly original landforms—those here that Charles and Maggie Jencks had together striven to construct.

Portrack ultimately stands to provide a new set of aesthetic experiences to the visitor. The garden epitomizes a response to the numerous imponderable, universal, and cosmological ambiguities that confront society at large, in seeking to resolve new queries about our position in the universe. This response is experienced by the visitor, first, effectively on the aesthetic level of the form of art that the garden presents, and, second, at a deeper level, through the new scientific realities that its creator has assiduously researched and that form the intellectual and philosophical basis for the creation of the garden. The experiential perception for the visitor is episodic, in that identifiable parts and elements within the garden can be "read" separately (e.g., the Garden of the Sixth Sense, the mounds): there is consequently no closure to this temporality. Certain elements will be experienced as "inspiring" (e.g., the Universe Cascade) and others, confusing to the visitor. In expressing this overall process, which is deliberately constructed by Jencks, the visitor may become aware of natural phenomena having a greater or lesser sense of nature, indeed, of foreboding. At the same time, the visitor can, with the garden's creator, experience a sense of release. One can find here a direct yet scientific experiential basis for the necessary speculation hereabouts about the human condition, and the future of the universe, which hopefully will persist as long as this remarkable and pioneering garden exists. Here the various installations, large and small, organic, natural, or metallic, can be "read" by the visitor always on their own terms, episodically; or else cumulatively and collectively so, for the more intellectually proactive visitor providing a new set of experiences in terms of garden art—but also, perhaps helping metaphorically at least, to unravel the mysteries of the universe as viewed today. Furthermore, Portrack offers a new extension to the traditional role of the garden in history. There is perhaps little sense of garden sanctuary (as distinct from Little Sparta), but there is in contrast a raised level of speculation about the universe, and therefore of the "three natures," proposing a challenging new definition of this time-honored categorization.

NOTES

[1] John Dixon Hunt, *Greater Perfections: The Practice of Garden Theory* (London: Thames and Hudson, 2000), 51–70, 181–206.

[2] G. A. Jellicoe and J. C. Shepherd, *The Italian Gardens of the Renaissance* (London: Ernest Benn, 1925), 26–27.

[3] Charles Jencks, *The Garden of Cosmic Speculation* (London: Francis Lincoln, 2003), introductory texts, 1–9.

[4] Charles Jencks, "Nature Talking with Nature," *Architectural Review* (January 2005): 71.

[5] Following the references to the garden of Cosmic Speculation C. Jencks as given below, also the author does not deem necessary to reference further quotations taken out of his texts. All non-referenced quotations are excerpted from C Jencks writings.

[6] Yves Alain Bois, "A Picturesque Stroll around Clara-Clara," trans. John Shepley, *October,* no. 29 (1): 32–62.

[7] Ron Graziani, *Robert Smithson and the American Landscape* (Cambridge: Cambridge University Press, 2004), 120–21.

[8] Jencks, *The Garden of Cosmic Speculation,* 89.

[9] Benoit Mandelbrot, *The Fractal Geometry of Nature* (San Francisco: W.H. Freeman, 1982).

[10] Andrew Wilton, *American Sublime: Landscape Painting in the United States, 1820-1880* (London: Tate Gallery, 2002), 11–12.

[11] Michel Conan, *The Crazannes Quarries by Bernard Lassus. An Essay Analyzing the Creation of a Landscape*, Dumbarton Oaks Contemporary Landscape Design Series I, trans. Karen Taylor (Washington, DC: Spacemaker Press, 2004), 8–9.

Contemporary Garden Aesthetics, Creations and Interpretations

Contemporary Garden Aesthetics, Creations and Interpretations

Contemporary Garden Aesthetics, Creations and Interpretations

Contemporary Garden Aesthetics, Creations and Interpretations

"To Make the Stone[s] Stony": Defamiliarization and Andy Goldsworthy's Garden of Stones

Jacky Bowring

I. One Possible Story

> One of the most powerful images I have of New York was staying in a hotel on Broadway. My room was high up in the building, I think on the 17th floor. I looked out of the window of my room and I saw a tree that had seeded itself, growing out of the side of the building opposite. It was for me a potent image of nature's ability to grow, even in the most difficult circumstances.
>
> —Andy Goldsworthy, Press Release for the Garden of Stones (2003)[1]

> I am afraid of towns. But you mustn't leave them. If you venture too far, you come to the Vegetation Belt. The Vegetation has crawled for mile after mile towards the towns. It is waiting. When the town dies, the Vegetation will invade it, it will clamber over the stones, it will grip them, search them, burst them open with its long black pincers; it will bind the holes and hang its green paws everywhere.
>
> —Jean-Paul Sartre, *Nausea* (1938)[2]

The evocation of the tragic is one of the most compelling responsibilities that the landscape has, as places where aesthetic experience becomes intensified and heightened. The memorial as object, as "monument," has transmuted into the domain of the garden, to a complex architecture/landscape/sculpture synthesis where new forms might be realized. Daniel Libeskind's Garden of Exile and Emigration at the Jewish Museum in Berlin and Peter Eisenman's Memorial to the Murdered Jews of Europe are two such examples of these garden-like forms that plumb the depths of experience in the name of tragedy. Andy Goldsworthy's Garden of Stones (2003) at the Museum of Jewish Heritage in Manhattan also seeks such a poetics of memory, honoring Holocaust victims and survivors (Fig. 1). The garden is composed of eighteen Vermont boulders, each with a dwarf oak (*Quercus prinoides*) growing out of a hollow cored and burnt into the stone. Both the Public Art Fund and the museum

1. *Garden of Stones*, Museum of Jewish Heritage, Manhattan. September 2003

itself immediately set about capturing the symbolic precision of the garden on their web sites, reciting a litany of symbols, including the resonances with Jewish stone grave markers, and the valorizing of Goldsworthy's tale of the origin of the trees-in-rocks motif during an earlier visit to New York. In *Passage,* Goldsworthy's most recent book, the symbolic significance of the number of stones is explained: "Each letter in Hebrew has a numerical value, and those that make up 'chai,' the Hebrew word for life, add up to eighteen, so this number always has special connotations."[3] Further, Goldsworthy crystallizes the symbolic nature of the stones and their trees: "Each stone had become a tomb upon which a tree was then planted—a poignant mixture of life and death."[4]

This story could stop right here, in the recounting of a symbolic armature, locking the "meaning" of the landscape experience safely in place. Following a well-beaten trail in the interpretation of Andy Goldsworthy's work, and the broader genre of land art, this story would set about recounting such aspects as the inherent symbolism, the romantic primitivism of working with the land, or the simplistic naïveté of the work. After all, modern culture predisposes the reader, or the "beholder," to an underreading of the world, to economize their effort, to seek rational explanations. The striving for an easy understanding quickly falls away to banality, and a cleaving of the subject from their potential place in the world. To accept ambiguity and mystery is to become empowered within one's self, in the manner suggested by Giambattista Vico in his *New Science:* "As rational metaphysics teaches that man becomes all things by understanding them, imaginative met[a]physics shows that man becomes all things by not understanding them ... for when he does not understand he ... becomes them by transforming himself into them."[5]

This, then, is a different story, prompted by visiting the garden two days after its opening in September 2003, a solitary encounter amid the ongoing construction work on the museum's new wing, an engagement with this group of stones, the tiny trees whipped about in the frenzied tail winds of Hurricane Isabel, which had just torn through the eastern seaboard leaving a trail of destruction. The language of land art, and the neat explanations of the symbolism, fail right at the crucial point of existential engagement, seeking closure when there is a need to simply stand, perplexed, at the edge of a void. This story is a questioning of the nature of potential experience, attempting to follow the trajectory opened up by the questioning of the relationship between form and content, to challenge the sufficiency of the symbol.

Our Callused Souls: Algebrization and Automatization

Classical works have for us become covered with the glassy armour of familiarity—we remember them too well, we have heard them from our childhood, we have read them in books, thrown them in the course of conversation, and now we have calluses on our souls, we no longer sense them.

—Viktor Shklovsky, "The Resurrection of the Word"[6]

The rehearsal of a mnemonic algebra reflects prevailing attitudes to memorials, a belief in the symbolic potency of information. Many contemporary memorials rely on an emblemization of the "data" associated with the tragedy—the numbers of dead, the volume of debris, the ages of victims. Memorial competitions for the September 11th terrorist attacks have operationalized the language of information as design, creating death datascapes. The most recent of these competitions, the Flight 93 Memorial for

Laurel Highlands in western Pennsylvania, which concluded its first phase in February 2005, continued the symbolization of the data of the tragedy, with the finalists focusing on representing the forty killed at this site, together with the 3,021 total deaths on September 11th.

Thomas Keenan suggests that this type of response aims for an "almost automatic machinery of remembrance," and this "can shield us from the powerful disorientation of the event the [memorials] seek to mark."[7] This is particularly true of a memorial for an event such as the Holocaust where the "data" are beyond comprehension, and to reduce it to an easily assimilated summary is to deny the very shock that is necessary. Terry Eagleton argues that such an event in fact signaled the "death of tragedy" for its extreme victimization and torment, with the hypothesis that "a monstrous excess of the stuff [tragedy] has finally obliterated our sense of the value by which it might be measured. We have supped too full of horrors, and even 'tragedy' is a shallow signifier for events which beggar representation. There can be no icons of such catastrophes, to which the only appropriate response would be screaming or silence."[8]

The collapsing of such desolation into data is an erasure of existential engagement, substituting a fascination with facts for a meditation upon tragedy, detaching ourselves from really feeling, so that, in the words of Shklovsky, "held accountable for nothing, life fades into nothingness. Automatization eats away at things, at clothes, at furniture, at our wives, and at our fear of war."[9] Shklovsky alludes to the deadening detachment of "sleepwalking" one's way through life, or "somnambulism" to use Tolstoy's description of his wife's disengagement with life.[10]

The "machinery" of remembrance can be compared to this sense of ennui, as found in the limiting effect of habituation in speech, where "things are replaced by symbols. Complete words are not expressed in rapid speech; their initial sounds are barely perceived. Alexander Pogodin offers the example of a boy considering the sentence 'The Swiss mountains are beautiful' in the form of a series of letters: *T, S, m, a, b.*"[11] Shklovsky's observation is that "this process of 'algebrization,' the over-automatization of an object, permits the greatest economy of perceptive effort."[12]

Although recourse to a symbolic summary of the Garden of Stones provides a "script" for the garden, there is a significant aspect of aesthetic experience that lies beyond this. A symbolic interpretation might be a safe, expected option within the current landscape architectural milieu, but a formalistic perspective has the potential to challenge and extend the design and interpretation of memorial gardens. The symbolic may provide a domain for the poetic, but it can become suffocating and insufficient. The development of Russian formalism was a reaction against such a situation, seeking the "emancipation of the poetic word"[13] from the symbolists' philosophical and religious entrapment. It is a search for those qualities that *resist* the seemingly inexorable process of the collapse into naturalization, a realization of Shklovksy's observation "We do not experience the commonplace, we do not see it; rather we recognize it."[14] It is via the formalistic route that the unsettling vein of defamiliarization, or strangemaking, is encountered.

On *Ostranenie*

The framing of the Garden of Stones as *ostranenie* or "strangemaking" is an effort to articulate the difference between this garden and many of the contemporary memorials that rely on an automatized engagement. *Ostranenie* is a word coined by Russian Formalist Victor Shklovsky in his essay "Art as Technique." The very meaning of the word has been troublesome; as with any neologism, the challenge to translate it carries some of the responsibility of transferring the conceptual as well as linguistic sense. Benjamin Sher translated one of several versions of the essay called variously *Art as Technique* or *Art as Device*. Sher writes specifically about the need to try and encapsulate the sense of Shklovsky's term: "It is a pretty fair assumption … that Shklovsky speaks of *ostranenie* as a process or act that endows an object or image with 'strangeness' by 'removing' it from a network of conventional, formulaic, stereotypical perceptions and linguistic expressions."[15] He recounts his struggle with possible equivalents, dismissing "estrangement" as too negative, "making it strange" as too positive, and "defamiliarization" as "wrongheaded." Sher's preference was for "*en*strangement," a neologism of his own, but all of these have a useful place in expressing the nature of experience.

Boris Eichenbaum signaled formalism as a freedom from "the traditional idea of form as an envelope, a vessel into which one pours a liquid (the content)"[16] and described the need, therefore, to show that "the perception of form results from special artistic techniques that force the reader to experience form"[17] such as defamiliarization. Shklovsky's essay "Art as Technique" described the way in which defamiliarization in literature is a means of overcoming the automatism of perception that comes with habitualization. Tolstoy's "pricking of the conscience," for example, is achieved through the defamiliarizing strategy of not naming the thing that is described, as in his treatise on flogging, and through providing an alternative viewpoint as in his story "Kholstomer," where the story is narrated by a horse. Such techniques produce an uncanny effect, adopted by the modernist avant-gardes, as a way to deal with the sense of exile from reality that came with the trappings of modernity, "as if a world estranged and distanced from its own nature could only be recalled to itself by shock, by the effects of things deliberately 'made strange.'"[18]

Shklovsky asserted that the role of art was to overcome habitualization and bring new freshness to aesthetic experience: "Art exists that one may recover the sensation of life; exists to make the stone *stony*. The purpose of art is to impart the sensation of things as they are perceived and not as they are known. The technique of art is to make objects 'unfamiliar,' to make forms difficult, to increase the difficulty and length of perception because the process of perception is an aesthetic end in itself and must be prolonged."[19] Kyrstyna Pomorska's translation of this passage infuses this point of view with further dimensions on the nature of aesthetic experience, that "in order to return *palpability* to life, to *feel* things … there exists something which is called art. The aim of art is to give a palpability to a thing, as a vision, not as a recognition; the device of art is a device of making things 'strange' and of a difficult form."[20] The yearning for a palpability within the ordinary, of finding the extraordinary within, is echoed in the subtleties of work such as that of Swiss landscape architect Georges Descombes, in constructing a landscape intervention in such a way that it "jolts its context, scrapes the ordinariness of a situation, and imposes a shift on what seems the most obvious."[21] Similarly, Goldsworthy's stones and trees are on one level resoundingly familiar, ordinary elements for a memorial garden, but the way in which they are composed, assembled, presented, makes them strange. The scale of the stones, their repetition, the aching void implied by the mass of the stones, the decontextualization of trees *in* stones, and the metaphorical resonances are garden parallels of linguistic techniques of "baring the device," or what Mukarovský terms "foregrounding." Such devices impeded the automatic, easy, conventional responses to what is perceived and thus create a more profound experience of the work. Mukarovský explained that "automatization schematizes an event; foregrounding means the violation of the scheme."[22] In poetry, for example, the Russian formalists sought sounds that would become foregrounded through their rhythm, and perception would be intensified as a result, through the effects of what Jakobson called an "organized violence."

Defamiliarization in poetry is a technique for revealing the familiar and predates the Russian formalists in the work of Romantic poets Wordsworth, Coleridge, and Shelley, and beyond to the German poet Novalis. In the eighteenth century Novalis (Friedrich von Hardenberg) described the foundation of Romanticism as "making the familiar strange, and the strange familiar," or more specifically of "investing the commonplace with a lofty significance, the ordinary with a mysterious aspect, the familiar with the prestige of the unfamiliar, the finite with the semblance of infinity."[23] Novalis expressed the necessity for estrangement within Romanticism, stating that "the art of *estranging* in a *pleasing* way, of making an object strange and yet familiar and attractive—that is romantic poetics."[24] This search for a revelatory alienation within the poetic was extended in turn by the English Romantics, described by Shelley in his *Defence of Poetry* as that which "strips the veil of familiarity from the world, and lays bare the naked and sleeping beauty which is the spirit of its forms."[25] The Romantics sought an understanding not so much of the perceptions themselves, but the nature of devices that produced defamiliarization. This is expressed in Coleridge's description of Wordsworth's ability "to give the charm of novelty to things of every day, and to excite a feeling analogous to the supernatural, by awakening the mind's attention from the lethargy of custom, and directing it to the loveliness and the wonders of the world before us; an inexhaustible treasure, but for which in consequence of the film of familiarity and selfish solicitude we have eyes, yet see not, ears that hear not, and hearts that neither feel nor understand."[26]

Wordsworth's ode to the "glory and freshness of a dream" was a lament for the "innocent eye" of childhood vision, an uncallused soul, beyond the state of quotidian consciousness. Saddened by the "shades of the prison-house" that close upon the growing boy, Wordsworth in *Ode: Intimations of Immortality* alludes to the loss of the freshness of youth, of the awareness of the nature of the eternal soul before it begins to fade with his passage away from innocence.[27] This prefiguring of defamiliarizing techniques in Romanticism sheds further light on the significance of estrangement in Goldsworthy's work. The grounding of alienation within Romanticism resonates with Goldsworthy's search for a poetic and lucid encounter with nature, and underscores his expression of a need for an unclouded innocence. Strickland-Constable calls attention to Goldsworthy's "induced 'innocence of eye'"[28] and elsewhere he speaks of a striving for "seeing something you never saw before, that was always there but you were blind to it."[29]

One of Goldworthy's means of effecting disorientation is through undoing the apparent closure of his work through demystifying it via captions. The captions to the photographs of his ephemeral works are often lengthy and "lay bare" the devices of their construction, listing the materials and techniques. For example,

> Dead hazel sticks
> collected from nearby wood
> partly burnt
> laid on old bracken
> in anticipation of the new
> revisited from late winter through to summer.[30]

He writes how the captions are part of the work itself and in essence could be apprehended as a device of strangemaking: "The dis-orientation is necessary to provoke a response uncluttered by previous knowledge; the information is essential to persuade us that this color is, truly to be found in nature."[31]

Although poetry was the primary focus for the work of the Russian formalists, strangemaking and disorientation haunt a range of artistic practices, including literature, cinema, painting, and sculpture, all of which cross back and forth into the realm of the garden and the nature of aesthetic experience. In literature, Marcel Proust achieves this sense of strangemaking through renewing a "genuine existential contact with things and the world."[32] As an antidote to the modern world's dislocation with experience, Proust strives for a renewal of perception, through not only what is said, but the shocking way in which it is said, to achieve a sense of disorientation. For example, Proust juxtaposes Madame de Sévigné with Dostoyevsky, drawing an unlikely comparison between the seventeenth-century doyenne of French society, who was known for her epistolary elegance, and the existential intensity of the nineteenth-century Russian novelist. Proust revealed what he called the "Dostoyevskian side of Madame de Sévigné's *Letters*,"[33] and through this he found a way to see her anew, "as though for the first time."[34]

Jameson cites Shklovsky's "Theory of Prose" to identify the technique for seeing an object anew, "to place the object in a new semantic row, in a row of concepts which belong to another category."[35] Shklovsky offers a range of literary devices that echo profoundly with the experience of landscape, which are summarized by Jameson as: to not *name* an object, but only describe it in its "empirical inertia"; to render it from an unusual angle, or over a great distance; or microscopically as by Swift; or in slow motion; or juxtaposed to cause certain qualities to stand out; or tampering with conventional expectations of cause and effect. Although such devices refer to an *object,* Shklovsky also looks at plot devices, which might be analogous to the experience of motion within the landscape, the orchestration of experience: retardation; the decomposition of action into episodes; double plotting, such as the interpolation of heterogenous anecdotes and stories; and baring the device through attracting the reader's attention to the basic techniques of narration.[36]

Defamiliarization influenced the cinematographic techniques of Sergei Eisenstein's montage,[37] as well as Jean-Luc Godard's jump-cutting,[38] and the legacy of non-narrative film such as the otherworldly works of Russian filmmaker Andrei Tarkovsky. In theater, defamiliarization became realized in Berthold Brecht's disrupting strategy of "alienation" through the denaturalization of perception, seeking what has been termed a "critical distance." Brecht's "estrangement" effects (*Verfremdungseffekte*) act against complacency and the very automatization that is at the heart of the necessary shock of defamiliarization. In the context of the Garden of Stones, this emphasis resonates with the need to demand a consultation with the self, away from the easy shield of objectivity and distance one encounters the shock of subjectivity.

In the visual arts of painting and sculpture, the *dépaysement* (literally "to expatriatate" or in this sense to decontextualize) techniques advocated by the Russian formalists are echoed in the oneiric imagery of the surrealists, notably in the work of artists such as René Magritte, and in Salvador Dali's investigations *de l'autre côté de l'oeil.* As a counter to the automatized apprehension of imagery, these works were unnerving, even shocking. In sculpture, Marcel Duchamp established the idea of the readymade, which echoes with Goldsworthy's work in terms of presenting the most ordinary of objects as works of art, infusing them with new perception, making them strange. Although Goldsworthy often is described as "getting in touch with nature," trying to "understand" it, a reframing of his work as "strangemaking" finds parallels with the work of Duchamp. Goldsworthy's "readymades," *objets trouvés,* are from nature rather than the domestic landscape of Duchamp's urinal and bicycle wheel, and he observes, "apparently ordinary places yield extraordinary things."[39] In his exhibition, decontextualization, and juxtaposition of these ordinary elements, Goldsworthy transfigures them in the same way as Duchamp with his readymades, drawing attention to them so that they are apart from their setting and somehow unnatural.

2. *Garden of Stones*, Museum of Jewish Heritage, Manhattan. September 2003

Devices make a work "literary" rather than "ordinary," and in the Garden of Stones, the devices of repetition, placement of the rocks in close proximity, the planting of trees *in* the rocks extract the stones from their ordinary stoniness and into the realm of aesthetic experience (Fig. 2). In Goldsworthy's ephemeral works, also, it is precisely the nature of the devices employed that aestheticizes them, finds their literariness, their poetry, amid the prose language of nature.

Many of Goldsworthy's works rely on the setting up of paradoxical conditions, and paradox is a prime revelatory figure of defamiliarization. Midsummer Snowballs, a project in London, for example, is a paradox upon paradox: "First there is the paradox of the spherical snowball making a flat line in the snow, resulting in the equation ball versus line. Then there is the white of the snowball leaving behind a dark trail of bare earth, marking the contrast of light versus dark, white versus black, negative and positive."[40]

The formal devices of the decontextualization, the readymade, and the play of paradox all contributed to the defamiliarized sensibility of the Garden of Stones. The stones appear to hover on the graveled terrace, defying their apparent size and weight in an oneiric manner, and a surreal quality is achieved so that they seem like something from a dream, producing a retardation of experience that enables the beholder to "extend and intensify the perceptive process."[41] They take on a Magrittean feel, and the resonances between Goldsworthy's Garden and Magritte's paintings such as *The Glass Key* (1959) and *Castle in the Pyrénées* (1959) are striking. The stones feel almost too large for the space in which they are confined, echoing *The Listening Room* (1958), where an enormous apple pushes against the sides of a stone chamber. This strangemaking of the stones transports them toward becoming poetically tragic, in the sense of what Shklovsky termed the "palpableness" of construction.[42] "Palpableness" is Matejka and Pomorska's translation of Shklovsky's *osčutimost'* in his striving to differentiate between poetic and prosaic language. Lemon and Reis's translation falls back on the sense of "perception," where "Poetic language is distinguished from prosaic language by the *perception* of its structure."[43] However, the notion of *palpability* acutely captures the impression of form upon the reader/beholder, even beyond that of "perceiving." In language Shklovsky identifies acoustics, articulation, and semantics as the means by which palpableness is achieved, terms that can be transferred into the realm of the experience of landscape. It is here that a distinction between the apprehension of a memorial as a mere marker of events and as an experience of the tragic might be realized. The former is essentially a prosaic experience, a reading of dates and data, a habitualized and easy underreading of the site. To experience the tragic, however, the "language" of the landscape must transcend this, into the domain of the poetic; the tragic is something to be *felt*. Although a prosaic response to memory might offer a script of sorts, a poetic articulation aspires to the palpable, such that any script may actually dilute and detract from this existential frisson, and the recognition of self as subject.

Encountering these stones amid the swirling gales of a solitary September visit required no script. Their very presence within the Museum of Jewish Heritage was enough of a "caption," and more important was the form of the experience (Fig. 3). The long walk

3. *Garden of Stones*, Museum of Jewish Heritage, Manhattan. September 2003

through the museum itself, claustrophobic, introspective, alarming in its sheer intensity of information, then the exterior, a sense of gravity suspended with the realization that the rocks sit not on the ground plane, but on a cantilevered terrace. Even the presumption of weight and rest is thus undone, made strange, held aloft in the air in a Magrittean sense. Time spent alone with the stones allows for their repetitive dreamlike hovering to become palpable, their stoniness, their gravitas. The absence of prescribed content allows for a magnitude of feeling that somehow acknowledges Eagleton's observation on the Holocaust as beyond the tragic, that here was a place for silence, a place for screaming, and not for the impassive act of reading.

The extraction and reworking of nature in this way is what allows a seizing of formal qualities, and via this to poetics. Vinokur described how the poetic word is rooted *within* language, exists within it, but "the poetic word grows in the real word as its particular function, exactly as poetry grows out of the surrounding world of reality."[44] This resonance between the perception of the stones in a Magrittean sense continues throughout Goldsworthy's oeuvre. The improbability of the forms of construction, ordinary materials made strange, things out of place. There are many uncanny echoes between the paintings of

4. *Elective Infinities*, collage, Jacky Bowring

5. *The Art of Conversation*, collage, Jacky Bowring

6. *The Unexpected Question*, collage, Jacky Bowring

Magritte and the photographs of Goldsworthy's ephemeral works, and the montaging of these two artists' work seeks to see them both anew, through that very same act of defamiliarization. Magritte's image of an egg within a cage, *Elective Affinities* (1933), finds a parallel surrealistic tension in Goldsworthy's snowball contained within a cage of barbed wire (Fig. 4). Challenges to gravity resonate between Magritte's *The Art of Conversation* (1950) and Goldsworthy's *Balanced Rocks* (Fig. 5). The play of depth, the plummeting voids, occur in both artists' work as gaping holes within familiar environments, a rent in the fabric of the everyday. Whereas Goldsworthy constructs his holes in stone, soil, and twigs, Magritte creates uncanny apertures to other worlds (Fig. 6). Goldsworthy says that looking into a deep hole unnerves him, his "concept of stability is questioned and [he is] made aware of the potent energies within the earth. The black is that energy made visible."[45]

Beyond the collages offered here, there are many further echoes between the artists' work, including similar efforts to make materials strange through their decontextualization, as in the (extra)ordinary sight of Goldsworthy's midsummer snowballs within the city of London and the huge, imposing sphere of Magritte's *The Monumental Shadow* (1932). Weightlessness and gravity are paradoxical partners in Magritte's *The Battle of Argonne* (1958), where a rock hovers next to a cloud, a similar paradox to Goldsworthy's feather-wrapped rock. Magritte and Goldsworthy both transfigure materials, as the visual analogue equivalent to having a story narrated by a horse. Magritte transforms all things to stone in a range of works including *Memory of Journey* (1950), and Goldsworthy executes parallel transfigurations through wrapping elements in other materials, for example, a branch wrapped in leaves, a stone wrapped in petals. Morphing is a further technique of defamiliarization and is found in the change of state as in the boot becoming a foot in Magritte's *The Red Model* (1937), and Goldsworthy's transformation of a tree into sandy drapery in his work in Schoorl in North Holland.[46]

The use of the *objet trouvé,* the found object, the readymade, is seen in Magritte's work in the curious representation of the most mundane of daily objects, a pipe, a shoe, a mirror. In Goldsworthy, the objects are found in nature, transformed by their exhibition, decontextualization and juxtaposition. The rock is a readymade, existing in nature, but here exhibited, so that the stoniness of the stone might come forth, away from an automatized, habitualized way of seeing rock in a memorial setting, where it is shorn of its rockiness, polished, inscribed with names, dates, data.

The Knight's Move: "The Magrittean Side of Andy Goldsworthy"

Moving diagonally like a knight, I have intersected your life.
— Viktor Shklovsky, *Zoo, or Letters Not about Love*[47]

This interfacing of Russian formalism, Goldsworthy, and surrealism is in itself something of a formalist experiment, of decontextualizing things to see them anew, "to place the object in a new semantic row," or as Shklovsky explains elsewhere, to "make an object into an *artistic* fact, it has to be removed from the series of real-life facts. … You have to tear the thing from the row of habitual associations in which you find it. You have to rotate it like a log on the fire."[48] This juxtaposing of Goldsworthy with Magritte is a Proustian gesture, in the manner of the shock of Madame de Sévigné juxtaposed with Dostoyevsky to see her as though for the first time, her "Dostoyevskian side." The search for the "Magrittean side of Goldsworthy" is for a way around the habitualized response to his work, to try to plumb the depths of why it might provide some existential significance. This paper is therefore in itself a formalist work, advocating a cleaving of the work from its contextual ties, rather than relying on the given readings. Shklovsky speaks here and there of the idea of the "knight's move"— the oblique move where things that are not linearly connected are combined, with a sense of surprise, unexpectedness. It is such a knight's move that is being attempted here, a reading against the grain, eluding authorial intention. In keeping with one of the incarnations of the formalists' belief in suppressing concerns with content and context, the notion of "intent" is not considered as significant as the form itself.

The placing of Goldsworthy within the frame of formalism, and beyond this into the estranged domain of surrealism, is a gesture toward the unexpected, and in fact something that the sculptor himself has resisted, stating, "Surrealism doesn't interest me generally," although he does acknowledge that "Magritte really does question how we see things."[49] This "knight's move" therefore leaps to a square that is not in a linear sequence from the sculptor's perspective, but one that provides a different strategic position. Turning from a following of authorial intent, away from the sculptor's claim on his work, is to liberate it, accepting that there are other interpretations that have their own value. It is in a sense the elevation of the beholder of the landscape, the "reader"; as Roland Barthes wrote, "we know that to restore to writing its future, we must reverse its myth: the birth of the reader must be at the cost of [in some translations 'requited by' or 'ransomed by'] the death of the author."[50] This work is therefore intentionally provocative in its swerve away from diachronic exegesis, which is often called into play in the discussion of gardens and landscape design, walking away from the scene of the crime, as Jakobson described: "The situation has been that historians of literature act like nothing so much as policemen, who, out to arrest a certain culprit, take into custody (just in case) everyone and everything they find at the scene as well as any passers-by for good measure."[51]

The birth of the reader, the critic, the beholder therefore becomes a route to a perception of the site. The designer or artist is in a sense abandoned at this point, and the forms remain. There is no "correct" symbolic exegesis, and the challenge that this paper explores is to follow a different path, as signaled by the chiasmatic epigraphs in the introduction. The presentation of the trees as symbols of the struggle for life is trite and tired already, but through recognizing them as elements made strange, perhaps even menacing, the existential potential is amplified. Such a displacement of received meanings could be paralleled to the Situationists' technique of *détournement,* or diversion, in terms of the replacing of recognized elements, and thus a renewed apprehension of things already known.

Goldsworthy's rejection of connotations of surrealism therefore is bracketed in the aspiration for finding something else as part of the experience of his work. The Russian formalists contended that it was "literariness" or *literaturnost,* rather than the referents and all contingent elements of history and context, that were significant. Similarly, this has been a search for the "literariness" of the garden, to find the poetic devices that are foregrounded in this memorial. It is an effort to take a leap of faith, turning away from the easy read of content, and toward the difficulty of form.

Goldsworthy's Garden of Stones is only a beginning and not an end to this evaluation and elevation of formalism as a means of potent experiences. The garden opens out a field of possibilities stemming from the surreality of Goldsworthy's oeuvre. Within his work the ordinary is made extraordinary, echoing the defamiliarization and retardation of experience sought by the formalists, as in an early stone work from the mid-1970s, where the stones apparently defied gravity, where the "suspension of probability is exploited … not altogether as an end in itself but as much as device to make the spectator look harder."[52] The Garden of Stones captures some of this sensibility, yet it is also flawed in its execution, with the apparent surreality in part the product of a sleight of hand, where the bases of the stones are concealed within a matrix of gravel, disguising their connection. This is more in the manner of classical art, where it was believed that processes should be concealed in the name of product, as opposed to the formalists' desire to bare the devices and reveal process. However, Goldsworthy wrote, "The most profound thing I can say about a sculpture is how it's made."[53] This reflects the formalists' concerns with the categories of *material* and *device,* which in some ways they viewed as more instructive than the distinction between form and content. At the same time, it also lays the work open to Jameson's criticism of Shklovsky's attention to technique, saying that "his insistence on technique seems to reflect a nostalgia for an older handicraft culture"[54] Indeed, Goldsworthy's work easily slides into the realm of the decorative, a factor that contributes both to its widespread popular appeal, and to its being spurned by institutions such as the Tate Modern. Simon Schama observes that Goldsworthy's work is seen as "unfashionable," because of its moral intensity, the Ruskinian devotion to work and craft, scientific curiosity, and connection with the long history of land use.[55] Schama feels the Garden of Stones offers an "encounter with the elemental" and "a poignant metaphysical conceit strongly realized."[56]

The Magrittean side of Andy Goldsworthy brings us some way toward an exploration of surreal forms in the landscape as a means of aesthetic experience. The path toward a truly uncanny, defamiliarized landscape experience beckons. Goldsworthy opens the gate, perhaps without wanting to do so, yet his path leads to a different place. Even the sleight of hand attempted by the concealed bases of the granite boulders questions an authentic concern with form. The divergence is evident in the captions of the works of Magritte and Goldsworthy, where he seeks to "demystify" his works, giving literal descriptions of the components, and Magritte seeks to mystify his. While Schama defends Goldsworthy as conceptually as rich as Robert Smithson, and offering compressions of space and water as metaphysically suggestive as Anish Kapoor, it seems that Goldsworthy primarily seeks concert with the physical, his repeated concern to "understand" nature, so that "leaves teach me about stone and stone about leaves,"[57] whereas Magritte courts the metaphysical, and it is here that existential intensity is amplified, en route to a place of melancholy, tragedy, sublimity. There is a significant distinction between the petit-surrealism often conjured up in the fetishized objects such as dripping clocks and gloves, and the uncanny sense beyond that of a sensing of space and form. This uncanniness in an architectural setting is articulated by Anthony Vidler, as an *experiential* uncanniness, underscoring that it is the very rootedness of the strange within the familiar that is at the heart of such a feeling, as epitomized in Ernst Bloch's comment on the detective novel: "Something is uncanny—that is how it begins. But at the same time one must search for that remoter 'something,' which is already close at hand."[58]

The Garden of Stones represents something of a sea change in Goldsworthy's work, perhaps not of his own making. Although his ephemeral and permanent/semipermanent works have largely eschewed symbolic dimensions, the Garden of Stones is predominantly becoming received as a symbolic work. The reports of the artist and the museum are elevated within the discourse of interpretation, in what Juan Pablo Bonta phrases a phase of "official interpretation." Within the anatomy of criticism, Bonta explains, with reference to Mies van der Rohe's Barcelona Pavilion, the "official interpretation" is the message presented by figures of authority and is part of how "pieces of architecture reach their meaning."[59] Bonta's constructed anatomy illustrates how the role of the received commentaries and critiques on built works help shape the understanding of them, and he states, "The ultimate incorporation of architecture into culture is the result of the work of critics no less than of designers."[60] The naturalization of the official interpretation and its subsequent canonization can obliterate different readings of sites, and the criticism of built works sometimes must disrupt this uncritical reception of views. This paper is an attempt to resist this symbolic slippage, to allow the "sensing of the stones" to travel via formalistic routes. Symbolism is a significant component of existential richness, of providing hooks and triggers for emotional response, yet it is not enough. In her critique of a near neighbor of the Garden of Stones, Brian Tolle's Irish Hunger Memorial in Battery Park City, Cynthia Davidson described how the "obviousness of its symbols" were essentially salvaged through the defamiliarizing strategy that ensures that "playing the known against the unknown creates the ambiguity necessary for a work of art."[61] This underscores the question of whether tragedy can reside in symbolism alone. The tendency of symbolism to reduce all experience to the habitualized and automatized can prevent a denial of engagement, experience, of the existential freshness which is necessary most of all in a memorial garden. There are interesting parallels with the work of Swiss designer Georges Descombes, whose work explores a counterposition to that of a neat symbolic language, believing that rather than filling things with meaning, it is more powerful to leave a "semantic void" that allows for the beholder to participate in the work. Opposing the deadening effect of the analytical is the awakening possibility of synthesis. This reinforces the potential of a formalistic approach in the striving for experience, as Robert Maxwell says with reference to abstract objects in the context of an architecture of the tragic, they are enigmatic, and *because* of this "[resist] being emptied of meaning."[62] Symbolism is insufficient, it shields ourselves from our selves, where such an encounter is the very thing of aesthetic experience; it is here that we might *feel* the tragic. As Magritte observed, beholders tend to search for symbols as a means of protection, as a safety net, and thus avoid the fear of the unknown. He said, "They hunt around for a meaning to get themselves out of a quandary, and because they don't understand what they are supposed to think when they confront the painting … they want something to lean on, so they can be comfortable. … They want something secure to hang onto, so they can save themselves from the void."[63]

The question is, therefore, how the dance between form and content might be addressed in contemporary gardens, in this case a memorial garden. The embracing of the experience of form as aesthetic experience promotes particular ideas over the ways in which gardens, and in this case particularly memorial gardens, might "work." An overattention to the embedding of content can lead to habitualized responses to gardens, limiting access to compelling aesthetic experiences. Significantly both Magritte and Goldsworthy have denied the presence of the symbolic in their work, counter to much of the literature produced on both artists. Following her long-term dialogue with Magritte, in her presentation of his work and his life as an artist, Suzi Gablik wrote that "people have always looked for symbolic meanings in Magritte's pictures, and in some cases managed to find them. Nothing caused him greater displeasure."[64]

A shift in the balance toward formalist considerations embraces recognition of the richness beyond prescribed content. The encounter with the Garden of Stones induced an experiential epiphany, which revealed not only the significance of defamiliarized form in the pursuit of the tragic, but also about Goldsworthy's work in general. The recognition of the defamiliarizing strategies he adopts illuminated the potential contribution of such an approach to the experience of landscape. Although his work is widely copied, what is generally lost is this sense of the decontextualization of elements, of the transcendence into the poetic. Ironically, the criticisms of technique in the Garden of Stones are aspects that are strengths in Goldsworthy's ephemeral works. The disguising of the stones' bases beneath the gravel runs counter to his "baring of the devices" in his ephemeral works, where the thorns and structural elements used to hold things together are part of the piece itself.

Through defamiliarization, the Garden of Stones offers aesthetic experience that produces both minor illuminations (the stoniness of the stones) and major illuminations (an uncanny, dreamlike mode that connects to the necessary disorientation for the memorialization of tragedy). The interpretation of such epiphanic experiences via the route of formalism is an effort to explore the terrain beyond automatized, algebraic, symbolic certainties. The Garden of Stones paves the way for the elevation of the sensing of stones as a prime garden experience, beyond the deadening nature of decoding, to find what Jameson spoke of, that gardens realized in such mode could, like art, be a means of "restoring conscious experience, breaking through deadening and mechanical habits of conduct … and allowing us to be reborn to the world in its existential freshness and horror."[65]

NOTES

[1] www.publicartfund.org/pafweb/projects/03/goldsworthy_release_03.html.

[2] Jean-Paul Sartre, *Nausea,* trans. Robert Baldick (Hammondsworth: Penguin Books, 1965; originally published as *La Nausée* by Librarie Gallimard, 1938), 221–22.

[3] Andy Goldsworthy, *Passage* (New York: Harry N. Abrams, 2004), 62.

[4] Ibid., 69.

[5] Giambattista Vico, *New Science* [1725] cited in Steven Holl, Juhani Pallasmaa, and Alberto Pérez-Gómez, "Questions of Perception: Phenomenology of Architecture," *Architecture and Urbanism* (July 1994 special issue): 84.

[6] Victor Shklovsky, "The Resurrection of the Word" (1914), in *Russian Formalism: A Collection of Articles and Texts in Translation,* ed. Stephen Bann and John E. Bowlt (Edinburgh: Scottish Academic Press, 1973).

[7] Thomas Keenan, "Making the Dead Count, Literally," *The New York Times,* 30 November 2003.

[8] Terry Eagleton, *Sweet Violence: The Idea of the Tragic* (Oxford: Blackwell, 2003), 64.

[9] Victor Shklovsky, "Art as Device" (1925), in *Theory of Prose,* trans. Benjamin Sher (Elmwood Park, IL: Dalkey Archive Press, 1990), 5.

[10] Eric Naiman, "Shklovsky's Dog and Mulvey's Pleasure: The Secret Life of Defamiliarization," *Comparative Literature* 50, no. 4 (fall 1998): 333–52.

[11] Victor Shklovsky, "Art as Technique" (1917), in *Russian Formalist Criticism: Four Essays,* trans. Lee T. Lemon and Marion J. Reis (Lincoln: University of Nebraska Press, 1965), 11.

[12] Ibid., 12.

[13] Boris M. Ejxenbaum, "Theory of the Formal Method" (1927), in *Readings in Russian Poetics: Formalist and Structuralist Views,* ed. Ladislav Matejka and Krystyna Pomorska (Cambridge, MA: MIT Press, 1971), 7.

[14] Victor Shklovsky, "The Resurrection of the Word" (1914), in *Russian Formalism: A Collection of Articles and Texts in Translation,* ed. Stephen Bann and John E. Bowlt (Edinburgh: Scottish Academic Press, 1973).

[15] Benjamin Sher, Translator's Introduction, in Viktor Shkovsky, *Theory of Prose,* trans. Benjamin Sher (Elmwood Park, IL: Dalkey Archive Press, 1990), xix.

[16] Boris Eichenbaum, "The Theory of the 'Formal Method'" (1927), in *Russian Formalist Criticism: Four Essays,* trans. Lee T. Lemon and Marion J. Reis (Lincoln: University of Nebraska Press, 1965), 112.

[17] Ibid., 113.

[18] Anthony Vidler, *The Architectural Uncanny: Essays in the Modern Unhomely* (Cambridge, MA: MIT Press, 1992), 8.

[19] Shklovsky, "Art as Technique," 12.

[20] Shklovsky as translated in Krystyna Pomorska, *Russian Formalist Theory and its Poetic Ambiance* (The Hague: Mouton, 1968), 36, my italics.

[21] Georges Descombes, "The Swiss Way," in *Recovering Landscape: Essays in Contemporary Landscape Architecture,* ed. James Corner (New York: Princeton Architectural Press, 1999), 76.

[22] Jan Mukarovský, "Standard Language and Poetic Language," in *Linguistics and Literary Style,* ed. Donald C. Freeman (New York: Holt, Rinehart and Winston, 1964; original essay published 1932), 19.

[23] Novalis, cited in Martin Jesinghausen, "The Sky over Berlin as Transcendental Space: Wenders, Döblin and the 'Angel of History,'" in *Spaces in European Cinema,* ed. Myrto Konstantarakos (Bristol: Intellect Books, 2000), 77.

[24] William Arctander O'Brien, *Novalis* (Durham, N.C.: Duke University Press, 1994), 317.

[25] Percy Bysshe Shelley, "A Defence of Poetry," in *Shelley's Poetry and Prose: Authoritative Texts and Criticism,* ed. Donald H. Reiman and Neil Fraistat, 2nd ed. (New York: W. W. Norton, 2002; original essay published 1819), 533.

[26] Samuel Taylor Coleridge, *Biographia Literaria* (1815), vol. 1, chap. XIV. Cited in William Golding, *Romantic Poetry and Prose* (Oxford: Oxford University Press, 1973), 645.

[27] William Wordsworth, "Ode, Intimations of Immortality from Recollections of Early Childhood," in William Wordsworth, *William Wordsworth: Selected Poems* (London: Penguin, 1994), 141.

[28] Miranda Strickland-Constable, "Beginnings," in *Hand to Earth: Andy Goldsworthy Sculpture 1976-1990* (New York: Harry N. Abrams), 18.

[29] Andy Goldsworthy (2001) in Thomas Riedelsheimer (director), *Rivers and Tides,* Germany, 2001.

[30] Andy Goldsworthy, *Time* (London: Thames & Hudson, 2000), 34.

[31] Andy Goldsworthy, Frontispiece, *Hand to Earth: Andy Goldsworthy Sculpture 1976-1990* (New York: Harry N. Abrams).

[32] Frederic Jameson, *The Prison-house of Language: A Critical Account of Structuralism and Russian Formalism* (Princeton, NJ: Princeton University Press, 1972), 55.

[33] Marcel Proust, *À la recherche du temps perdu,* 3 vols. (Paris, 1954), vol. 1, 653–54, cited in Jameson, *The Prison-house of Language,* 54.

[34] Ibid., 55.

[35] Ibid., 60.

[36] Ibid., 60–61.

[37] As Eisenstein describes it, "the collision between shots"; see, for example, *The Montage Principle: Eisenstein in New Cultural and Critical Contexts,* ed. Jean Antoine-Dunne and Paula Quigley (Amsterdam: Rodopi, 2004), which relates Eisenstein's principle of montage to broader aspects of a poststructural apprehension of texts and films, and could be extended to gardens.

[38] Jump-cutting defamiliarizes the viewer by jumping to the next scene before the previous scene has been played out in the way that would be expected in conventional film or theater.

[39] Goldsworthy, *Time,* 96.

[40] Judith Collins, Introduction, in Andy Goldsworthy, *Midsummer Snowballs* (London: Thames & Hudson, 2001), 9–10.

[41] Robert Sherwood, "Viktor Shklovsky and the Development of Early Formalist Theory on Prose Literature," in *Russian Formalism: A Collection of Articles and Texts in Translation,* ed. Stephen Bann and John E. Bowlt (Edinburgh: Scottish Academic Press, 1973), 36.

[42] Shklvosky's "Potebnja," cited in Ejxenbaum, "Theory of the Formal Method," 14.

[43] Shklovsky, cited in Eichenbaum, "The Theory of the 'Formal Method,'" 114, my italics.

[44] G. Vinokur, quoted in Krystyna Pomorska, *Russian Formalist Theory and Its Poetic Ambiance* (The Hague: Mouton, 1968), 25.

[45] Andy Goldsworthy, *Andy Goldsworthy: A Collaboration with Nature* (New York: Harry N. Abrams, 1990), no page numbers.

[46] "Damp sand pressed into tree trunk difficult to stick several collapses took all day," 1999, in Goldsworthy, *Time,* 123.

[47] Viktor Shklovsky, *Zoo, or Letters Not about Love* (Elmwood Park, IL: Dalkey Archive Press, 2001), 23.

[48] Shklovsky's "Theory of Prose," cited in Jameson, *The Prison-house of Language,* 70.

[49] Andy Goldsworthy talking to Kenneth Baker in Andy Goldsworthy, *Wall at Storm King* (London: Thames & Hudson, 2000), 19.

[50] Roland Barthes, "The Death of the Author," in Roland Barthes, *Image, Music, Text* (New York: Hill and Wang, 1977), 148.

[51] Roman Jakobson cited in Ejxenbaum, "The Theory of the Formal Method," (In Ladislav Matejka and Krystyna Pomorska (Eds), Readings in Russian Poetics: Formalist and Structuralist Views. Cambridge, Mass.: The MIT Press, 1971), 3.

[52] Miranda Strickland-Constable, "Beginnings," in Goldsworthy, *Hand to Earth,* 20.

[53] Goldsworthy, Frontispiece, in Goldsworthy, *Hand to Earth.*

[54] Jameson, *The Prison-house of Language,* 81.

[55] Simon Schama, "The Stone Gardener: A Land Artist Comes to Lower Manhattan," *The New Yorker,* 22 September 2003, 126–32, 130. (This article has subsequently become an "official interpretation," to use Juan Pablo Bonta's term, through its republication in Andy Goldsworthy's *Passage*).

[56] Ibid., 132.

[57] Goldsworthy, *Hand to Earth,* 108.

[58] Ernst Bloch, "A Philosophical View of the Detective Novel," cited in Anthony Vidler, *The Architectural Uncanny: Essays in the Modern Unhomely* (Cambridge, MA: MIT Press, 1992), 3.

[59] Juan Pablo Bonta, *An Anatomy of Architectural Interpretation* (Barcelona: Gustavo Gili, 1975), 57.

[60] Ibid., 67.

[61] Cynthia Davidson, "Irish Hunger Memorial" *Architectural Record* 7 (2003): 102–5, 104.

[62] Robert Maxwell, "Approaching the Void: Can the Tragic Appear in Architecture?" *Architectural Design (The Tragic in Architecture)* 70, no. 5 (2000): 8–14, 11.

[63] René Magritte, quoted in Suzi Gablik, *Magritte.* London: Thames and Hudson, World of Art Series edition, 1985. p.11.

[64] Ibid.

[65] Jameson, *The Prison-house of Language,* 51.

Contemporary Garden Aesthetics, Creations and Interpretations

Contemporary Garden Aesthetics, Creations and Interpretations

Contemporary Garden Aesthetics, Creations and Interpretations

Contemporary Garden Aesthetics, Creations and Interpretations

Cardada by Paolo Burgi: The Experience of the Gaze

Massimo Venturi Ferriolo

Man, by beginning with Nature, which is for him the source of all stimuli, renders himself spiritual.
—G. W. F. Hegel, *Lessons in the Philosophy of History*

The Artist and Nature: The Interpreter of Place

The artist has been called upon to interpret a site with a vast horizon, where the power of the gaze extends into the far distance (Fig. 1). Cardada is sheer poetry, an expression of art in its highest form, which lends force to the imagination through its arrangement of the elements that make up the visible.

The eye, as it sweeps over the landscape, takes in the primal beginnings of nature in the outline of the mountains, in the burgeoning life of its plants, in the sensitive, instinctive life of the animals that leave faint traces of their passing in the earth and snow, in the flow of waters, in its vast visible expanses, and in the silences and sounds that nourish our idea of the infinite spaces of nature, our memory of the imaginary (Fig. 2). Its outline takes shape before the observer's eyes in all of its aspects—tangible, concrete, distant—hovering between immanence and transcendence in the space of our thoughts, an idealized natural order in which we are no longer participants but spectators.

The eye also grasps where nature has been "humanized" and order has been imposed upon its chaos, canceling the deep abyss that the poet explores through landscape, creating two levels of observation: two profound superficies. The whole unfolds during the arc of a day, ending in the luminous beam of artificial light that protracts itself into the night, illuminating the path of Bürgi's *landscape promontory*.

The span of our lives—according to a pre-Socratic fragment—is as the duration of a single day with our eyes turned toward the light (Fig. 3).[1] It is this light that permits us to project our gaze through space, the panorama of the veiled majesty of the visible world. Light is the totality of the world; without light and without the human eye the cosmos would not be visible but invisible, and hence nonexistent. It could not even be depicted (Fig. 4). Light and the power of sight have the same

1. *The Large Horizon* (photo: Massimo Venturi Ferriolo)
2. *Idea of the infinite spaces of Nature* (photo: Massimo Venturi Ferriolo)

divine origins, as is suggested by the Greek word *thea*—light, the luminous goddess of a thousand names, is translatable into landscape forms, aspects of vision. Light is the indispensable medium that allows us to see landscapes and grasp their limitless visibility, it embraces the invisible; the profound capacity of the gaze is the source of our aesthetic formation, grounded in both myth and history.

At Cardada we discover, in the foreground, two levels of knowledge linked to our sense of sight. Up above, in the context of a broader panorama, is Cimetta with its *geological observatory,* where we may study the history of nature and the geological materials that form the foundations of the earth and the abode of man in proximity to the divine, the place (*ethos*) of Heraclitus and the *visible and flowing theos* of Plutarch (Fig. 5).

The majesty of the visible world testifies to the activity over millennia of the diligent constructor of dwelling places; it reveals mankind's landscapes and their ethics, beginning in the deep well of the past when we were born into an environment hostile to our survival. Mankind, like all other animals, is an element of nature, but not armed with specialized tools or dependent upon a specific environment. An animal can flourish only in its natural habitat, whereas mankind can and indeed must construct the places for inhabiting an abode. Construct and inhabit. Inhabit and construct. Creating and sojourning in a specific place represent parallel activities.[2] This activity is incessant; continually transforming, the world belongs to the human order of things, as was underlined by Giambattista Vico when he wrote: "Proceed: so that first there was the wilderness, then villages, next cities, and finally the academies."[3] Each phase represents a different mode of inhabiting the world.[4] By adapting the environment to their needs, humans create their own landscape: an eternal construction site devoted to the project of building their world.

This project and its ecological prerequisites are visible from the *landscape promontory*—the history of the landscape, of mankind, and of the spirit, expressed in the form that infuses these materials of the demiurge. The two levels open onto a third with a dual and multiple contemporaneity, onto the notions of transformation with its issues, the architecture, historical places, and places untouched by history. This completes our vision of the world, rendering it *definitive* in form: the universe of the visible, the totality of the cosmos symbolically enclosed in the *logo,* with names assigned to places from the summit to the valley in this landscape—Cimetta, Cardada, and the city of Locarno (Fig. 6).

3. Ray of light (photo: Massimo Venturi Ferriolo)
4. Luminous Whole of the World (photo: Massimo Venturi Ferriolo)

We will not focus on "what is a landscape," but on the manner and way in which landscapes are as they are, asking ourselves exactly what their significance is today. *De-finire* (defining-finishing) would then signify: to find the place and bring it to fruition, to enter into the landscapes. In this way the unfolding of events discloses its relationships, the "being in the world" of creator and project. *Occurring,* in fact, is a mode determined by the presence of things and their relationships. Places and regions, proximities and distances, states of mind and ambiences: in the unfolding of events all these elements form part of a specific, predetermined unity, a univocal image. The key moments in the composition of places, of

visible entities, are at once univocal and multiple. They make up the reality that presents itself to the gaze in its immediacy and its distance. A boundless visibility. The spectator can grasp the relationships in the unfolding, and perceive by means of the gaze all that belongs to the present age, to life *now,* as hidden or evident in the forms of landscape. At the same time the spectator can grasp the tradition and the space of one's own life through the study of the outward aspects of a place.[5]

The gaze presumes the existence of a stage, a spectacle, a visual horizon, and its object is the universe encompassed by vision, a world composed of images with their functions and formative levels, capturing the *web of events,* its unfolding in the landscape and its multiple plots. In this context the sense of sight, the spectacle, and the appearance of things reflect, in their

5. Visibility and Knowledge (photo: Massimo Venturi Ferriolo)
6. Ascent to Cardada (photo: Massimo Venturi Ferriolo)

rich language, the power of the gaze and demand the capacity to observe the contingent. Herein lies the true excellence of the landscape artist, capable of foreseeing as if one already had in mind the complete story of the spectacle from beginning to end.

The intelligibility of the whole in a single glance is the essence of the project of our world—visible and hence comprehensible. It exposes itself to our view in its entirety. The gaze leads to knowledge, and from there to judgment, to discernment. The act of looking demands attention, an *attentio, tensio, tendere ad* ("reaching out for") in the present, a present marked by the simultaneity of that which is, that which was, and that which will be. The future, in its relationship with the already existing, is *Aus-bildung* and lies in the landscape, in the formation of a consciousness, a propositional wisdom.

The constant tension of the present is the indispensable condition for an entity to manifest itself to us over time or in time. We distinguish between that which "not yet is," that which "is now," and that which "is no longer," because we reach out for a power that *attracts* us and unveils reality: the eternal. We are gripped by the place and by a creative emotion (*Ergriffenheit*) that sends through us an electric current, the magnetic charge needed to act. The origin of every work of art, the experience of divine harmony, the principle of every artistic activity lies in the *originative tension* that is the source of every form of poetics.

To this originative force generated by tension we must add a state of mind, a *Stimmung* or *spiritual tension*. In this way we may realize the interaction between subject and object, to borrow the words of Rosario Assunto, who wrote that the relationship man–nature is configured as "a modality of the subject–object rapport in its most sublime and definitive moment."[6] The object becomes subjectified, the subject recognizes itself in the object, and they become commingled; thus we arrive at the objectifying of the human spirit, and the expression of nature. The landscape becomes a place destined in the final analysis for contemplation, a work of art, the space in which a conjunction between ethics and aesthetics can take place.

In this way the original relationship that existed between harmony and the divine becomes visible, immortal, constantly present, the Platonic cornerstone that, as we already said, Plutarch defined as *visible and flowing*—existing outside of time while at the same time forming part of it. We may also view this as a reaching out for the infinite and the eternal, while at the same time looking back to rediscover a dimension of the romantic *Sehnsucht*.

In the constant tension of the present, the subject *subjugates* him- or herself to the

7. The uniform tension of the Present (photo: Massimo Venturi Ferriolo)

object (I–landscape), to nature, or more precisely to the rediscovery of the oneness into which one is absorbed (Fig. 7). The artist does not begin with the self, but with the mastering of the divine within, with enthusiasm, intense spiritual emotion, with one's openness to the world; the poet is inspired by the *visible,* by a god, and therefore is consumed with *enthusiasm*.[7] The artist does not, however, project ideas in an arbitrary, subjective manner; he or she is responding to an appeal that springs from the creative tension within: "Being the subject of the poet, of the artist—in the sense of being-subjected (*subiectum*)—sends down its roots of being-outside-of-oneself."[8] The eternal, or that which exists outside of time and is the condition of time, the necessary tension within which—and only within which—we may distinguish the "not-yet" from the "no-longer" and from the "now," is the sphere wherein we may explore our relationship with that which was in the beginning.

The artist becomes detached from the self and immersed in the originative harmony that constitutes the prerequisite of inspiration: a specific state completely free of all intentions, the true spirit enrobed in subjective elements, in *Stimmungen,* in states of mind and spiritual tensions. This produces the constitutive equilibrium that is the preliminary condition of creativity, which makes the spiritual experience universal. The spirit is made world through a merging of the natural and the spiritual— the world as an open totality upon which we may turn our gaze. The distinction between internal and external disappears in a dimension that is at once totally human, completely spiritual, natural: a dimension that we have lost and can find again only through a renewed capacity to see.

The spirit pervades Cardada—living reality and myth. With the dizzying verticality of its horizon the site offers a perfect vision of the whole, allowing us to understand its interwoven myths, to discover the connections between interlacing stories, where the *occurring* represents the true subject-object of a poetic form. Art has at its disposition different levels of themes that do not form a single evolution, but are visible above and beyond the limit posed by the horizon. It offers the aesthetic experience of visibility with its multiple levels of knowledge, beginning with the original forms of the world and their unfolding in time, where the history of nature gives way to the history of mankind and our modes of comprehension.

The world has as many forms as the numbers of eyes that can contemplate it, forms arranged and offered to the cognition. The constellation of landscapes has well-defined borders within which man may accumulate the knowledge linked to seeing and to the conjoint capacity to distinguish, beginning with the gaze, to observe the forms of a place.

The *eminent visibility of the whole* is an ancient theme. It allows the comprehension of places in their totality and immense complexity. Its horizon is knowledge: to observe is to know. Visibility has two distinct, yet convergent forms: one directed toward a universal, the *theoria,* and the other focused on the particular, the *aisthesis.* This imperative dominates the spectacle that Cardada offers, like a theater in which we find the most skillful presentation of the visible, through an unadorned arrangement that takes into account events and evaluations through the language of its various elements.

The gaze of the spectator measures distances and horizons that are always new, discovering the deep abyss of nature that is one with history; it explores new possibilities in the time and space delimited by the act of observation. This is the significance of Bürgi's *Project for the Reclamation of the Territory.* It exposes the possibility of modifying the environment that surrounds mankind, a faculty upon which our survival depends: to act upon nature, foresee, make provisions for, to plan, arrange, and organize its many elements, is the mode of being and acting of one accustomed to exploiting possibilities.

This project represents the expression of a desire. Its gaze is focused on both the past and the future, on a world that may be transformed, on the reality of the possible. To reclaim a territory signifies reappropriating that which has been lost or dispersed: it is mankind's battle against oblivion, against despoilment, against the loss of our roots. Without memory there is no future. The antique lessons of history are written in the *diffuse aestheticity* of the visible, the source of all learning and formation.

Mankind receives instruction from the immediately visible, and at Cardada an artistic project of immense verticality unfolds in a space with an incalculably vast horizon, a project that organizes a temporal order with sublime lightness, guiding the gaze of the spectator through a succession of forms unveiled and made manifest in the totality of the visual space. Our desire to impose order on chaos by means of an art made up of hidden forms is thus realized, in an example of landscaping that does not conclude with the project itself, but that draws the spectator into a continual process of discovery and rediscovery, transforming us once again into a participant: a student of landscape with an informed eye.

Information, or *Bildung,* springs from *Bild* (picture), from the elaboration of the visible elements required for the *Ausbildung* (formation) of the spectator, in a gradual process with a beginning and an end, but one that is completely open to the range of human possibilities and to the representation in the imagination of worlds both real and possible. At work here is the representation of human action and the consequent reflections: an ethic of contemplation.

As Thomas Mann affirmed, deep is the well of the past, too deep to sound, but the prospect for the future is not unfathomable if one respects certain rules of behavior, for the world exists with mankind as its arbiter. This is why the study of the different threads of unfolding events is so revelatory. It awakens the capacity to observe the contingent reality, a reality subject to transformation, and to gather the positive with the negative, the beautiful with the ugly, the good with the evil.

Mankind, as the constructor of places and the dweller therein, can foresee the entire unfolding of this action, as if the creator had the entire plot of the spectacle—the landscape project—complete in one's mind. Underlying this is an ethical assumption consonant with the place, which must always respect the mythical signification of *ethos.* The faculty to see ahead is foresight itself and manifests a clear link between foreseeing and the knowledge acquired by the experience of acting, of casting one's gaze over a landscape. The object of the vista is the *visible.* It may be expressed through the discourse of a language that captures the reality perceptible to the eyes, parallel to the myth and to the eternal present—*divine* in the Plutarchian sense.

The object of the narrative is the world of action, mankind with its project of incommensurate visibility. The poetry and the representation provide mankind's vision of the landscape of the *theatron,* the scenography of events, the gaze focused upon the cosmos to grasp the complexity of its forms. Thus the picture, the *Bild,* contains the plot of the action—that which has happened, the events, their taking place in the landscape, an ever-present unfolding. The ordering of events becomes the true foundation of the panorama of Cardada, of the arrangement of the visible and its language springing from the depths of nature. The story is myth, revealed to our sight by the composition of events that stimulate thought and reflection (*Ausbildung*) born of our astonishment at the hidden miracle. The gaze that pierces the horizon encompasses all: places, events, music, harmony, song, thought, reflection, and playfulness. A poetics of events is traced, stimulated by the emotion arising from a sublime comprehension of the fascinating mystery of the sacredness of place.

The sacredness of the eternal present is

8. The woodland path (photo: Massimo Venturi Ferriolo)

sublimated by the project through its connection with the myths and events that constitute the elements in its ordered unfolding on three levels of the gaze. Let us traverse these levels, let us look at the images (*Bilden*) and comprehend them by studying and evaluating every one of its particular aspects, beginning with that which has been realized and that which has not. For example, the point of departure at Orselina with its cableway, symbol of the climb toward the vast and dynamic temporal spaces of Cardada, was to have been marked by a *laminar cascade.* Thus a beautiful work of art would have signaled the beginning of an itinerary, an exploration in space and time, with its sounds—the flow of water marking the flow of life and time in its consecutive eras and different levels; levels marking an evolution in stages, laminars, thin layers that are the formations of time. This cascade, which would have constituted an initiation into knowledge, prepared the gaze, stimulated

curiosity and enchantment, was never realized, perhaps because of the modern world's baffled incomprehension of beauty.

The symbolic departure point here is a place consisting of many places with superimposed levels: Locarno, Cardada, Cimetta. The first question posed by the landscape architect must be: "What can a place on multiple levels offer?". Of necessity this forms the theoretical cornerstone of the architect's research, the own point of departure. Cardada offers a horizon, space for discovery face to face with nature and landscape, an entity that is divided today but that was united in a distant, mythic past, long before the present divorce between nature and history.

9. The playful itinerary (photo: Massimo Venturi Ferriolo)

10. Communication for Knowledge (photo: Massimo Venturi Ferriolo)

The space of discovery, as already mentioned, is encompassed in the breadth and depth of the horizon. We must discover what can be perceived beyond the visible: the appearances that allow us to grasp what is hidden from our view. Phenomena can reveal hidden things. From this arises the need to "sublimate that which is" in relationship to the genius loci, as Paolo Bürgi wrote in his preliminary reflections, *Progetti Proposte Interventi* (Projects Proposals Actions): a *raising* supported by the catching (*Ergriffenheit*) of the *mysterium tremendum et fascinans* emanating from the place and from the primal, mythic font of creativity. The necessity for a dialogue with places seen from predetermined points of view and animated by a sequence of propositions is affirmed: to see = to recognize = to respect = to understand = to know = to form = *Ausbildung* = *Bild* = plot = events = time = depth = past = unfolding = when = geological periods = formation of the earth's crust = the Insubres line = to see = to recognize = geology = ecology = levels = beyond the horizon.

This dialogue with the horizon produces degrees of knowledge linked to the act of seeing, reveals its evolution and poses questions regarding the contents of nature. It becomes the ideating concept for itineraries created to reveal a methodology for investigation, a progression forward and beyond, with the goal of in-depth research (*methodos*) conducted to disclose the winding ravines and lines of nature. The journey goes forward under the banner of fear and respect—that ancient, reverent sense of wonder that will allow us to recuperate the "peripheries," spaces that have been degraded by tourism, and hence to recover the pristine, natural landscape in its most essential sense.

Itineraries

Cardada has three itineraries, departing from the arrival point of the cableway and traversing as many concepts: the sun, the landscape, and the sense of play. The actor is nature—subject and object with the visitor—nature that unites and diversifies everything in its manifold aspects: plant, animal, and mineral. Three levels can be reached in succession by these itineraries, from the lowest to the highest or vice versa, and the observer is completely free to choose, with different options at one's disposal linked by the common denominator—their point of origin.

Emerging from the cable car we find ourselves in the square, where originally there stood a fountain carved from a single tree trunk—symbol of time and of life.[9] There we may choose between two paths of knowledge, each leading to a different level; to the left lies Cardada with its *landscape promontory,* while to the right is the *via del sole,* the "strong link" that brings us to Cimetta and the *geological observatory.* These two itineraries form an integral part of the *woodland path* (Fig. 8).

Across the chosen space of the mountain runs the *play path,* which allows us to "discover by playing." Accessible to all, it

11. Contemplative break (photo: Massimo Venturi Ferriolo)
12. Aspects of a pleasurable discovery (photo: Massimo Venturi Ferriolo)

unfurls around Cardada. A marvelous idea animates this itinerary: the exploration of a wild forest that has become a woodland, no longer alien but hospitable, which welcomes and teases the visitor with the possibility of learning, beginning with its dense plant life: "We discover an alternation of different types of groves—beech, fir, larch, hazelnut, birch—which trigger different sensations—warmth-coolness, darkness-light, dense-transparent, dry-damp. Nature and perception: through significant experiences that strike the five senses—colors, scents, tastes, sounds, textures (Jorge Luis Borges' 'partial and already lost echoes')—a sensorial pleasure towards nature is stimulated."[10] Here the power of the sense of playfulness and its capacity to reveal the world are confirmed (Fig. 9).

The games scattered along the path encourage us to rediscover forgotten sensations, unveiling a sound- and light-spangled landscape made up of darks and brights, colors and reflections, still pictures and pictures in movement. Communication via the simplest of instruments—fun-house mirrors, the playground swing—is aimed at the rediscovery, the reappropriation of the senses of touch, hearing, taste, smell, and, of course, sight, *the* sense par excellence (Fig. 10).

The sensations received through the eyes are aesthetic (*aisthesis*) and are the messages that we prefer, because "the sight furnishes us with more knowledge than the other senses and reveals to us many differences"[11]—the infinite variety and diversity of the perceptible world (Fig. 11). The real and the ideal forms of nature stand out in all their splendor, sensorially complete, each with its name and "membership card" pertaining to its final form: the particulars of a universal idea. Once again the concept of embracing with the gaze includes all the significations of seeing, "the most acute of the sensations that we can receive through the body."[12]

The role of the body in its broad, fundamental sense is reevaluated and assigned a place within the landscape and nature, for without the body these could not exist. Sensory reality stimulates reflection, which in turn is tied to movement, and in particular to the movement of the body in space. Things appear in relation to the movements of the observer, in a choral action that springs from the rapport between mind, body, and place. To play reveals itself as a mental exercise in addition to its purely pleasurable aspect: a *re-creative* bridgehead of discovery (Fig. 12).

Thus creativity, stimulated by the senses and above all by the sight, receives a vital impulse. Sight is the most precious of our five senses and is connected to light, in both myth and reality: it elaborates images. The imagination—*phantasia*—takes its name from *phaos* or light "because without light it is not possible to see."[13] As Jean Starobinski wrote:

> Innate in perception itself, intermingled with the operations of the memory ... imagination is much more than a faculty for evoking images that transcend the world of our perceptions: it is the capacity to discard, in virtue of which we depict things that are far away and detach ourselves from things that are present and real. From this [arises] the ambiguity that we find everywhere: the imagination, when it anticipates and foresees, serves action, it shows how the realizable might be configured even before it is realized. In this first sense, the imagination collaborates with the "function of the real," in as much as our adaptation to the world requires that we exit from the present instant and leave behind us the data of the immediate world, to take possession—in thought—of a future that is at first indistinct.[14]

This function, we can affirm, is central to a poetic process that manifests itself gradually, and in a way that is both aware and unconscious, beginning with the *play path* as its re-creative antechamber.

The visible belongs to the mutable world of the sensations, to nature that is in continual transformation that creates and re-creates itself. Nature is the birth of "becoming," as is comprised in the meaning of *physis,* the elemental term from which all things spring.[15] This mutable world feeds the imagination through re-creative movement.

We are now ready for the games of the imagination prepared by the artist: for a process of discovery that bifurcates with the two paths that lie before us, two roads of knowledge. The *geological path* is directed upward and appears more universal because it concerns the origins, the structure and composition, and the history of the earth. On the same plane, the even more universal and at the same time specific *ecological path* lays bare the relationship between living things and their environment, enucleating mankind and our landscape as far back as their primal origins. Let us first direct our steps upward, to the *origin* of things, following our natural impulse to discover the originating principle and the key moment from which all was derived. *Origo* is birth.

The *via del sole* as originally conceived by Paolo Bürgi has not been entirely realized; what we find is an itinerary based on the idea of a strong link between the entrance—initially imagined as a red wall, a rectangle following the inclining slope—and a yellow disk at the summit symbolizing the sun and guiding our eyes toward the light to discover the landscape and to read it. "Along the path which links the cableway station to that of the chairlift is a *trait d'union* realized in stone: 24 fragments of

13. A glimpse at a place of encounter (photo: Massimo Venturi Ferriolo)
14. Path to the garden of Time and Origins (photo: Paolo Bürgi)

15. Gaze at the garden (photo: Paolo Bürgi)
16. The Platform of Cimetta, the garden of origins (photo: Paolo Bürgi)

roughly polished stone on which have been incised signs that are references to the past, and hence to movement. This passage is intended to serve as a stimulus, to guide persons, to arouse a certain curiosity (materials: stone, cement, color). A pedestrian link between two stations, conceived as an important connecting element and realized as a surface of stone laid on the ground. On either side is nature, intact."[16] This sustains the notion of signs of the past, traced on the ground. At its origin is the curiosity that leads us to discover an "intact nature."

Here begins the *woodland path,* a new link replacing the initial idea of the *via del sole,* which winds through the verdant forest and conducts us into the very heart of nature. As we walk along this path we cross a stand of fir trees, pass by a small church, and continue to the chair lift. Along the way, through the birch trees one may glimpse a clearing, a space that extends an irresistible invitation to pause, to encounter people and nature in a meeting that may be transformed at any moment into a celebration, the possibility of inventing new, yet antique "natural" relationships. Bürgi originally intended to cut into the hillside and create a level surface of exposed rock, a constellation of potential activities (Fig. 13).

The *Geological Observatory* of Cimetta

Remember that thou magnify his work, which men behold. Every man may see it; man may behold it afar off.
—Job 36:24–25
Hearken unto this, O Job: stand still, and consider the wondrous works of God.
—Job 37:14

Once we arrive at Cimetta, the artist has drawn for us a path that leads directly to a new space with a limitless horizon, where majestic mountains rise and inspire untrammeled thought, knowledge that soars far beyond their luminous range. This is a garden of concentrated diffuse aestheticity (Fig. 14).

A platform—nothing more than a thin disk of reinforced concrete, the most contemporary of materials—poised on the summit and traversed by rocks eroded with time, juts out on two sides into the void, hanging over the valleys, and as we step onto this platform we find ourselves in a *geological observatory,* a *garden of time* floating over the surrounding landscape: a well whose almost unfathomable depths we may sound (Fig. 15).

The *geological observatory* of Cimetta is a garden that offers an invitation to scientific reflection and to the contemplation of the natural and human events encompassed in the gaze. It invites the visitor to study with respect, to observe by looking attentively, to *preserve* or to *store,* to act as the custodian of the event, of that which has occurred and could repeat itself: an important, *mythic* event, a phenomenon that has taken place. This is the discovery of the unfolding of events on which landscape

17. Deep is the Well of Past (photo: Massimo Venturi Ferriolo)

thinking is based, entering into the landscape to understand the series of events that created it. One *contemplates,* with concentration and admiration, meditating on what has happened, and enquiring into geological origins to understand the composition and history of the earth's crust—its geological periods. The beginning of all visible and invisible things enters into a system of coordinates that begins from the platform of the *garden of origins* (Fig. 16).

Railings and contours help us to orient ourselves. "Interlacings and inlays of rock visible on the horizon introduce geology and geological time. A line drawn on the sheet of stone invokes the exceptional nature of the Insubres line, visible to the satellite's eye and made perceptible from the observatory. It fascinates rather than instructs."[17]

The consequences of this fascinating vista are immense, open. Knowledge draws nourishment from the sense of

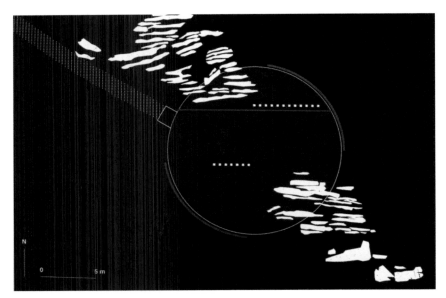

18. The Insubric line (drawing: Paolo Bürgi)

wonder and is strengthened by the formative nature of the garden, with its representation of images that encourage a continual interplay between the intellect and the fantasy. The aesthetic quality of the garden, its formal arrangement, gathers within its panoramic view (*Ausblick*) a truth waiting to be revealed, one that demands an imaginative capacity (*Einbildungskraft*). Its openness to the world, its contents and its symbols are an invitation to reflection. Thought springs from admiration, from the marveling fascination of the gaze.

The platform at Cimetta represents a *new garden,* an original and wholly contemporary form that proposes a design that goes beyond classical schemas without, however, abandoning them; instead it inserts them into a more up-to-date prospect of discovery of the horizon and beyond, surpassing every limit of depth and distance.[18] Existence and a new aesthetic experience in the art of landscape and the garden commingle in this space of limitless visibility: a profound reflection on art and history with a clear sense of the forms of the place and their evolution (Fig. 17).

Let us enter the garden and read its manifest and hidden geometries. The first element that captures our gaze is the panorama, the *Bild,* the entire picture of this ample and complex spectacle: the *one thing distinct in itself* described by Hölderin.

There is an orderly sequence to the spectacle, which begins with the discovery of the panorama and with the immediate relationship between the name and the thing that orients our gaze, disclosing the identity of the places and the mountains. The word is *divine,* which comes from the visible and allows things to appear, and is *true,* like myth; it is the thing itself, the mode and the space in which the thing presents itself as such.[19] Things become real and living thanks to their names, which allows us to recognize the place where we find ourselves with respect to other places. They orient the spectator in relation to visible reality by identifying its forms, its particular places, and this is an important step toward their disclosure.

A hermeneutics of place reveals their soul: a spiritual entity to be evoked, but an entity couched in a difficult and complex language that needs to be interpreted: an art of the place with an artist able to grasp and explain its human roots. Every place possesses a soul that can be revealed by the artist.[20] This is the sense of the garden, a space for origins and discoveries.

The *geological observatory* of Cimetta "is situated above a much trafficked area of the Alpine chain, where it is possible to observe the geological processes of two distinct regions; these processes are perhaps not very obvious, but their appearing before our eyes, their discovery can stir our imaginations, sustaining emotion and humility in the face of geological time and space."[21] The Insubres line, which descends from the Marobbia Valley and continues toward the region of the Centovalli, crosses our garden, a red line that cuts the circle in two, a circle that allows us to scan the periods in the evolution of the African and

European tectonic plates (Fig. 18).

The two sections of the circle represent geological periods in the formation of the panorama and are of different widths that reflect their relative ages. In these spaces symbols are arranged in a temporal sequence:

The rocks arranged on the platform of the geological observatory of Cimetta come from every area included in the panorama; the processes that generated the Alpine mountain chain had their beginnings in the Jurassic Age (about 195 million years ago) and are still active today. Its uplifting was the result of the corrugation and superpositioning of layers of rock often several thousands of meters thick. The Insubric line traversing the circle from east to west represents the scar of the collision between the African plate to the south and the European plate to the north. The rocks located to the south of the line date to periods preceding the formation of the Alps, around 300 million years ago, and were practically unaffected by the Alps' formation. In contrast, enormous pressure and heating metamorphosed the rocks situated to the north of the line: most of these are just a few tens of millions of years old. 1–7: samples of rock

19. From trilobite to dinosaur (photo: Massimo Venturi Ferriolo)
20. From esquiseto to Man (photo: Massimo Venturi Ferriolo)

originating from sites south of the Insubres line; 8–19: rock samples from sites lying to the north of the Insubres line.[22]

The platform is therefore divided symbolically into two sections. The one positioned over the hemisphere of the African plate is dark gray in color and much broader due to its greater age. This plate was formed about 300 million years ago, and its rock samples are located a greater distance from the Insubres line because they are so ancient. The section of the platform hovering over the European plate is lighter in color, being more recent and closer in time to the formation of the

21. To the landscape promontory (photo: Massimo Venturi Ferriolo)
22. The capability of the gaze (photo: Massimo Venturi Ferriolo)

Alps and to the Insubres line, the period that produced the "young" rocks that are arranged on this side, close to the line of demarcation. The Insubres line is a red streak crossing the disk.

The samples of *rocks on the horizon* reflect the specific depth of each: not only the tectonics of their structure and composition (integrated into the project and explained in the panels posted on the railings), but their movements, coordinated with the places of their formation and with their use by the demiurge to construct dwellings capable of defying time. A history of materials for construction and decoration, materials of both utility and beauty like that of the stone itself, with its stratified millennia here provides fuel for our imaginations. That is the lime for the furnaces of antiquity, stones for the churches of Rome and Zurich, pavements, columns, and chimneys, the Church of Saint Paul without the Walls, the millstones of oil presses, *beole* (translator's note: a fine-grained, homogenous stone with a high quartz content), the decorations of castles, the marble of the collegiate chapter of Bellinzona and of the Kunsthaus of Zurich, the exteriors and interiors of the post offices of Bellinzona and the banks of Milan—all are legible from the suspended platform of our garden. With the power of the gaze we can grasp the occurrence of that "one thing distinct in itself" that is the particularity of specific places in a global panoramic context.

This specificity stands out within a broad picture representative of the formation of a particular *cosmic* geographic area, its evolution over incalculable periods of time. We have come in fact a great distance and may ask ourselves, like Thomas Mann: "Where do the principles of human civilization lie? How antique are they? ...When we speak of 'antiquity' we mean for the most part the Greek and Roman empires and therefore a world that, by comparison, is of the freshest modernity."[23]

Let us look back on the *events in time,* starting with the possibilities offered to our vision-knowledge by this garden, going back 400 million years. The story of nature begins, of life with its process of becoming. We discover that nature is not simply a picture, but an uninterrupted flow of visible things, *divine:* eternity. A temporality beyond our habitual perception of the limited time span of man's experience since antiquity manifests itself in all of its density, as thick as the kilometers of certain rock layers.

The question is once again, as always: How antique? What was there before antiquity? What events characterized the cosmos long ago? The roots emerge of the numinous *mysterium tremendum et fascinans* of the sacred that inspires our reverent astonishment, fear, and respect as we reconsider today our use of these ancient materials and reflect on issues of transformation, globalization, the ethical-aesthetic identity of places: on movement, and on time.

The line of time crosses the garden with its symbols of the slow but constant evolution of life. Nine stages are incised in stone, separated from one another by the epochal spaces of *occurring,* of that which has taken place: trilobite ... ammonite ... fern ... equiseta ... dinosaur ... ginko ... rat ... birch ... man. We also know that there are periods in which "nothing happened," "moments" composed of millions of years (Figs. 19 and 20). Paleontology, prehistory, legend and myth, mountains and history are all displayed for those wishing to learn: "He who saw the depths, [even unto] the foundations of the earth: he who learned everything, making himself expert in all; Gilgamesh saw the depths, [even unto] the foundations of the earth, in everything he reached complete knowledge! He saw secret things, discovered hidden things, he spoke of the legends of the time before the Flood."[24]

The *Landscape Promontory*

"Nostalgia for the Present"

At that precise moment the man said to himself:
What would I not give
to be with you in Iceland
under the grand immobile daytime
and share this now
like sharing music
or the taste of fruit.
At that precise moment
the man was together with her in Iceland.

—Jorge Luis Borges[25]

Let us return then to Cardada and take the *woodland path* in the opposite direction to reach the *landscape promontory*, preparing ourselves for the contemplation of a new horizon (Figs. 21 and 22). As we walk along the footbridge of titanium that passes over the trunks and branches of the forest, we find signs of the mythic abyss of existence from which the cosmos drew its

23. Gaze into the world (photo: Massimo Venturi Ferriolo)

origins traced upon the paving stones (Fig. 23). The *hidden miracle* is incised in the stones that we tread upon to reach the platform of the horizon, a trampoline into the past that is inserted in the present. Before reaching this landscape, this history and culture, however, we must plunge into the primordial, into a time before the geological origins of Cimetta.

The Semitic civilization has left a singular image of the *abyss,* which in the ancient city of Ugarit was a goddess when the earth was still deserted, veiled in shadows, and without order.[26] At that time: "No blessed dwelling place, no temple for the gods in a holy place had yet been constructed. No cane-brake had yet sprung up, no tree was yet created. No brick had yet been produced, a mould to make bricks had not yet been created. No house had yet been built, no city constructed. On the face of the earth there was only water."[27]

The echoes of an *incipit* from the primal waters of life had not yet completely faded away, like the feminine presence of the abyss, the autogenerative *physis* and universal mother. This profound echo is present in the spirit of the artist: "Three billion years ago, during the dawn of life, there was a torrid heat in the atmosphere, which contained no oxygen but plenty of gases such as methane and ammonia. As these were whirling and mixing, they united to form more complex structures which enriched the seas. What actually sparked the beginning of life remains a mystery to this day."[28]

Physis, the totality of the cosmos, draws its lymph and language from water, from the generating principle contained in the verb *phyo.* It indicates the *source* or *font of all things,* the *river mouth* or *terminal point,* the *permanent support of all things:* this is water in its quality as substance and matrix. Thales offered this picture of the myth of the origin of the world: *Water is the principal of elements. The cosmos is animated and full of demons.*[29]

Paolo Bürgi takes as his starting point the birth of the first *molecule of DNA* in water, in a study conducted with the biologist Guido Maspoli: "In the primordial seas, something magnificent happened: the development of a DNA molecule. Today we know that DNA contains all the construction plans of living organisms: the shape of leaves, the color of the eyes, the wing span."[30] The subsequent stages then unfolded from the *cell,* the fundamental building block of life, to *tissues* and organs, followed by the *organism-individual,* captured in the leaf of a maple tree or the print of a buzzard's clawed foot: living things such as the maple tree growing beside the footbridge, the ant that crosses it, and the person that walks along it. All are living entities and therefore can generate offspring of the same species, transmitting their parents' DNA to their descendants in a chain that grows ever longer. Thus we arrive at *populations:* "A species consists of groups of individuals, of populations which always remain in the same meadow, the same forest, the same rock or lake, i.e. in the same ecosystem."[31]

The observer is now in possession of knowledge of the *ecosystem* within which every species has its function and every individual exploits the resources offered in a vital rapport between interdependent elements, designed with traces of Leonardo Fibonacci's numerical series. Mankind forms an integral part of a *universe* in which "the Earth is a living system, perhaps even a single organism. Air, water and earth are life itself. For life on Earth, air is as important as the flower to the butterfly, grass to the deer, the snake to the buzzard, the river to trout. We as well belong to this community of creatures."[32]

Now there suddenly opens up before our eyes a horizon composed of places and a culture of extraordinary intensity: a boundless landscape with a double, multiple contemporaneity. Observers arrive fully informed, their imaginations stimulated by the various itineraries traversed; they know that they live in an ecosystem and on a planet that forms part of the universe. They know that they are humans, individuals, living beings subject to a stringent temporality, but that they are also the constructors of landscapes in which their own histories may be read. Here they can cast their gaze over their works and see the final form of the world.

Art, the exercise of our liberty of expression on nature, projects us beyond the limited time span of our individual existence into a present of quality, through the incessant activity of constructing—inhabiting—thinking. The action is simultaneous and continuous: to create and characterize *ethos,* the dwelling place, in a process that approaches perfection through our freedom to act. In this way culture is born, the human world, history, the work of the demiurge, finding its place in the living, visual landscape. The platform of the *landscape promontory* directs our gaze across a panorama that embraces the project of the human world, a heritage at once visible and invisible, material and spiritual, the heritage of every society that exists in a specific place and of which we form an integral part with our ethic values: from *ethos,* the mythic word for *place, dwelling.*

Mankind shapes the living reality: the abode where one dwells, lives, and leaves one's works. Dwelling places are the mirror of our culture, the result of a creative art in a world marked by the presence of the past and present, which receives myth, the memory of antiquity and the acting in the present. This history of the distant past is visible in the aestheticity, that is, in the formal, foreshadowing aspect of sensations.

We, as spectators, therefore can scan, by virtue of the legibility of this limitless landscape, everything that belongs to us, hidden or evident in the forms that lie before us. At the same time we can apprehend the traditions and spaces of our lives through the study of the outward aspect of a place, be it primeval or of our own creation or extraneous to us. The native and the outsider are both engaged spectators to whom these references—designed to prompt the imagination—are addressed.

The discovery of a vast visual horizon also reveals the depth of the well of the past into which we must gaze. It discloses the inspiration of the artist, whose hand is able to impose order on perceptible phenomena: an aesthetic experience that bespeaks a tension in the temporality bound up in the present. Aesthetics—*aisthesis*—is the awareness of phenomena, and perception is the sensory aspect of our *affectivity.*[33]

The eye captures the aestheticity that permeates the landscape, not only its value as a work of art, but also the story that it has to tell, concentrated in the space encompassed by the platform of the *geological observatory,* a story that narrates the profundity of nature, "that which can be seen from the place."[34] The deep well of the past becomes contemporaneous with the

24. The Aesthetics of Promontory (photo: Massimo Venturi Ferriolo)
25. Nature and Art (photo: Massimo Venturi Ferriolo)

observer, because of the sense of wonder created by the poetic art used to describe the visible, an art that, as Giovanni Boccaccio wrote: "*prende origine dal seno di dio e riceve il suo nome dagli effetti*" tied "*all'ammirazione dell'opera di madre natura*" (originates in the bosom of God and takes its name from its effects ... [linked] to the admiration of the works of Mother Nature).[35]

Poetry is the free play of the imagination, unleashed as it contemplates forms—art as a game that is also most pleasingly realized in the ludic itinerary (the *play path*) that traverses the landscape; a manifestation of the creative act, a representation whose goal is to instruct, to display the beauties of the sylvan wilderness, and to promote an awareness of the environment. This is true *beautiful art* in the Kantian sense,[36] appearing in the form of nature regulated by *genius, that natural gift,* the creative faculty innate in the artist that also belongs in the most profound sense to nature. This concept is embodied in the Latin word *ingenium*—"the innate disposition of the spirit *by means of which* nature shapes art."[37] Its inextricable ties with *physis* and the *naturalis proprietas* of the earth, mankind's *ingenium loci,* the particular nature of the terrain and its vegetation, the natural characteristics of a site, allow us to recuperate a tradition that has fallen into oblivion.

This eternally sacred and eternally present tie remains manifest—the temporality of nature that embraces the fleeting nature of human life and is expressive of the tension of the artist. Art projects the ephemeral figure of mankind, that living being, beyond the landscape of time.[38] Space and time therefore open up existence and the aesthetic experience of a tension that makes visible the "before" and the "after," granting us knowledge of the process of becoming within the frame of eternity. It is the tension of the originative harmony of creation unfolding in three acts: not yet (the future), no longer (the past), and now (the present). The past is composed of the memory and impressions left behind by the *occurred,* by "that which has taken place." The present is the theme of a dual and multiple contemporaneity. It contains the past, the present, and the future, constantly present during the unfolding of temporal events in time, within a frame in which events can be chronologically ordered.

The *occurring* is that which "takes place" and reveals its specific, local identity through our reading of it, beginning with the present and projecting toward the past or into the future. Its comprehension requires thought processes that—like landscapes—have no regard for boundaries and focus on places of every form and aspect, testing their depths, entering into their spaces and opening up new perspectives: a powerful gaze like a luminous ray coming from afar that can shed light both on what has happened and on the unknown that is still to come. To enter a place, and discover its tangible and its immaterial contents, signifies abandoning every delimiting ontological definition of the nature of landscape.

26. The Occurring (photo: Massimo Venturi Ferriolo)

Our attention is displaced to the process of occurring, to the content, to the character of places.

As one looks out on the island of Brissago the memory of historical personages is evoked: Stefan George, Graf von Stauffenberg, the Baroness Saint Leger, Franz Liszt. They too form a part of this itinerary without boundaries that can be traversed starting from the platform at Cardada, our trampoline into the past (Fig. 24). On one side, the artist is responding to the demands of the contemporary world for a "new, yet antique" configuration of the landscape that will express the sensibility and spirit of the present time in its relationship with the past and future (Fig. 25). The *occurring* with its many intertwining threads finds expression in Paolo Bürgi's project for Cardada. He reveals to us that which is visible beyond the imaginable, beginning with the creation of the world, followed by the primordial origins of life, up until the modern-day ugliness of Locarno, image and global reality embodied in a place—salvaging tradition (Fig. 26).

Tradition represents neither a turning back nor traditionalism; it is something that belongs to the history of the relationship nature–liberty, which belongs to places and landscapes. Our manner of being, our customs and religion, our relationship with the divine, all of that which characterizes landscape as an environment that includes life and ourselves as individual elements belonging to a given place, our physical and social environment, our real nature and our imaginary one, our culture—all of this is tradition, and landscape in its diffuse aestheticity. All of this is in continual transformation, a dynamic work of art made up of shifting, changing elements, but with fixed sanctuaries from which the history of these mutations may be scanned. All of this is visible within a totality of unfolding events characterized by a dual, multiple contemporaneity. The events of millennia and of centuries all form part of the present picture.

The eye gathers in history, tradition, a notion of place. Every landscape is inseparable from the culture and the community that formed it. Its visibility underlines the succession of events: it offers, therefore, an image without confines for those with the patience and desire to peruse it.

The contemplation of a landscape is more than an aesthetic experience, more than an end in itself, an image of abstract beauty. It embodies a profound and universal truth for philosophers, architects, men of letters, and lovers of beauty, but above all for the common man who lives and acts daily within the context of a specific landscape. Let us embrace the ethics of contemplation. Let us observe what has been made and done. Let us scrutinize the past and the present: let us read what a place has to tell us and judge those who constructed it. Let us then make projects for the future, for a potentially better and more desirable world. To project is ideation, desire, deliberation. Let us judge the past and work toward the future.

NOTES

[1] *Antiphons,* DK 87B50.

[2] As Martin Heidegger clearly demonstrates in "Bauen Wohnen Denken" (Darmstadt: Mesch und Raum, 1952, 72 ff. ("Building, Dwelling, Thinking" in Martin Heidegger, *Basic writings from Being and time (1927) to The task of thinking (1964),* edited, with general introd. and introductions to each selection by David Farrell Krell, (New York: Harper & Row, c1977).

[3] Gianbattista Vico, *Principi di scienza nuova d'intorno alla comune natura delle nazioni,* (Napoli: Nella stamperia Muziana a spese di Gaetano, e Steffano Elia, 1744), 239.

[4] As Robert Pogue Harrison noted in *Foreste. L'ombra della civiltà,* (*Forests: The Shadow of Civilization,* [Chicago: University of Chicago Press, 1992]), Italian translation by Giovanna Bettini (Milan: Garzanti, 1992), 269.

[5] On the same theme see Ute Guzzoni, "Landschaften. J'aime les nuages … ," in Ute Guzzoni, *Wege im Denken, Versuche mit und ohne Heidegger,* (Freiburg: Alber, 1990), 8, 25–59.

[6] Rosario Assunto, *Ontologia e teleologia del giardino,* (Milan: Guerini e Associati, 1988), 28.

[7] From the Greek *enthousiasmos,* derived from *enthousiazein* (to be possessed by divinity), which is derived from *entheos* (divinely inspired), composed of *en* (in) and *theos* (god).

[8] Ernesto Grassi, *Arte e mito,* (Naples: La Città del Sole, 1996), 137. This paper owes much to that text, as these pages demonstrate.

[9] With a total lack of sensibility, during the re-landscaping phase the fountain was moved to a new position that seriously compromised the original intentions of the architect, obliterating the message that he wished to convey. This decision betrays the complete absence of an appreciation of landscape as a work of art on the part of those supposedly responsible for safeguarding it. The formation of an awareness of landscape on different levels, from the custodians to the visitors, remains an unrealized project in Europe.

[10] As Paolo Bürgi wrote in his project.

[11] Aristotle, *Metaphysics,* 1.1.980a21–27, *De sensu,* 1.437a4–17.

[12] Plato, *Phaedrus,* 250d.

[13] Aristotle, *De anim,* 3.3.429a3, *De sensu,* 2.438b3.

[14] Jean Starobinski, *L'occhio vivente. Studi su Corneille, Racine, Rousseau, Stendhal, Freud,* trans. G. Guglielmi (Turin: Einaudi, 1975), 277–78. Originally published as *L'oeil vivant* (Paris: Gallimard, 1961).

[15] Aristoteles, *Metaphysics,* 4.5.1014b15–16.

[16] As Paolo Bürgi wrote in his project.

[17] Ibid.

[18] This was a constant thread running through the work of Bernard Lassus: the *démesurable.*

[19] Cf. Walter Friedrich Otto, *Le muse e l'origine divina della parola e del canto,* ed. Susanna Mati (Rome: Fazi, 2005), 96. Originally published as *Die Musen und der göttliche Ursprung der Singens und Sagens,* (Düsseldorf-Cologne: Diederichs Verlag, 1956).

[20] Cf. James Hillman, *L'anima dei luoghi. Conversazione con Carlo Truppi,* (Milan: Rizzoli, 2004).

[21] From *Relazione geologica* in Paolo Bürgi's project.

[22] Ibid.

[23] Thomas Mann, *Le storie di Giacobbe,* trans. B. Arzeni (Milan: Mondadori, 1990), 36. Originally published as *Die Geschichten Jaakobs,* (Berlin: Fischer, 1933).

[24] *Saga di Gilgamesh. Epopea classica babilonese, Tavola I, Prologo,* in *La saga di Gilgamesh,* ed. Giovanni Pettinato (Milan: Mondadori 2004), 5.

[25] From *Jorge Luis Borges. Selected Poems,* ed. Alexander Coleman (New York: Viking Press, 1999).

[26] The version from Genesis.

[27] *The Cuneiform Texts from Babylonian Tablets,* Cuneiform texts from Babylonian tablets, &c., in the British Museum. (London: The Trustees, 1896). XIII, 35–38, Italian translation in Massimo Baldacci, *Prima della Bibbia. Sulle tracce della religione arcaica del proto-Israele* (Milan: Mondadori, 2000), 88.

[28] From the explanatory text to be found posted on the railing of the Geological Observatory: "Three billion years ago, at the dawn of life, there was a dry heat in the atmosphere and it contained no oxygen, but plenty of gases such as methane and ammonia. As they were whirling and mixing, they united to form more complex structures which enriched the seas. What actually sparked the beginning of life, is a secret to this day."

[29] DK 11A3.

[30] "In the primordial seas, something magnificent happened: the development of a DNA molecule. Today we know that the DNA contains all construction plans of living organisms: the shape of leaves, the color of the eyes, the wing span."

[31] From the illustrated text posted on the railing of the Observatory: "A species consists of groups of individuals, of populations which always remain on the same meadow, the same forest, the same rock or lake, i.e. the same ecosystem."

[32] Ibid.: " Earth is a living system and maybe even a unique organism. Air, water and earth actually mean life. For life on earth, the air is as important as the flower to the butterfly, grass to the deer, the snake to the buzzard, the river to the trout. We too belong to this community of creatures. 'Thanks to space travel, we can see the world with our own eyes. This may help us to behave more responsibly.' James Lovelock."

[33] In Immanuel Kant, *Critique of Practical Reason,* First Part, "Transcendental aesthetics, study of the perception of space and time as *a priori forms* of our sensibility."

[34] In Paolo Bürgi's project.

[35] "Dei gremio originem ducere et ab effectum nomen assumere," in Boccaccio, *Genealogie deorum,* XIV, 7e8.

[36] Immanuel Kant, *Kritik der Urteilskraft,* mit einer Einleitung und Bibliographie herausgegeben von Heiner F. Klemme; mit Sachanmerkungen von Piero Giordanetti.

Contemporary Garden Aesthetics, Creations and Interpretations

Contemporary Garden Aesthetics, Creations and Interpretations

Contemporary Garden Aesthetics, Creations and Interpretations

Contemporary Garden Aesthetics, Creations and Interpretations

The Planetary Garden, Garden Unknown: On the Work of Landscaper Gilles Clément

Jacques Leenhardt

Translated by Unity Woodman

Gilles Clément formulated the notion of the "planetary garden"[1] some 20 years ago—a fine oxymoron when you think about it, as this notion links what could not be more local—the garden—with the global—the planet.

Clément's starting point came from personal experience—an experience shared by a whole generation that saw an epistemological break erupt in the representation of the world: the earth seen from the moon. This planet on which the human race plants its feet and whose spatial organization was determined from a point of view rooted in a local feeling of belonging, which held all the way up to the sixties of the twentieth century, was suddenly, from one day to the next, perceived from the outside as a composite whole, and its horizon became henceforth the whole universe. A technical event essentially changed their vision. Equipped with this global perspective of the territory they inhabit, human beings have had to renew the conceptual frameworks they used to elaborate this *world vision*. And out of this decentralizing experience, the idea itself of the local vacillated.

However attached the gardener feels to his or her plot of land, he or she no longer can consider it within the framework of a traditional view of landscape. In a sense the gardener has been stripped of his or her horizon, or else it has assumed a different form, namely, that of the entire planet. Gilles Clément felt strongly that these considerations, however generally accepted, should have very concrete consequences on the way in which we conceive of the garden and, likewise, on how we formulate the question of landscape.

Up until then, the questions pertinent to the occidental garden and to its conception rested on how to make use of a perceptible space in relation to the subject gazing at it, and how to make use of the different botanical elements we had available to us in this space. We have been aware for quite some time now of the historical and geographical variations in these plant materials as they came to us. The history of the Western garden in particular has been especially marked by a curiosity for exotic plants and the problems concerning their acclimatization. However, what the vision of the earth from the moon produced was a singular intellectual and emotional shock. All the developments in the science of ecology for at least a century were suddenly ineluctably altered and gained an unprecedented impact. What was once the repository of a few specialists of the ecosystem is now open to the entire population of the globe, a population newly sensitive to the possibility and necessity for new representations of the very elements that constitute nature: vegetable, animal, and human.

Yet the absence of conditions that would enable us to develop new fields of knowledge—concepts and images capable of providing a framework for this new world vision—has hampered the spreading of this new consciousness to ever wider circles of the population. Between scientific knowledge and cultural representation there need to be icons sufficiently powerful to galvanize our aims and choices of social practice.

It is clear to everyone by now that the symbolic and technical processes linked to globalization consider the ultimate questions of local versus global as central to the debate. But we can hardly say that this epistemological turning point has significantly altered or revolutionized the technical aspects of the garden. Seen from this angle of ecosystems, biodiversity highlights the importance of the biosphere's dynamic rather than its distribution on the surface of the planet.

What, therefore, would be the appropriate form of a garden if its logic is no longer to be that of distributing the vegetation in space but that of providing the life of nature with the conditions that will allow it to follow its own course—the dynamic relationship of ecosystems as opposed to the order imposed on them by an architect's work or conception of a garden? What form are we to develop that does not first draw from the characteristics of space, such as the planted bed, the pathway, the ha-ha, but instead from the principles of growth and spontaneous association at work within nature? And how is that form to speak to our deepest feelings, to install its dynamic at the very point that touches the foundation of our existence: life?

The notion of the planetary garden develops around these very questions. A singular characteristic of Gilles Clément is to have placed an interdisciplinary activity at the heart of his practice as a gardener, one that embraces seemingly disparate domains: a theoretical work on the dynamic of ecosystems, which he analyzed in his work *The Moving Garden;*[2] the practical work of gardening, which led to the creation of the Parc Citroën and the garden of La Vallée and to the creation and supervision of the botanical garden of Rayol;[3] a systematic investigative approach to the diversity of biotopes, which has turned him into a relentless traveler; and, finally, an activity of diffusion through events such as the exhibition "The Planetary Garden," held in La Villette, Paris, from September 1999 to January 2000. This exhibition offered the general public access, both on an intellectual and on a sensitive level, to approaching such questions about life on earth and its transformations. And last, Clément is also a writer who explores through the form of literature, in *Thomas et le Voyageur* (Thomas and the Voyager),[4] yet another means for understanding what is at stake in this work and what are the processes underlying our concerns about gardening. A multiple strategy thus unfolds in which different aspects converge in constructing a contemporary representation of the garden, as seen from the new angle of a planetary dimension to life on earth. This strategy aims not only at making a new *style* of garden but also at formulating how we are to conceive of these new representations. It relies on the most up-to-date knowledge we have on botany and biology and sets its goals on transforming our civilization's current notions about the garden. For Clément, therefore, this is about finding, within an aesthetic order, the corresponding principles for governing life.

Now, to come closer to what such a form of aesthetic and cultural action might look like, I will first use an example taken from literature: *La nouvelle Héloïse* (Julie, or the New Eloise),[5] published in 1758 by Jean-Jacques Rousseau.

Letter XI of the Fourth Part of this epistolary novel is centered on the description of the garden that Julie—the narrator's former lover who has since married and had children[6]—conceived as a real utopia, a refuge of nature and happiness that presents itself as an image of a harmonious, reconciled world. Such harmony, for Rousseau, clearly depends on the establishment of a new relationship between Man and Nature, which prefigures a happier society based on friendship.

According to the book, the particularity of this garden draws from three essential points, the effects of which I wish to elucidate in showing the enhanced rapport between the garden and what we could call the vital principle:

As opposed to aristocratic gardens, to those plans inspired by Le Nôtre, expressing the power of money, the megalomania of the artist, and the resolve to illustrate and pay homage to man's mastery over nature, the Elysium, as Julie calls it, is the product of her work alone, the work of a person who attempts to establish a relationship to nature that is at once personal, constant, and restrained.

This garden lets nature unfold in its own guise, following its own processes that Julie directs and contributes to for the benefit of its living evolution and development. She does not attempt to substitute herself here; she is its gardener, not its architect. From an aesthetic point of view, the Elysium has more in common with wild and uncultivated nature than with what we would usually call a *garden,* described by the narrator: "In the more open spots, here and there, without order and without symmetry, I saw roses, raspberries, currants, lilac bushes, hazel trees, elders, syringa, broom, and trefoil, which embellished the ground by giving it the appearance of lying fallow."[7]

Here Rousseau has given us a metaphor for reconciled life through the invention of a garden, which, one could say, turns its back on the usual practices, putting the emphasis instead on life itself, the life of the gardener who is dedicated to caring for it and the life of nature as living processes. For these processes are what gives meaning to the act of gardening, as they are equally a source of pleasure in making a garden and the pleasure one experiences in strolling through it.

Rousseau's discussion holds the seeds of our growing consciousness of modern science's tendency to isolate the objects of its findings from the circumstances of their environment, and consequently from their vital dynamic. In this logic of abstraction, things belonging to nature become *objectives,* inert (not living) and unorganized. Such objects are, properly speaking, *unreal* to how we see in our daily perception. In exchange, if you like, we have a strong hold over them: they are available, quantifiable, and susceptible to experimentation. Viewed from what is clearly a reductive angle, they enter exactly into the world of utility and efficiency, while they remain divorced from life. As Edgar Morin says,[8] simplification has reduced the idea of body to that of matter and this last to atom, an elementary and useable unit. The energy that powers the industrial and technological ideology of the modern era is that of the laborer's output of work or the financial flux: a useable and exploitable principle, a general and abstract equivalent. Yet in neither case do we truly find nature (physis) or human beings, but only an approximate reality, almost a metaphor, a state of affairs defined scientifically or socially by our dominant values and always reducible to utility.

Of course, Clément is fully aware of what we traditionally term "garden," defined, before anything else, by its formal visual repertory of enclosures, flower beds, pathways, planted borders, and hedges but not by any biobotanical process. Classical thought based its "gardening culture" on such "forms," making them stand in opposition to "wilderness." But the "garden" that appears as fallow or wild, "Julie's garden," or the "moving garden" belongs to none of these categories. They simply do not apply as its concept lies in a spontaneous order at the heart of a complex system of interdependencies.[9]

What might come to be called *beauty* in such a garden would not simply be the result of a human-imposed order or rational arrangement of the botanical elements in geometrical designs. Rather its forms, always in a state of transformation, would produce the movements of metamorphosis and vital shifting true to biotopes, including those that human activity instigates. Travelers, farmers, botanists, and gardeners are all participants, although often unawares, in the metamorphoses of nature, on the same level as birds, the wind, and insects.

Thomas et le Voyageur (Thomas and the Voyager)

But as long as we have not formed or formulated a new world vision for the contemporary era with its primary concern of promoting and protecting the vital process, there cannot be any new garden *aesthetic* or gardener's *ethic*.[10] From now on, we are confronted with the question: How should we promote representations that will facilitate the birth of such a world vision? This is the question at the heart of *Thomas et le Voyageur.*

Hence a gardener writes a story that takes the form of an epistolary exchange. This is how Gilles Clément makes his language operate from a double decentralizing mode: instead of speaking in his own name, he projects himself in his two characters and puts them both into contact but from two distinct places. On the one hand there is Thomas, who lives in Saint-Sauveur, a village in the heartland of France, and on the other a multiplicity of places that the Voyager travels to and analyzes. Each of these diverse territories, like so many points of view, presents a specific organization that has something in common climatically with Saint-Sauveur, but that remains distinct.

Furthermore, the story takes into account the transformations that its characters undergo, instigated by their "adventures," in meetings, discussions, and reflections. This dramatization allows these different points of view to collide and their experiences to provoke changes; in other words, how the landscape and nature is experienced enters into the process of forming and transforming the characters.

From the point of view of the resolution of the contradiction between the local and the planetary, which is at the origin of this intellectual enterprise, the narrative form puts knowledge in the position of permanent experimentation. Intellectually, the two protagonists are not on the same level: the Voyager is versed in botanical, anthropological, and ecological science and puts himself into situations, during his peregrinations, that constantly renew his experience, using his knowledge to put them into perspective. But he has made a pact with Thomas, the man of the *terroir,* of the local terrain: *together* they intend to produce the image of the planetary garden, that is, to make it representational.

The erudite Voyager, however, knows only too well that knowledge can *explain* but not *constitute a picture,* that the laws governing the environment—laws he masters perfectly—correspond to an abstract observer, with neither hearth nor home, a vagabond, whereas Thomas, the artist, the man who knows how to draw, knows only the particular—the local—and that this knowledge, in line with his artistic *habitus,* stems more from the senses than from understanding.

Here we encounter one of the philosophical issues put forth by Kant, who reserved for the concept, for knowledge, all that takes its cue from *determinant judgment,* across categories. Yet Clément's position could be interpreted as refusing that Kant's *reflective judgment,* which constructs itself out of intuitive, sensitive experience, is incapable of producing concepts. Hence, the concept of the planetary garden, under the guise of the theoretical modesty implied in the literary form, is invoked in an affirmation of a wholly new conceptual framework for reflecting on the notion of garden and landscape for the upcoming century.

This framework finds its form in the two sides to the story's contradiction: Thomas informs the Voyager that their vision of a planetary garden[11] may be purely illusory and utopian, that the garden necessitates a direct and personal engagement—even physical—dependent, therefore, on our sense of what is pleasing or not. For there to be garden it is necessary to feel, to have the body and its senses meet the garden's colors, aromas, and soft breezes, its metamorphosing and transforming play of light. Then, on the other hand, are the laws that govern the environment that are universal and do not depend on place—the erring of the Voyager being its concrete narrative sign. The distance he takes in relation to Saint-Sauveur, to being anchored to a particular terrain, symbolizes a narrative point of view where all identity, all that is aboriginal, is relativized, at times to the point of irony.

From this point of view, the narrative device gives form to a growing complexity, at least from an epistemological standpoint: although the story begins with the two solitary dialogistic figures who incarnate the two terms of the underlying contradiction, by the end of the story their importance has shifted to what we would call the book's minor characters: Madeleine, the student, and last, Bryan, the artist-voyager. In Bryan we have a concentration, in his *ethos* and in his person, of the two perspectives incarnated, respectively, by Thomas and the Voyager:

> We are getting ready to reconcile the irreconcilable" says Thomas to the Voyager: "the state of
> things on the one hand, the environment that you seem to know and the feeling it arouses, and on
> the other, the landscape, where I am most at ease.
>   See the woven complexities; who could possibly untangle the subject from the object, the
> mood from its cause[12]

The choice of expression of the literary form to approach this experience of the landscape, at once the foundation of the story and its contradiction, paves the way to the language and the work that must address it: not simply language as the ordering principle of taxonomy or connections that relate to biotopes, but one of a poetic lexicon and rhetorical tropes. In this lexical profusion, Gilles Clément succeeds in articulating a variety of sensations that conjugate the thing and the effect it produces on the Voyager. But for that experience to be of literary efficiency it must be inscribed within the story of a sense encounter, an initiatory moment that can potentialize these effects. Hence, the Voyager reminds Thomas, in a letter sent from Chile, of an experience he is indebted to him for. And here lies the origin, no doubt, of their common project:

> The Voyager:
> Behind your house, only a few steps away, is a low wall. Not far is the hill, itself not very high.
> All the same, what I began was a long journey: to recognize with each step the ground's
> unevenness, its every detail, its ruggedness, how I was avoiding the pointy stones or learning not to
> lay my foot too heavily on them (the soles of the feet can orientate themselves like a sail, I
> discovered). … How, I wondered, is it that this insignificant ground has gathered so much density,
> that it manifests itself overall more by its population than its consistency. I was walking on a
> population; no one had told me that, not you or any book. … The grasses. They were in the

hundreds, animated by an imperceptible motion. … Each blade offered itself up to being received or stroked, crushed, pushed back, brushed over or halted; each behaved differently on me, on my body, and sometimes I put my hand there to get a better understanding—to get closer to the encounter.[13]

This page describes in more detail than I have in this quote the experience of this exposure of the body to the landscape. The story of the initiatory night whereby the cognitive skills are subjected to the mediation of the feeling body indicates the path to follow in the task of drawing, of producing the image of the planetary garden. It encapsulates all the distance that exists between the herbarium, the collection, taxonomy, and this immediate knowledge through the senses of nature and landscape.

The story of *Thomas et le Voyageur* plays on this opposition between knowledge and the senses in many different instances. I will take just one example: the room Thomas has set up to create the image of the planetary garden, the imagining room. In the middle of the room, a large white canvas awaits his first markings of the pencil. On the wall, there is a universal lepidopteran collection and an ample supply of scientific documentation. But what assistance can this taxonomy in boxes and this bookish knowledge lend? In this sense, the room stages the overall question being explored in the story.

The dynamic of the story ends up demonstrating that knowledge and sense experience can perform their true function only through the double articulation of the narrative itself, in the confrontation of the Voyager's experience and the issues of the garden, the one and the others anchored in the living through the body placed in actual situations.

The icon of a *cosmos* such as a Hildegaard von Bingen was able to dream in her medieval times is no longer conceivable today; no one could invent or draw it in the open world of the planetary garden. And yet, the whole issues of *Thomas et le Voyageur* are engaged in its production, in finding such an expression.

To bring about a new configuration of the world a new type of representation is needed. But what shall it take as its image?

Thomas writes to the Voyager:
The imagining room [where the image is to be created] has become a true picture of display: You will see, the walls are covered … covered all around. In the middle there is nothing. It's true, each time I think a sketch treating our research is almost finished, I see it as somehow lacking the resolve to serve as a model. There's not one that matches the revision of how you are coming to see the universe. They resemble it too much—old. The landscape isn't taking shape; I fear we're on the wrong track. What we need is a drawing that can extend the field of all visions, and to find the most accurate 'subject' to represent it, the one and only, what all these elusive factors we have been talking about have in common; we have to return to the entomological notebooks, 'knowledge clouds the acquisitions of experience': it's not in enumerating the beings and phenomena in nature that we come any closer to finding its uniqueness; it is in their relationships to each other, in what links them, what brings them closer together, in the unique and the

indissociable. You fell into it, you say, the universe is ostensible and baroque, 'enveloping,' above all alive, its identity is not a figure or a form but behavior.[14]

The solution to this problem of representation, already embarked upon in the choice of the narrative form, depends on the emergence of a new form of visual experience, homologous to the form of experience brought about in the story. If there is to be a possible image or expression for this, it must perform the same polyphonic and interactive effect as that produced in reading the epistolary novel. But who will conceive of this image, this future icon, the icon of a garden—itself only a possible garden?

The answer to this question begins to take shape around the character of Bryan, a solution one could qualify as provisionary or incentive. As for all artistic engagement, Bryan's work does no more than anticipate what will be its common sentiment. Bryan is an artist-voyager, whom the Voyager meets in Australia. He accumulates images, builds them up in installations, in videos and other works of art. He constructs machines, machines that function on the basis of multiplication, of displacing images. With this he does not produce a *reality,* per se, as much as transformable *schemata* that are capable of engendering just about everything. But by the end of the story Bryan is ill, and if he has been taken over by the madness of his project, like Frenhofer in Balzac's *The Unknown Masterpiece,* it is because he has constructed nothing but virtualities through the manipulation of his store of imaginative processes in what amounts to a world devoid of palpable reality, a world ruled more by the logic of thinking and desire than the logic of making. At the end of his work, something virtual and therefore mad is produced, much as the idea itself of the planetary garden. *Thomas et le Voyageur* concludes in a question. It is not altogether certain whether we are even capable of writing our own legend. Our conceptions, which allow us to dream the planetary garden today, have not perhaps sufficiently honed our senses to the point of being able to live or feel such a utopia, or even for us to imagine it, let alone represent it.

The abstract nature of the idea itself of planetary garden still gets in the way, it would seem, of producing any perceptible, concrete idea. And yet… The different gardens designed by Gilles Clément develop one or another aspect of this agenda. None of them produce exactly the planetary garden, which is and will always remain, in the philosophical sense, an Idea, a horizon, and a provocation, as well, to think and feel differently these metaphors for our relationship with nature and what we term "gardens." In terms of horizon, what the planetary garden draws for the century of ecology that we have entered upon is a new and varied landscape.

Let us attempt in conclusion, then, and as a way of confirming that Gilles Clément is first and foremost a gardener, the outlining of a few of these aspects that might afford this Idea its concretization. I will approach four of them, of which each can be subsumed in the following principle: "A history of landscapes that classify themselves by their life and not by their aspect, a territory of Man in which the individual's place is neither in the middle nor above, but within."[15]

I. Logically speaking, the biosphere must come first. Missing are the corresponding cultural or aesthetic elaborations for this priority. Considering that the history of gardens and landscapes was written in compliance with the conceptual framework that governed cultures of modernity, which saw Man's relationship to nature as instrumental—the planetary garden aims at ridding itself of this dominating role, as well as of the constraining forms it imposes on the field, on the enclosure. It strives to open up its territory to the great winds of change and exchange. Not with the approach of the ethnographic museum that attempts to integrate the "exotic" cultures of others, but with the trend toward decompartmentalization, whereby the aboriginal or exotic no longer belongs to any distinct category, and whereby there is no longer any hierarchy between what is and is not recognized as *value*. Its value must lie in what is rendered perceptible to the eye, in the beauty of the cultivators, the surprises of successions.

The Parc Citroën in Paris embraces this effort by offering, in the limited setting of an urban park, an experience of the *moving garden*.[16] This involves providing a new representation of the internal dynamic of the garden, more than leaving nature to produce, following its own logic, unpredictable groupings or assemblages. The moving garden of the Parc Citroën is above all a moment of pedagogical astonishment, to which the planetary garden stands on the horizon. The Parc Citroën, which may be considered, mostly by its localization in the heart of the city, as a "manifest" garden, denies the idea of a proper movement of natural life in a suite of gardens whose artificiality is clearly shown (the white garden, the black garden), stating again the question of life under the horizon of passing from nature to artifice. One must imagine here that the gardener addresses him- or herself to a new form of sensibility in the very experience of the garden. Flowers and bushes, mosses and perennials are not there for their aesthetic value. The white garden's "beauty," for example, is only experimented, is only moving if it is able to evoke, through the cast of the paradox it presents to sensibility, ideas emerging of the singular gathering that constitutes it. It is known that the value of a floristic gathering and the capacity to resent it as beautiful (i.e., to recognize it as such) depends on the traveler's mastering a code of sensibility to the garden. It is also known that these codes vary with time. From this point of view, the Parc Citroën takes part in the building of new codes of sensibility, when the still abstract "ideas" of today will become ordinary forms of sensibility. For those already engaged in these new questions, the "idea" itself is already source of pleasure.

As Julie said, all that work done in the Elysium garden has no other object than pleasure (in opposition to utility). But the codes of pleasure must not be built only on objects, as those, for example, Burke classified to support his definition of the sublime. The codes of pleasure to which Rousseau refers implicitly do not pertain to a register of forms and objects: they refer to the capacity of sensibility to grasp the spectacle offered by nature. And there is no place here for Mother Nature, whole and sacred, but, modestly, for what is shown of nature in the building of the garden. This sensitive capacity must be a new occasion to think and resent, to enjoy, joyfully or in distress, this moment when, in the garden, man is confronted with nature, his own and that which he organizes before his eyes. These codes, both aesthetical and that refer to a more largely anthropological perception, will probably take a long time to become partaken by a majority.

Gilles Clément has also created in the garden he calls La Vallée a life-sized experience of the moving garden. Here he has engaged in a dialogue with wild or uncultivated nature, letting surprises emerge, but never losing sight of an eventual structure pleasing to the eye, that which is not automatically produced by biotopes. Hence the mower has its role to play, as do the sheers and the watering can—instruments of culture par excellence. Here we cannot avoid seeing the competition between two principles: that of the haphazard aesthetic of revealing life as it comes and that of the form that is designed to provide a fixed framework and supporting structures both for making this spontaneity visible and perhaps also for making the link with more traditional structures, those pertaining to agreeable perception and the contrasts that bring them about. At the heart itself of this planetary awareness is an anchoring in the local and in the anthropological or cultural structures of the spatial, gardening imagination.

II. The principle of method: the movement inherent in the dynamic of biotopes instigates an order that still appears disordered. Our eye, our consciousness has been formed by the classifying act. Our pleasure, if it does not exhaust itself in the symmetrical, nevertheless rests there. The welcome of unpredictability and surprise is, or may well be, a source of joy. But to be able to recognize in the unpredictable the inherent beauty of the living, one must first let the dynamic of the biosphere express itself fully. Looking, here, takes on a particular value, that of curiosity and admiration. But the gardener's ability to magnify and strengthen these effects will only come later as their emotional power over us has been severely eroded by the admiration we have for the technical instruments and artifices that have so greatly extended the field of life itself; these aesthetic effects that emphasize the living will require a whole new approach to reading, to awakening our senses to what has been deadened.

III. We begin to see that the aesthetic dimension to the planetary garden is no more distinct from the development of a new ecological ethic, in the wider sense of *oecumene,* or the whole of the inhabited part of the earth, than the forms of the classical seventeenth-century garden were from the ethic of being "masters and protectors" of nature. In this new concept or framework, biological movement is seen as inseparable from the gardener's presence, a presence that must inversely bow down to its logic. The gardener no longer fights against the disorder that this movement provokes, if only within the limits of an acquired global ecological consciousness. Such modifications involve, no doubt, a vigorous *aggiornamento,* which will take time: that every actor of the aesthetic of gardening operate from a deep sense of being a gardener of the biosphere and that they develop this sense in how they envision their practice. Already in his time, Rousseau understood this: it is as a protector of life in its singular dynamic that Julie manages to create and take care of her Elysium garden, and it is likewise as such that she gives it its meaning and beauty. Her ethos is necessarily the basis of her aesthetic.

IV. The planetary garden is a new thinking for the age of globalization, inferring a practice that is abject to uniformity. This idea of the planetary garden espouses the evolution of a world that passes from a mosaic of cultural and biological monads, systems closed in on themselves, to what one might choose to represent as a large archipelago of multiple interconnections. But although it fits wholly into the natural and cultural process of globalization, the idea of the planetary garden opposes itself to the globalizing logic of reducing difference and of the standardization of solutions that the power of money seeks to impose everywhere. It is also for this reason that the planetary garden does not preach any determined aesthetic, not even that of wild, untouched nature, with which it is often confused. "The Planetary Garden views globalization from the angle of the diversity of beings and practices … it integrates biological, political, and social data that interact on the planet by taking into account that a single model of organization has never existed or even been possible."[17] This is why the notion of the "gardener" takes on such an ethical and political dimension in Gilles Clément's exercise, which is well captured in his book's title *La sagesse du jardinier*[18] (The Wisdom of the Gardener).

Once again, one cannot take an actual realization of a garden to illustrate the ideas tackled here. Nevertheless one can speak of *Les Jardins de Valloires* where Gilles Clément planted a collection of more than 5,000 bushes gathered by the nurseryman Jean-Louis Cousin. This collection is composed of a great number of subjects of Asian origin, which follows in this logic of decompartmentalization. The fact that they are all particularly resistant to limestone, for the pH in Valloires is higher than 8.5, creates a necessary ratio between the site and the plant and presents to the eye a particular form of biotope. The idea of a collection induces a more attentive and comparative look, either because it imposes itself by reference to the botanical knowledge, and in particular to its planetary dimension, or because it offers to the eye unexpected combinations. One could eventually note that Gilles Clément did not develop his project as if it were in any ordinary site: Valloires is an ancient abbey, and it is known that Saint Benoît gave the Cistercian regulations this principle: "*ora et labora,*" which very early converted the

Cistercian monasteries into high places of agriculture and medicinal plants. In the eighteenth and nineteenth centuries, botanist monks traveled the world and brought back from China and North America many plants nowadays acclimatized. By using the form of a monastery in the garden, Clément rejoins this past; he valorizes it according to the logic of the garden and awakens our attention toward this rule that could be seen as the primitive formulation of what will become the laic form of the "*sagesse du jardinier.*"

After reading the different works by Gilles Clément, a question remains, raised by the notion of "style," a term I used in passing in these reflections. Can I or should I accompany these reflections with images? Should I show examples of a style or of a particular aesthetic? Indeed, one might find it somewhat paradoxical that no images correspond to his work—it is about creating gardens after all. His publications on the garden do offer numerous drawings and illustrations, especially of spontaneous "gardens." But I have decided not to include images because of a concern, which I would like to develop in conclusion.

Thomas et le Voyageur is a book about the impossibility of producing the image or representation that is needed, the *icon* of the planetary garden. It would be very interesting to confront the arguments of the iconoclasts with this absence. In the field of the visual arts, that in which garden also belongs, the exemplary force of images and their capacity to be utilized from a superficial comprehension poses a true danger when they are taken up merely in their academic by-products. The romantic garden and land art generated multiple picturesque or sublime by-products, or at least that tried to be such. The importance, if there is one, of Gilles Clément's gardens is in their manner of provoking *feeling* and *thinking,* more important than whatever eventual shape or form they assume. And we have seen that this reflexive sensibility takes its roots in an anthropology of man in nature.

To show you a picture of an uncultivated site, whether intentionally devised as such or purely spontaneous, would make this discourse run the same risk of fixing in an image what should provoke, for he or she who walks in it, various sensations and questioning. The how and the why must not be limited to the intellectual field of questioning; on the contrary, they should perfuse our senses as we stroll through the garden by mixing our memories of frolicking in the open meadow with the frustration of not being able to actually organize the elements of that singular moment of existence within any acquired framework and learned experience of the garden.

This brings us again to Gilles Clément's strategies as someone who makes full use of the story. Our century has kept its distance to the scientist modernity, which we once believed capable of pinning down reality itself. But now we know that reality, far from existing in and of itself, is what we say of the world. This is what Stephen Jay Gould wanted to express when he said it would have been more fitting to name humans *homo narrators* than *homo sapiens.* For we know of nothing beyond the stories we can make of the world. But once again putting into story is the form par excellence that enables us to speak, not of the thing or the object itself, but of the relationships that exist between them and us.

To recount through gardening artifices and through the artifices of the gardeneer, as, for example, in writing an espistolary exchange, and to recount in a thousand ways what real and imaginary rapport we can have with the biosphere are the basis on which Gilles Clément has made is choice.

NOTES

[1] *Le jardin planétaire* was the theme advanced for the 1996 symposium under Claude Eveno and Gilles Clément's direction at Chateauvallon (the proceedings were published by Éditions de l'Aube in 1997). In addition, l'École régionale des Beaux-Arts in Valence published in their Collection 222, under the title *Contribution to the Study of the Planetary Garden,* a little book in which the following pages of *Thomas et le Voyageur* are foreshadowed.

[2] Gilles Clément, *Le Jardin en Mouvement* (Paris: Pandora Éditions, 1990).

[3] It deals with the creation of several gardens under a preexisting forest cover. Each of these conjures up a landscape of Mediterranean climate from one of the world parts. The creation work lasted for five years, and Gilles Clément still goes there four times a year to follow this realization commissioned by the *Conservatoire National du Littoral.*

[4] Gilles Clément, *Thomas et le Voyageur* (Paris: Albin Michel, 1997).

[5] Jean-Jacques Rousseau, *La nouvelle Héloïse (Julie, or the New Eloise)* (Philadelphia: Pennsylvania State University Press, 1968).

[6] This is a detail important for understanding the general structure of the work. Julie's garden is not made for just anyone in terms of being a utopia; it is influenced by the presence of strong personal relationships but that are not exclusive, which is what Rousseau calls *friendship.*

[7] Rousseau, *La nouvelle Héloïse,* 306.

[8] Edgar Morin, *La méthode/La nature de la nature* (Paris: Le Seuil, 1977) (English translation as *The Method/The Nature of Nature* [New York: Peter Lang, 1981]).

[9] *Le jardin de Julie* is a largely commented upon text. Louis Marin emphasized the way in which, at the border of the world of economical efficiency embodied by her husband Wolmar, Julie outlines the development of a cut of the world island, a utopia of nature in which would emerge the mythic theme of the woman-nature as a garden. Cf. Louis Marin, "L'effet Sharawadgi ou le jardin de Julie: notes sur un jardin et un texte (Lettre XI, 4e partie, *La nouvelle Héloïse*)," in *Traverses,* no. 5, Centre Georges Pompidou, Paris, 1976.

From a more pragmatic point of view, closer to Gilles Clément's concerns, Raphaël Larrère emphasized that Julie's garden, as natural as it appears, is the fruit of a work of construction of nature, that it is by dint of artificiality that the "natural" effect is obtained. He thus focused his purpose on the quite actual question of the "construction of nature," of its pedagogical, touristic, or urbanistic aims. See Raphaël Larrère, "L'art de produire la nature, une leçon de Rousseau," in *Courrier de l'environnement,* no. 22 (June 1994).

[10] Gilles Clément would undoubtedly prefer the idea of "wisdom" rather than that of *ethic.* See *La sagesse du jardinier* (The Wisdom of the Gardener) (Paris: Éditions l'Oeil Neuf, 2004).

[11] Gilles Clément, *Le jardin planétaire: Réconcilier l'homme et la nature,* Exhibition at the Grande Halle de La Villette, Paris 1999–2000. Catalog published by Parc de la Villette-Albin Michel, Paris, 1999.

[12] Clément, *Thomas et le Voyageur,* 24.

[13] Ibid., 56–57.

[14] Ibid., 83.

[15] Ibid., 188.

[16] Clément, *Le Jardin en Mouvement.*

[17] Clément, *Le jardin planétaire,* 126.

[18] Clément, *La sagesse du jardinier.*

Contemporary Garden Aesthetics, Creations and Interpretations

Contemporary Garden Aesthetics, Creations and Interpretations

Contemporary Garden Aesthetics, Creations and Interpretations

Contemporary Garden Aesthetics, Creations and Interpretations

"A Garden of the Hesperides": The Landscape Initiative of the Musée Gassendi, Digne, and the Geological Reserve of Alpes de Haute-Provence

Stephen Bann

My concern in this essay is to raise a question about the contemporary garden that is in itself quite simple, but benefits from the opportunity to look carefully at an unusual initiative that has taken place over the past few years. This is the unique joint venture between a provincial museum specializing in both arts and sciences, the Musée Gassendi at Digne in southeastern France, and the protected area of chiefly wild landscape that forms its surrounding environment, the Réserve géologique des Alpes de Haute-Provence. The question with which I am concerned can be simply stated, before I begin my commentary on the experiential aspects of this remarkable and productive joint venture. It is this: Where can we find in the contemporary world the same richness of symbolism, the same diversity of features, and the same ambition to achieve a distinctive synthesis between nature and culture, science and the visual arts, that we observe in the great European gardens of the early modern period—Versailles, Herrenhausen, Stowe (to name just a few). This question does not imply any wish to devalue what is rightly seen as the main focus of many of the papers being published in this collection, which are directed primarily to what might be called "auteur" gardens—the product of the vision of a single practitioner, or indeed the "landscape approach" of a particular contemporary artist. Undoubtedly this is where the most substantial achievements of the present day do lie, and this has been the case at least since the end of the eighteenth century when professional individuals began to take over from the multidisciplinary enterprises of the earlier period. Of course, it would be perverse to try and return to the circumstances of the early modern period, which has bequeathed us innumerable puzzles concerning the degree to which prominent theorists actually engaged in gardening. But I still want to ask where we can look to observe something broadly comparable to the earlier model. This might mean that we were considering a designed landscape that derived from essentially different though complementary practices, within the overall framework of a distinctive vision of the place of nature in the contemporary world.

Again, I have no doubt at all that several contemporary landscape designers, and not surprisingly those who have especially close connections to poetry and the visual arts, achieve this distinctive vision. Ian Hamilton Finlay's garden of Little Sparta, now happily conveyed to a trust that will safeguard its existence, is surely the most striking example.[1] Indeed, the fact that Finlay has used the talents of a large number of stonecarvers and other craft specialists to achieve the densely interwoven

1. Per Barclay, sculpture for the Nordland project, Norway

texture of plants, objects, and inscriptions is a germane one here. There is a real sense that he has responded to the possibilities of a stone-carving tradition distinctive to the British Isles, and so introduced a diversity of voices. Yet in other cases the conventions of architectural authorship, which rely on the prestige and authority of a single name, have been carried over into landscape architecture. It is significant that, almost alone of contemporary landscape designers, Bernard Lassus has recognized the problem of heterogeneity as one to be assumed, rather than simply ignored. Indeed, he has specifically incorporated his own subtle theory of the "heterodite" into his ongoing practice.[2] But Lassus, whose remarkable recent achievement is considered by Michel Conan in chapter five, is untypical in coming from a background in the plastic arts. He is the exception that proves the rule. As a general rule, the threat of heterogeneity is something to be averted at all costs.

Of course, there is a genre, or subgenre, of the garden in which heterogeneity of authorship is admitted, and indeed welcomed. This is the highly popular development of the "sculpture park," of which any number of prominent examples could be named. Conceived originally as an outdoor room for the display of museum collections, the sculpture park has taken off on its own and requires now no more than a token building to offer information on the works displayed. Spectacular natural sites—forests, lake-girded islands, and upland pastures—have been developed as sculpture parks. I make no comment on the quality of the individual works exhibited there. In some cases, they are among the most impressive examples of sculpture by the most distinguished contemporary artists in three dimensions. In other cases, the standards are not so high. Yet, as regards to the argument that I am pursuing, this is simply not the point. The fact is that the sculpture park, as a general rule, fails to offer the kind of overall vision of unity in heterogeneity that concerns me here. Only in the rarest cases does the sculpture park succeed as a garden, or as an example of designed landscape. Whether it be a fine tract of mainly untouched open country, as at the Storm King Sculpture Park, or an intensively planted area, like the garden next to the National Gallery in Washington, the integration between landscape design and the sited objects remains a matter of arranging

2. Steel engraving after J.M.W. Turner, *The Goddess of Discord in the Garden of the Hesperides* (Royal Academy, 1806)

individual objects on the purely functional basis—no more and no less attentively than if they were being juxtaposed in a sequence of rooms. Hence we lose the many possibilities of subtle accommodation between the individual features and the overall design that is the glory of the great Renaissance and Baroque gardens.

To take one (admittedly hyperbolic) example, we lose any sense of the thrilling discoveries that are possible when one deserts the main axis of paths at Versailles for the delights of the individual *bosquets*. When I wrote briefly on the sculpture garden in the compendium *Architettura dei giardini d' occidente* some years ago, I could single out only the inspiring case of the Villa Celle, near Pistoia, as a counterexample, and this exception was surely the result of its inclusion of at least three garden types within its compass: an Italian villa garden, a nineteeenth-century English garden, and a section planted traditionally with olive groves.[3] Again Ian Hamilton Finlay showed how this potential heterogeneity could be galvanized when he chose to make an olive grove, rather than the adjoining "forests of the avant-garde," the site for his intimate Virgilian contribution. Finlay indeed has developed a rare skill for making what I once termed "strategic interpolations in the secular spaces of modern sculpture parks."[4] But this resourcefulness can serve only to emphasize their failure elsewhere.

I should mention here that I have nothing but admiration for the Nordland project in northern Norway, and greatly admire the persistent concern for synthesis between existing elements of the scene, both manmade and natural, and the artist's individual contribution. I notice this particularly in the work of the Norwegian sculptor Per Barclay, who made the rehabilitation of an ancient fisherman's hut the starting point for his measured visual exploration of the landscape and its geology[5] (Fig. 1). But the Nordland project extends over many hundreds of square miles, and in no sense could it make any claim to be a centered initiative. In this respect, as we shall see, it is radically different from the museological and landscape project based at Digne.

Before passing to Digne, however, I need to explain the phrase used in my title. The "Garden of the Hesperides" is not the name given to this creation by its sponsors or authors, and indeed there is no name as yet that satisfactorily describes the whole project. However, this is the name that I have already used when writing about the venture, because of what appears to me to be an illuminating connection with the title of a painting by Turner—the "most important picture of [his] first period" according to Ruskin: *The Goddess of Discord in the Garden of the Hesperides,* first exhibited at the Royal Academy in 1806 (Fig. 2). It is, of course, a commonplace in the historical study of Western gardens that we look for guidance as to their symbolic function and the iconography of their individual features in the great landscape paintings of the post-Renaissance period, those by Claude and Salvator Rosa, among others. Turner's *Garden of the Hesperides,* as interpreted by Ruskin in a virtuoso essay published in the last volume of *Modern Painters,* could be seen as a paradigm for the many-layered symbolism and momentous social message that was carried by historical landscape painting as late as the nineteenth century, and thus a challenge (as I would interpret it) to any present-day initiative seeking to endow landscape with symbolic, social, and scientific significance. Ruskin, whose insistence on direct experience is coupled with a profound sense of the Western landscape tradition, can serve here as a valid precursor to John Dewey.[6]

To put it concisely, Turner's painting condenses, for Ruskin, natural and allegorical readings of landscape. Its mythological theme is the visit of the Goddess of Discord, Eris, to a garden notionally set in the western section of the Mediterranean world, where the beneficent tree that grows the golden apples has been blighted by the hot breath of the dragon that stretches out its length along the nearby mountain top. It is an apple from this blighted tree that will be offered by Paris to Aphrodite in the mythical Judgment of Paris and so trigger the process of division between peoples that launches the Trojan War and the conflict-torn history of the West. Ruskin thus interprets Turner's message in the broadest of terms as an allegorical representation of the internecine war that has inevitably dogged the development of the Western world—not least in the period of the Napoleonic wars that were contemporary with the early stages of Turner's career. But he also directs our attention to the supreme genius of Turner as a student of natural landscape. Turner has (it would appear) transposed on to this mythical garden the vision of Alpine landscape that he gained during the interval of the Peace of Amiens in 1802 when the continent was briefly open to British travelers. Ruskin himself had returned to the Alps in 1860, just before the last volume of *Modern Painters* was published, and he had taken the opportunity to paint the Alpine glaciers. He used this direct experience to discern in the form of the dragon's body "a representation of a great glacier, so nearly perfect, that I know no published engraving of glacier breaking over a rocky brow so like the truth as this dragon's shoulders would be, if they were thrown out in light."[7] But he also detected in that monstrous form—which he himself engraved as an illustration for *Modern Painters*—an extraordinary inspiration from the discoveries of contemporary natural science: "the adoption of the head of the Ganges crocodile, the fish-eater, to show his sea-descent (and this in the year 1806, when hardly a single fossil saurian skeleton existed within Turner's reach)."[8] In other words, the "imaginative intellect" of Turner (to use Ruskin's own words) has conjoined the findings of contemporary geology with an acute perception of natural phenomena in the form of an allegory that advances this mythic landscape as a portent of the destructive forces inherited by the Western world from its remote, ancestral past.

Ruskin's many-layered interpretation could detain us for a good deal longer. But I want it to stand here primarily as an indication of the multiple meanings invested in landscape—historical, scientific, and experiential—and their relevance to the landscape initiative under discussion. I also need to characterize this now in terms of its complex origins. Digne, an ancient bishopric and regional center, lies at the heart of a region of spectacular mountain scenery that is also of considerable geological significance, since it lies along a fault where the original seabed of the Mediterranean has risen to the surface and so exhibits a remarkable profusion of fossil remains. This is one of the largest, and the most recent, areas in France to receive special designation as an area of scientific importance, being classified as a "Réserve naturelle géologique." It is out of the ordinary not only in its vast extent, but also in having numerous inhabited parts within the designated area. The museum at Digne, founded in the nineteenth century and installed from 1905 onwards in the old Hôpital Saint-Jacques in the center of the town (Fig. 3), possesses important scientific collections as well as some notable examples of the fine arts. Nadine Passamar-Gomez, who was originally trained as a geologist, took over as curator of the museum in the 1990s with the brief to renovate it completely and made two major decisions.[9] On the one hand, the museum, now christened the Musée Gassendi in tribute to the distinguished seventeenth-century philosopher and scientist long associated with Digne, was to be completely redesigned. It was to exhibit the existing collections, but also to develop the links between science and the fine arts as demonstrated by the activity of

3. Exterior view, Musée Gassendi, Digne-les-Bains

contemporary artists.[10] On the other hand, a joint venture was initiated with the Réserve géologique, drawing in a broad range of such artists who could exhibit at the nearby CAIRN gallery (Centre d'art informel de recherche de la nature). In certain cases, they were also invited to submit plans for permanent work in the extensive surrounding territory of the reserve itself.

This collaborative strategy began around 1995, and the "reinvented" museum finally opened in 2003. It has involved the residence at Digne of artists such as the American Marc Dion, who created a spectacular modern "cabinet of curiosities" now installed in the museum—and planned to install a lifesized bear in a local cave in the course of 2005, and the French artist Hubert Duprat, whose residency has generated the extraordinary project of vitrifying another cave, in accordance with the concept originally developed in the papers of the Renaissance ceramicist Bernard Palissy. My own recent visit in the spring of

4. Andy Goldsworthy, Sentinel, at Les Clues de Barles, in the river valley of the Bès

2005 coincided with the opening of an exhibition of the work of Paul-Armand Gette. Gette was himself originally trained as a geologist, and on this occasion he showed work derived from a photographic study of the springs in the surrounding area.[11] I mention these examples only to stress the careful judgment with which the choice of artists has been made, although such individual practices do not in themselves amount to the creation of a designed landscape. What is noteworthy, however, is the way in which such favorable conditions of working have inspired other artists to work in a more coherent way, as far as the design of the landscape is concerned. Instead of punctuating the area with individual works—which is still the approach employed in such comparable contexts as Vassivière in the Haut-Limousin, the Domaine de Kerguehennec in Brittany, or the Forest of Dean in Gloucestershire—they have responded to the exceptional qualities of the local landscape with schemes that genuinely advance the potentialities of this unique collaboration between the museum and the protected region. The two artists who have most consistently pursued such strategies—while representing very different, indeed almost antithetical approaches to landscape—are the British sculptor Andy Goldsworthy and the Dutch artist herman de vries.

Goldsworthy's itinerary has been the most sustained, extending from 1998 onwards, and embodying a series of clearly defined stages that illustrate his progressive shift from an episodic use of the landscape to a fully structural engagement. On his first visit to the region in the summer of 1998, he made use of its natural resources to create some of his striking but ephemeral transformations of natural elements into manmade forms, which are perpetuated for a wider audience by color photography: thus a square formed by leaves casts a shadow as it turns with the stream's current, and a delicate chain of hazel leaves is held together by a blade of grass for a few brief moments. The cairn that he created in the bed of the River Bès on the occasion of this visit was designed to be swept away eventually by the winter flood. But, as early as 1998, Goldsworthy also created the first of his cairns, a stone structure built over a stream, whose rushing sounds it magnified and translated to ground level. This was situated in the vicinity of the CAIRN gallery and the Réserve of the museum. Over the next three years, Goldsworthy then made his decisive move into the surrounding landscape. His cairns took the form of "Sentinels," marking the three river valleys that have historically been the major channels of communication throughout the reserve, and consequently the locations for the main roads leading outwards from Digne in a northerly direction. It is important to underline, however, that these roadside sentinels are adapted to their sites in rather different ways. In contrast to the two that could be described in traditional landscape terms as "eye-catchers," which stand at the roadside and provide a sense of human scale and artifice by contrast with the distant mountain peaks, the second sentinel is slipped into a cleft in the high rock face at Les Clues de Barles (Fig. 4). This is a stretch where the Bès River cascades through a dramatic gorge, so that the visitor is always aware of the crashing noise of the turbulent river when approaching the hollow, dry-stone construction along the side of the roadway. The sentinel stands there upon an informal podium of last year's golden leaves.

Not far from this sentinel, and once again in a steep-sided passage between sheer rock faces, is the site developed by another artist, the Spaniard Juan Foncuberta. This is perhaps the work that most ingeniously concretizes the message of the reserve as an extraordinary geological spectacle, precisely by intruding upon its ammonite-rich rock faces with a hybrid creation scarcely less audacious than Turner's dragon. On a rock clearly visible from the road, there stands out the relief of a fossil identified by an official roadside panel as "La Sirène du Bès," a creature technically described as a *hydropithèque,* or type of mermaid, which possesses a mammal's body and a prominent fish tail (Fig. 5). The official panel, similarly designed and endowed with the same authority as other panels installed by the reserve, dilates upon the significance of this unique discovery, only adding the suspect rider: "Ayez un doute"—Be a little skeptical. If the visitor to the site pursues the conundrum as far as the Musée Gassendi, they will find their doubts temporarily allayed, maybe, by an extensive photographic display covering the entire life history of the (supposed) palaeontologist who discovered this prodigy— and even a plausible explanation for its not being very widely known.

5. Juan Foncuberta, 'La Sirène du Bès,' in the river valley of the Bès.

Alas! It was deprived of the appropriate publicity because its discovery happened to coincide exactly with the revelation in faraway Britain of that other marvel of science exposed to the world in 1947, the remains of "Piltdown Man."[12]

Foncuberta's two-part intervention nicely encapsulates with its poetic pseudo-science the interdependence of the areas of discourse that the Musée Gassendi, in collaboration with the geological reserve, brings into surprising conjunction. His work has typically involved the age-old practice of inventing monsters, as with the aquatic denizen of the Château d'Oiron that he has conjured up through the device of showing a murky videotape. At Digne, however, the presence in the landscape of the fake fossil not only enhances the interest of the genuine geological panorama, but also gently subverts the role of the museum display as a purveyor of authority. Yet another, no less distinctive way in which an artist's contribution to the landscape exploits and explores this scientific connection needs to be taken into account before returning to Goldsworthy's later participation in the ongoing collaborative program around Digne. The scholar after whom the museum is now named, Pierre Gassendi, was the son of a peasant from a village in the vicinity of Digne who became a noted humanist and scientist.[13] His distinctive achievement lay precisely in his searching critique of Aristotelianism, and a return to the materialist philosophy of Epicurus. Indeed, this emphasis on an empiricist approach to history, archaeology, art, and science brought him directly into conflict with the great Descartes, who jocularly accused him at one point of rejecting the well-known principle of the "*Cogito*"—I think therefore I am—and putting in its place the heretical statement "*Ambulo ergo sum*"—I walk therefore I am (Fig. 6). Gassendi did

6. herman de vries, '*ambulo ergo sum*,' inscription placed beside the track leading to the '*bois sacré du sanctuaire de la nature de roche-rousse.*'

not protest against this imputation, and it is surely appropriate to claim him as a forerunner of the empiricist thinkers of the succeeding centuries, of Hume and, perhaps ultimately, of Dewey. Certainly it is the case that "*Ambulo ergo sum*" provides a suitable motto for the landscape project of the Musée Gassendi at Digne in association with the geological reserve. I take it that the designed landscape that is emerging there is increasingly seen as enhancing the experience and serving the special needs of walkers. As will be seen shortly, this realization has brought about a distinctive new strategy in Goldsworthy's work around Digne. But initially, and in part for chronological reasons, it is important to acknowledge the special contribution of herman de vries.

The Dutch artist de vries (who foregoes capital letters in his name and works) was born in 1931 and so qualifies as the senior of the main artists who have contributed to the Digne project. He is also distinctive in having had (like Gette) a scientific background. He studied at the National School of Horticulture in the Netherlands and published on zoological topics before becoming an artist in the early 1950s and subsequently editor of the review *nul* and promoter of the group of the same name in the early 1960s. From the late 1990s, his work has increasingly adopted the form of enclosed spaces, conceived also as nature sanctuaries. His 2001 creation in the vicinity of Digne, the "*bois sacré du sanctuaire de la nature de roche-rousse*," must surely rank among the most extraordinary. The visitor must climb steadily for about half an hour, by steep and difficult pathways, up the side of a mountain situated above the valley of the Bès before suddenly coming across the reassuring presence of a stone bearing the inscription "*ambulo ergo sum*," and then discovering the single, gold-tipped iron stake that demarcates the access to the "sacred wood" (Fig. 7). The enclosure installed by de vries is an enclosure and nothing more: a fence of identical iron stakes surrounds a ruined building that was used in the past by shepherds and still clings to the side of the mountain. It protects nothing, in other words, except the space that it encloses, and the vegetation that is now able to grow there unchecked. The site itself does not offer any special view—though the crest of the mountain is close and provides a suitable resting place to pause and enjoy the landscape. The work is, as it were, defined by its very contingency—by the foregrounding of the simple act of enclosing, rather than the special status of what is enclosed. de vries's current scheme for the Digne landscape is a series of stones inscribed with gold-lettered texts from a number of languages, which he describes as "traces." Starting from Wittgenstein's idea that "points" in an argument can be fruitfully compared with "points" on a map, he intends to place these individual stones bearing philosophical texts throughout the entire reserve. But they will be difficult, perhaps almost impossible, to find—since they hardly draw attention to themselves, even when the visitor is very close to them.

Any view of the significance of the Digne project that I have described as a "Garden of the Hesperides" must take into account the creative antithesis established on site between the contributions of de vries and those of Goldsworthy. Other artists, such as Fontcuberta, have contributed a great deal to the richness of the overall experience, and the Musée Gassendi continues to exhibit a range of different work and displays embodying the message of the connections between art and science, as they are emblematized in the representation of the natural world. As is entirely appropriate for a museum dedicated to a scholar of the seventeenth century, there is a significant stress on the present-day understanding of the concept of curiosity. Artifacts by contemporary artists are cleverly juxtaposed with specimens and works of art from the permanent collection. Thus one of Hubert Duprat's superb coral constructions is displayed in the midst of the room that includes the museum's small but choice holdings of Renaissance and Baroque paintings. Marc Dion has compiled his contemporary "cabinet of curiosities" from the reserve collections that would not ordinarily be on display; it reflects upon the museum's classification systems and introduces unexpected juxtapositions of his own devising. But even within the museum itself, it is again de vries and Goldsworthy who have

7. Herman de Vries, '*bois sacré du sanctuaire de la nature de roche-rousse.*'

intervened in ways that most effectively connect to the possibilities of representing the natural world beyond the museum's walls. For example, de vries has installed a "*Cabinet de Botanique*" in honor of Dr. Honnorat, a local nineteenth-century figure whose herbalist collections are shown in glass cases, while the surrounding walls are covered with de vries's own labeled specimens, discovered in the course of his walks around the countryside of the Haute-Provence (Fig. 8). He terms the Haute-Provence "the only place in the world where I have found nothing but pure poetry."[14] Goldsworthy's large wall piece consisting of dried mud, *River of Earth,* fills up one end of the large gallery where the late-nineteenth-century landscapes by the effective founders of the museum are put on display. In effect, it covers up what might have been a "magnificent view on to the surrounding countryside," as Goldsworthy acknowledges, but in his opinion this denial of the expected vista obliges the visitor to think more deeply about the different strategies for representing the processes and effects of the visible world.

Before I proceed to discuss the structural contribution of Goldsworthy to the Digne initiative, which is his extensive network of "art refuges" (*refuges d'art*), I want to clarify further the way in which this designed landscape might be understood in the light of the broader transformations of the contemporary idea of the garden. As I have already pointed out, the cardinal point about the general organization of the landscape is that it becomes accessible essentially through walking—*la marche*. In this connection, it is

8. herman de vries, 'cabinet de botanique,' installed in the Musée Gassendi, in honor of Dr. Honnorat

worth bearing in mind a few contextual details that make the realization of that objective in the area around Digne especially significant. A recent conference at Dumbarton Oaks discussed the practice of landscaping in relation to the acceleration of methods of transport from the railway age onwards, with special attention to the point that gardens are not in any sense refuges from the modern world, but earn their contemporaneity by creatively adapting to it. Annette Freytag spoke memorably about the urban parks constructed in the later nineteenth century in the vicinity of mainline railway stations, such as the Buttes Chaumont in Paris and the Türkenschanzpark in Vienna.[15] I spoke partly about Bernard Lassus's motorway rest area at Crazannes, which is also the main subject of Michel Conan's fine recent book.[16]

It is a paradox of our period, however, that the ever increasing rapidity of transport is by no means uniform in its effects, and that the topography as it is read from the map is subject more than ever to odd discrepancies and contortions of time and space. Approach Digne by train from Paris, and you will spend barely three hours getting from the capital to Aix-en Provence by TGV, and then around two hours proceeding by coach from Aix to Digne. The remoteness of the place of arrival is, of course, doubly emphasized by the relative depopulation of the surrounding countryside. The network of major roads, which pass almost exclusively along the river valleys already mentioned, is, however, superimposed on a much older network of communications that once criss-crossed the entire area and was predominantly used by human beings traveling on foot, or at best on horseback accompanied by pack animals. It is this configuration of ancient tracks that the program of nine "art refuges" aspires to uncover. The first of the refuges is, as stated earlier, the wall piece entitled *River of Earth* in the landscape room of the museum. From this central point, each stage in the ensuing sequence can be thought of as a staging point, offering both shelter and room for recreation, on a possible ten-day circuit that will ultimately lead all around the reserve. But each refuge is also conceived as an independent landscape feature. It usually incorporates a newly reconstructed building on a site specially chosen for its visual, historical, and other associations.

This becomes fully apparent in the case of the second refuge, incorporating the ruined Chapelle Sainte-Madeleine that overlooks the village of Thoard (Figs. 9 and 10). A new stone wall has been built to complement the old, with a distinctive niche that creates a sharp variation in the levels of light. A new relationship between inside and outside space is proposed. To quote Goldsworthy himself: "The experience of the chamber will be in stark contrast to the open mountains. I could think of no better primer for the refuges. The chamber at Sainte-Madeleine will be made more intense and intimate because of the walk preceding it, and the view that you have at your back as you enter the chapel. There will, I hope, be a dynamic counterpoint between the door opening out into space and the chamber opening into stone."[17]

9. Chapelle Sainte-Madeleine, overlooking the village of Thoard.
10. Andy Goldsworthy, refuge incorporating the Chapelle Sainte-Madeleine, under construction

It would be impossible to make a detailed assessment here of all of the refuges completed to date. The map provided indicates the scope of the project. (Fig. 11). At the time of writing, in the late summer of 2005, the ambitious scheme is progressing towards completion, with the *Refuge des Thermes,* illustrated here in the process of construction and conceived as the last in the circuit, now fully operational. Here a rather more modest building than the chapel, but still vested with human associations ripe for revival, has been rebuilt with a circular entry that offers a view of

a cairn of stones (Figs. 12 and 13). Simple seating arrangements have also been installed around the restored walls of the building. What seems appropriate is to conclude this report on an ongoing project by referring to two more of the remaining refuges. The illustrations will foreground the artist's original conception and the early stages of the process of rebuilding, as well as the ways in which the very process of the walk to the refuge is important. It is against the background of this directed and purposeful activity in the open air that we should set the revelation of each refuge's enclosed and inward-looking space.

The *Col de l'Escuichière* refuge is particularly striking because of Goldsworthy's search for a motif to mark the main

11. The scope of the project

12. Andy Goldsworthy, '*Refuge des Thermes,*' under construction

inward-looking wall, well documented through his fine series of pencil drawings that have been preserved and exhibited at the Musée Gassendi. A distinctive property of the rocks found in this part of the reserve is the white streak of quartz that shoots through the predominant grayish-black color of the stone. Goldsworthy conceived of several ways of reconstituting these abbreviated lines through juxtaposition of fragments that were found along the wayside. The scheme that was finally realized is, incidentally, congenial to an art historian, since it recalls Pliny's tale of the legendary Greek painters who competed to draw the finest lines with the brush![18] These streaks of quartz are recombined into elegant linear emphases that belie the fragmentary origins of the stones composing them. The motif also serves as a reminder that these refuges, which play a purely practical role in sheltering the visiting walkers, are also representational features, which interpret the physical environment of the site in terms of the artist's distinctive skills and sensibility.

Foremost in my mind, however, because it is the last refuge site that I visited in April 2005—and the one which required the longest walk—is the *Ferme Belon,* which also happens to offer the most substantial accommodation to potential visitors. The walk that I followed with Bruno Lochon as guide began with a distant view of the hillside on which the former farm is perched, as seen from the small adjacent village of Draix. The path up the hillside traverses a strange area where the ground has the consistency of dark sand, hard to walk upon and visually striking as it has been dramatically molded into wavelike shapes by erosion. After a walk of around half an hour, the farm itself is reached. It must have been originally quite a substantial establishment, and it offers a spectacular view on to the snow-capped mountain range opposite. Access is completely open, and the entire top floor has been provided with wooden bunks and basic equipment that permits small parties of walkers to stay overnight. There is a growing collection of other useful objects, like candleholders, that attest to the refuge's periodic occupation, over the summer months in particular. The choice of this farm for the refuge does, however, pose an important question about how the establishment of the walking circuit as a whole impinges on the ordinary life of the reserve, which (as noted before) is unusual in incorporating many farms and small villages. Goldsworthy himself has taken good care not to impinge on the region's small, but significant, tourist trade by creating refuges close to the villages that already offer accommodation. In this particular case, however, it was the mayor of Draix who proposed the Belon farm, not just because of its commanding position, but because it had served as a meeting point for the *Résistance* during the Second World War (Fig. 14). Goldsworthy thus had the difficult task of rehabilitating what would then turn out to be, in a real sense, a monument in the eyes of the local village community. He decided to dedicate the whole lower story of the building to this communal memory. By filling the space with a sequence of massive stone arches, he has created a spectacular and evidently nonfunctional feature that contrasts with the open space of the upper story—something that the casual visitor would inevitably come across,

13. Andy Goldsworthy, '*Refuge des Thermes,*' under construction
14. Ferme Belon, Draix

and perhaps understand as a sign that the reserved space had once been filled with visitors engaged in a very different sort of group activity. It would perhaps be pretentious to view this refuge primarily as a monument. But as the recent tendency among architects has been to emphasize the resonance of empty space in the context of monuments and memorials, it is worth signaling the fact that Goldsworthy has, by contrast, created a filled space—one whose impact is all the more powerful in light of the magnificent vistas of the open country all around it (Fig. 15).

15. Andy Goldsworthy, 'Refuge des Thermes,' lower story

Some final tentative remarks need to be made on the place that the Digne initiative might be seen as occupying in the broad spectrum of contemporary garden modes that is being investigated in this volume. What should be stressed first of all—and what is in fact very obvious—is the point that this designed landscape did not develop from any single, preconceived plan. Like all important gardens without exception, it has required a lengthy period of development, and a progressive adjustment to the existing conditions of the landscape that could not have been fully foreseen in advance. But, unlike the majority of the contemporary gardens discussed here, the ten or so years of its evolution up to now have depended on the providential conjunction of the activities of several people. Fundamental to its existence, of course, has been the original, pathbreaking accord between the Musée Gassendi in Digne and the geological reserve, with the further consequence that the reinvented museum could look at its collections of natural history and landscape painting in light of opportunities to commission new work from contemporary artists. This coordinated development, led by Nadine Passamar-Gomez, has been, as far as I can see, unique, despite being comparable in limited ways to initiatives like the "curiosities" collection of the Château d'Oiron in Poitou, and the landscape emphasis of the Contemporary Art Centre of Vassivière in Haut-Limousin. In both the latter centers, there has been a similar, productive entente between the artists and the site, although at Oiron the surrounding land has only recently become available for development, and at Vassivière, expansion is constrained by the center's presence in the middle of a manmade lake. The guiding feature at Digne has been the encouragement given to certain artists, in particular de vries and Goldsworthy, to make the region the focus of their continued engagement and commitment, so that for each artist the geological reserve has become an outdoor studio for the continuance of a program of integrated and purposeful work.

I began this essay by invoking Ruskin's description of Turner's *Garden of the Hesperides,* which the nineteenth-century critic interpreted as achieving the highest goals of historical landscape. For him, it was emblematic of the condition of Britain at the outset of the nineteenth century, and this achievement sprang from the fact that the artist had been attentive in different ways to the visual, intellectual, and scientific aspects of the known world. This is a difficult brief for any landscape project to set itself at the beginning of the twenty-first century. But the richness of the realizations achieved in and around Digne is already considerable. Fontcuberta's mermaid, de vries's sacred wood, and Goldsworthy's stone-tenanted farm are all memorable works that signify on several different levels. This creative diversity of approaches to the landscape, exemplified by such a high proportion of the collaborating artists to date, must surely inspire us to think in similarly ambitious terms.

NOTES

[1] The most recent publication on Little Sparta is Jessie Sheeler, *Little Sparta: The Garden of Ian Hamilton Finlay* (London: Frances Lincoln, 2003), which includes a full photographic documentation by Andrew Lawson.

[2] See Bernard Lassus, "The Heterodite" (1985), in *The Landscape Approach* (Philadelphia: University of Pennsylvania Press, 1998), 53. In this text, whose implications are developed in the succeeding project entitled "The Landscape Entity" (1987), Lassus quotes from his earlier visual experiments with the arrangement of "Glasses and Bottles" (1975/76), asking the question: "Is not heterogeneity more welcoming than homogeneity?"

[3] See Georges Teyssot and Monique Mosser, eds., *L'architettura dei giardini d' occidente* (Milan: Electa, 1990), 491–502.

[4] See Yves Abrioux, *Ian Hamilton Finlay: A Visual Primer,* with introductory notes and commentaries by Stephen Bann, 2nd ed. (London: Reaktion Books, 1992), 121. The case of the "Sacred Grove" in the garden of the Kröller-Müller museum at Otterlo is a good example. Invited to occupy a nondescript area relatively close to the building and other sculptural works, Ian and Sue Finlay determined to use the protected and so far unused area of woodland to create a "grove," where stone column-bases dedicated to figures from French revolutionary history were set around living trees.

[5] See Stephen Bann, "A Laid Table," in *Artscapes Nordland,* ed. Maretta Jaukkuri (Nordland County: Forlaget Press, 2001), 36–37. Barclay's contribution to the extraordinarily lakeland landscape at Vassivière, in the Haut-Limousin, is another surprising and creative development of the relationship between a built form and the adjacent water, which in this case employs a periscopic, mirrored effect. It should be added that the Nordland project also features Dan Graham's *Two-Way Mirror Construction* (1996), at a site where the artist's early interest in Caspar David Friedrich expresses itself through the framed reflection of a sublime mountain ridge. The heritage of the Claude glass is not extinct!

[6] For an interesting discussion of Dewey's aesthetics in relation to traditions such as the English "aesthetic criticism" that significantly departs from Ruskin, see Casey Haskins, in *Encyclopedia of Aesthetics,* ed. Michael Kelly (Oxford: Oxford University Press, 1998), 20–25. Dewey clearly shared Ruskin's aversion to German idealism and questioned the formalist critics (Fry, Bell) of the succeeding generation who repudiated Ruskin's insistence on the interdependency of art and life.

[7] John Ruskin, *Modern Painters,* new edition (London: George Allen, 1897), vol. 5, 338.

[8] Ibid., 339.

[9] I should take this opportunity to express my gratitude to Nadine Passamar-Gomez for originally inviting me to Digne in 2002, and encouraging my collaboration on the volume of essays *Nouvelles curiosités: New curiosities* (Digne: Musée Gassendi, 2003), whose publication accompanied the reopening of the Musée Gassendi in 2003. She has also been extremely helpful in advising me on my more recent visit, in April 2005. I would also like to express my thanks to Bruno Lochon, who guided me on various visits to the reserve and assembled visual documents for me with great goodwill and efficiency.

[10] For a concise statement of the history and current aims of the museum, see *Musée Gassendi—Un musée réinventé* (Digne, 2004).

[11] See Paul-Armand Gette, *La diversité des sources ou de l'optique à l'haptique* (Lyon: Fages Éditions, 2005).

[12] The "hoax" of the mermaid is fully covered in Juan Foncuberta, *Volte face: à l'envers de la science, les leçons de l'histoire* (Marseille: Images en Manoeuvres Éditions, 2000).

[13] See Anthony Turner with Nadine Gomez, *Pierre Gassendi, explorateur des sciences,* exhibition catalog, Musée de Digne (Digne-les-Bains, 1992).

[14] For this, and other, aspects of herman de vries's work in and around Digne, see herman de vries, *les choses mêmes* (Paris: Réunion des Musées Nationaux, 2001), esp. 34–36.

[15] See Anette Freytag, "When the Railway Conquered the Garden: Velocity in Parisian and Viennese Parks," 215–42, in *Landscape Design and the Experience of Motion,* ed. Michel Conan (Washington, DC: Dumbarton Oaks Research Library and Collection, 2003).

[16] See Stephen Bann, "Sensing the Stones: Bernard Lassus and the Ground of Landscape Design," in Conan, *Landscape Design and the Experience of Motion,* 53–74.

[17] Andy Goldsworthy, *Refuges d'art* (Lyon: Editions Artha, 2002), 51, 53.

[18] Pliny's description of the work emerging as a result of the competition between Protogenes and Apelles could be interpreted playfully as a celebration of the first abstract painting: "The work had previously been the object of wide admiration, containing, as it did, nothing other than barely visible lines." See Pliny, *Natural History: A Selection,* trans. John F. Healy (London: Penguin, 1991), 332.

Contemporary Garden Aesthetics, Creations and Interpretations

Contemporary Garden Aesthetics, Creations and Interpretations

Contemporary Garden Aesthetics, Creations and Interpretations

Contemporary Garden Aesthetics, Creations and Interpretations

Contributors

Stephen Bann

Stephen Bann is a Professor of Art History at the University of Bristol in (England) who has published extensively on aspects of contemporary gardening and landscape art. He is a Trustee of the Little Sparta Trust, which has recently taken over the running of Ian Hamilton Finlay's garden in Lowland Scotland. His articles and translations presenting the work of Bernard Lassus are included in *Bernard Lassus, the Landscape Approach* (University of Pennsylvania Press, 1999). In 2001, Bann published *Parallel Lines: Printmakers, Painters and Photographers in Nineteenth-Century France* (Yale University Press, 2001) which was awarded the R.H.Gapper Prize for French Studies. In the fall of 2005 he was Edmond J. Safra Visiting Professor at CASVA, National Gallery of Art, Washington D.C. He is currently a Senior Fellow at Dumbarton Oaks.

Jacky Bowring

Jacky Bowring teaches at the Landscape Architecture Group at Lincoln University in New Zealand. She has previously practiced as a landscape architect in Auckland (NZ) and in London, prior to pursuing her Ph.D. at Lincoln. Jacky's research and teaching interests are in the areas of design theory and critique and she maintains an active interest in design, undertaking a range of conceptual, competition-based projects. Her recent successes have included an honourable mention for her *Maison Métaphysique* in the Japan Architect Shinkenchiku competition, judged by Steven Holl, a Cavalier Bremworth Award for her *Thermal Baths Theatre* project, and finally, sixth place in the Pentagon Memorial design competition, with Room 4.1.3 and Peter England. Jacky's essay on Room 4.1.3, 'Textuality and Tattoos: Words and Room 4.1.3,' appears in the book *Room 4.1.3: Innovations in Landscape Architecture* recently published by the University of Pennsylvania Press.

Michel Conan

Michel Conan, Director of Garden and Landscape Studies and Curator of the Contemporary Design Collections at Dumbarton Oaks, is a sociologist interested in the cultural history of garden design. He contributed to a renewal of garden history in France in the mid-1970s with the publication of several reprints. He recently published the *Dictionnaire Historique de L'Art des Jardins* (1997) and *L'Invention des Lieux* (1997), and edited five Dumbarton Oaks symposia, *Perspectives on Garden Histories* (1999), *Environmentalism and Landscape Architecture* (2000), *Aristocrats and Bourgeois Cultural Encounters in Garden Art* (2002), *Landscape Design and the Experience of Motion* (2003), and *Baroque Garden Cultures, Emulation, Sublimation, Subversion* (2005). His most recent publications are: *The Quarries of Crazannes by Bernard Lassus, An Essay Analyzing the Creation of a Landscape* (Washington D.C.: Spacemaker Press, 2004); and *Essais de Poétique des Jardins* (Firenze: Daniele Olschki, 2004. Premio Hanbury, 2005).

Massimo Venturi Ferriolo

Massimo Venturi Ferriolo is *professore ordinario di Estetica* at the Facoltà di Architettura e Società at the Politecnico di Milano. He is the director of the "Kepos" e "Quaderni di Kepos" collections devoted to garden and landscape studies in philosophy, history and architecture, published by Guerini & Associati in Milano. Landscape (*paesaggio*) is at the center of his scientific interests linking ethics and aesthetics as well as theory and design. His own research approach, besides historical analysis taken in a broad understanding, concerns aesthetical philosophy mostly focused on the relationships between man and environment expressed through architecture, the arts, and geography. Massimo has published numerous articles—in Italy and abroad—on gardens and landscape, including: *Nel grembo della vita. Le origini dell'idea di giardino*, Guerini & Associati, Milano 1989; *Il giardino del monaco*, Semar, Roma 1991; *Giardino e filosofia*, Guerini & Associati, Milano 1992; *Giardino e paesaggio dei Romantici*, Guerini & Associati, Milano 1998; and *Etiche del paesaggio. Il progetto del mondo umano*, Editori Riuniti, Roma 2002. He edited the book by Joachim Ritter, *Paesaggio. Uomo e natura nell'età moderna*, Guerini & Associati, Milano 1994 (translated into French at Les Éditions de l'Imprimeur, Besançon 1997).

Susan Herrington

Susan Herrington is an associate professor of landscape architecture and environmental design. She is also a licensed landscape architect in the United States. Susan received her MLA from Harvard University and her BLA from the State University of New York. Her research concerns the history and theory of designed landscapes and the culture of childhood. Susan has conducted research concerning kindergarten gardens in Germany with support from the German Academic Exchange, in Boston through a visiting research position at Harvard University, and in Toronto through SSHRC. She has lectured throughout the United States and in Europe, orchestrated a thirteen-acre international design competition, and wrote *Schoolyard Park* (2003). In 2003, she began a five-year study called Outside Criteria, which studies the outdoor play spaces of childcare centers in Vancouver as part of the MCRI funded CHILD project. She was also awarded a UBC TLEF with Rick Kopak of UBC's Library and Information Science for Claude Glass: Creating a Digital Library. In 2004 her chapter "Taster Buds: Cultivating a Canadian Cuisine" was published in *Eating Architecture* (Paulette Singley and Jamie Horwitz, editors) from the MIT press. Susan was also asked to return to the International Garden Festival, "Les Jardins de Metis in Quebec" and brought MLA and ENDS students with her in June 2004 to build her garden, "Hip Hop."

Peter Jacobs

Peter Jacobs is a Professor of Landscape Architecture, at the École d'architecture de paysage, Faculté de l'aménagement, Université de Montréal. He has served as Professor at the Graduate School of Design, Harvard University on three occasions and has lectured widely in North America, Europe and Latin America. He is the recipient of the A.H. Tammsaare Environment Prize, the President's Prize of the Canadian Society of Landscape Architects, and the Governor General's medal on the occasion of the 125th Anniversary of the Confederation of Canada. Following his early practice in architecture, he has focused on landscape planning and urban design. He is a Fellow and past President of the Canadian Society of landscape Architects (CSLA), Canada's senior delegate to the International Federation of Landscape Architects (IFLA), and a Fellow of the American Society of Landscape Architects (ASLA). He is an Honorary Fellow of the Columbian Society of Landscape Architects, and has served as the Chair of the College of Senior Fellows, Landscape and Garden Studies at Dumbarton Oaks, Washington, D.C. He is a member of numerous scientific and professional editorial advisory committees, has written and edited publications related to landscape perception, and has devised theories and methods used for sustainable and equitable development. Current studies focus on the histories of the idea of landscape, the meanings assigned to landscape in different cultural settings and how these inform management strategies and actions over time.

Jacques Leenhardt

Jacques Leenhardt, philosopher and sociologist, is Directeur d'Études at the École des Hautes Études en Sciences Sociales (Paris, France). He is the Honorary President of the Internatonal Association of Art Critics (AICA), President of the Association of Friends of Wifredo Lam (Paris, France), Founding Member and President of Crestet Centre d'Art (1987-2002). Publisher of various books on artists and art critic. Jacques has organized of exhibitions staging the relations between art and nature: *Des Forêts et des Hommes* (Paris, Muséum National d'Histoire Naturelle, juin 1995-mars 1996), and *Villette-Amazone, Manifeste pour l'environnement au XXIe siècle* (Paris, Parc de la Villette, Sept-Dec 1996). Project Director for the *Themen Park: Umwelt* for HANOVER 2000 Universal Exhibition, Author of the The Green Square Project, and manager of the multidiciplinary team realizing the renovation of the Goitzsche Forest, near Bitterfeld (Sachsen-Anhalt, Germany). His publications include: *Lecture politique du roman* (Minuit 1973), *Lire la lecture*; nouvelle édition avec une Introduction, (Harmattan 1999), *La force des mots. Le rôle des intellectuels* (Megrelis 1982), *Existe-t-il un lecteur européen?* (Conseil de l'Europe1989), *Au Jardin des Malentendus. Le commerce franco-allemand des idées* nouvelle édition augmentée et actualisée, (Actes Sud 1997), *Les Amériques latines en France* (Gallimard 1992), *Dans les Jardins de Roberto Burle Marx* (Actes Sud 1994), "Playing with artifice: Roberto Burle Marx's gardens", in Jan Birksted éd., *Relating architecture to landscape*, Londres, E &FN SPON (Routledge), 1999 "Genius loci, le cas de Roberto Burle Marx", in *Le jardin planétaire*, Claude Eveno et Gilles Clément ed., (l'Aube1997), *Michel Corajoud, paysagiste* (V.Hartmann.2000), "Das Grüne Quadrat. Ein Park für Bitterfeld", in *Land Gewinnen* Heinrich Schierz ed. (Mitteldeutschland Verlag, 2000), and *Conscience du paysage. Le passant de Montreuil* (Ville de Montreuil 2002).

Priyaleen Singh

Priyaleen Singh is a Professor in the Department of Architectural Conservation at the School of Planning and Architecture, New Delhi. She holds a Masters' degree in both Landscape Architecture and Architectural and Urban Conservation and subsequently received the Commonwealth Scholarship to earn her Ph. D. from the Institute of Advanced Architectural Studies, University of York, U.K in 1998. As a Landscape Architect and a Conservation architect, teaching and practicing in India, Priyaleen has been involved in safeguarding and finding a sustainable future for the rich heritage of India as a consultant to INTACH (Indian National Trust for Art and Cultural Heritage) among other organizations. She has worked on: 'Conservation management plan for the settlement of Orchha (16th–18th century A.D.),' 'Interpretation of Chokhelao garden, Jodhpur (18th century A.D.),' 'Planning for tourism along the Buddhist sites of Kushinagar, Sravasti, Sarnath (4th-5th cent.B.C.), 'Restoration of gardens of Taj Mahal, Agra (17th century A.D.)', 'Conservation strategy for historic housing, Chanderi (15th century A.D.).' She is presently engaged in research on changing vocabularies in the history of the gardens of Taj Mahal, and studies of the lesser known Indian landscape design traditions from the sixteenth to eighteenth centuries to include the Rajput, Bundela and Jat garden design. She is also compiling a National Register of Historic Gardens of India, while remaining concerned with contemporary landscape design in India.

Michael Spens

Michael Spens was educated at Cambridge University (Corpus Christi College) and at the Architectural Association School of Planning where he completed regional landscape studies for his thesis in 1970. He qualified as an architect RIBA (1969) and practiced privately as an architect until 1980 when, following a number of design awards, he transferred to research to continue his work in landscape architecture. His parallel interest has been on the work of the architect Alvar Aalto and he is currently engaged on further research into Aalto's approach to Landscape. Following the published work on Aalto's 1935 Viipuri Library (1994), he was invited to participate in the International Committee supporting the restoration of this library. Since the building is now in Russia he was instrumental in bringing Russian and Finnish interests closer together. He was awarded the Knighthood (First Class) of the Order of the Lion of Finland by the President of Finland in 2002, for services to Architecture. He recently moved his research base to the University of Dundee, Scotland near his family home, and was appointed University Reader in Architecture in 2003. His publication *Modern Landscape* (Phaidon Press 2003) was published in French in May 2005.

Christian Tschumi

Christian Tschumi, who was a fellow at Dumbarton Oaks in 2004, grew up in Zürich, Switzerland, and became a licensed landscape gardener in 1988. After serving in the Swiss army, he studied landscape architecture at the Hochschule Rapperswil and graduated with a BLA degree in November 1993. He worked for Vetsch Landschaftsarchitekten in Zürich until 1995 when he started his own landscape architecture practice. That same year he was invited to be a visiting lecturer at The Department of Landscape Architecture at the Fachhochschule Anhalt in Bernburg, Germany. In 1997 he decided to pursue a masters degree in landscape architecture at the Harvard Design School. He later worked for Peter Walker and Partners in Berkeley and then as a project manager at Suzman Design Associates in San Francisco. In April 2000, he started his research on the modernization of the Japanese garden. While living in Kyôto, he wrote his dissertation under the guidance of Prof. Lampugnani (ETH Zürich) and submitted it in early 2004.

Udo Weilacher

Udo Weilacher, Prof. Dr. sc. techn. ETH Dipl.-Ing., was born in 1963. He was educated as a landscape gardener and studied Landscape Architecture at the Technical University Munich-Weihenstephan and at the California State Polytechnic University Pomona/Los Angeles from 1993–1998 he was the scientific assistant to Dieter Kienast at Karlsruhe University and at the ETH Zurich, Faculty of Architecture. Later he taught as a Lecturer at the ETH Zurich and finished his dissertation on Swiss modern garden architecture which received special recognition for excellence at ETH Zurich in 2001. Weilacher published numerous articles and several books on garden history, Land Art and landscape architecture such as *Between Landscape Architecture and Land Art* (1996/1999), *Visionary Gardens - The modern landscapes by Ernst Cramer* (2002) or *In Gardens - Profiles of contemporary European Landscape Architecture* (2005). Since October 2002, Weilacher has been a fulltime Professor for Landscape Architecture and Design at Hanover University in Germany.

Xin Wu

Xin Wu is the Assistant Curator of Contemporary Landscape Design Collection and Coordinator of Asian Programs at Dumbarton Oaks. Educated in China, Canada and the UK as an historian and designer, she has been involved in researching, teaching, practicing and exhibitions of architecture and gardens in China and North America. Her present research concentrates on contemporary landscape design criticism. Designed spaces and landscapes remain her primary focuses; meanwhile, she has developed great interest in minimalist art and land art. Parallel with her research on modern and contemporary Western art, she is a young scholar on Chinese garden history. Her recent publication, "Yuelu Academy: Landscape and Gardens of Neo-Confucian Pedagogy," examines afresh the Chinese academy landscape and gardens, which have long been downplayed in scholarship. Her argument proves that academy landscape and gardens are not only unique, but also crucial to the understanding of Chinese engagement with nature. She has also lectured on various topics at The Getty/The Huntington, the US Botanic Garden and Georgetown University.

Index